The Sexual Politics of Border Control

The Sexual Politics of Border Control conceptualises sexuality as a method of bordering and uncovers how sexuality operates as a key site for the containment, capture and regulation of movement. By bringing together queer scholarship on borders and migration with the rich archive of feminist, Black, Indigenous and critical border perspectives, it highlights how the heteronormativity of the border intersects with the larger dynamics of racial capitalism, imperialism and settler colonialism; reproductive inequalities; and the containment of contagion, disease and virality.

Transnational in focus, this book includes contributions from and about different geopolitical contexts including histories of HIV in Turkey; the politics of reproduction in Palestine/Israel; settler colonialism and anti-Blackness in the United States; the sexual geographies of the Balkan and Southern Europe; the intimate politics of marriage migration between Vietnam and Canada; and sex work in Australia, the United States, France and New Zealand. This collection constitutes a key intervention in the study of border and migration that highlights the crucial role that sexual politics play in the reproduction and contestation of national border regimes.

The chapters in this book were originally published as a special issue of *Ethnic and Racial Studies*.

Billy Holzberg is Lecturer/Assistant Professor in Social Justice at King's College London, UK. Billy's current research examines the role that emotions play in the reproduction and contestation of the European border regime. His research interests include theories of affect and emotion, gender and sexuality, postcolonialism, racialisation, critical migration and border studies and the politics of representation.

Anouk Madörin is Lecturer in Cultural Studies at the University of Potsdam, Germany. Anouk researches the surveillance and security architecture of the European border regime from a postcolonial perspective. Her research interests include visual and digital culture, media theory, postcolonialism, border studies, racial capitalism, the history of technology and gender and sexuality.

Michelle Pfeifer is doctoral candidate at the Department of Media, Culture, and Communication at New York University, USA. Michelle's research examines the role of media technologies in the formation, practices, affects and operations of European border regimes. Michelle's research interests include (digital) media studies, sound studies, gender and sexuality studies and critical border studies.

Ethnic and Racial Studies

Series editor: **John Solomos**, University of Warwick, UK

The journal *Ethnic and Racial Studies* was founded in 1978 by John Stone to provide an international forum for high quality research on race, ethnicity, nationalism and ethnic conflict. At the time the study of race and ethnicity was still a relatively marginal sub-field of sociology, anthropology and political science. In the intervening period the journal has provided a space for the discussion of core theoretical issues, key developments and trends, and for the dissemination of the latest empirical research.

It is now the leading journal in its field and has helped to shape the development of scholarly research agendas. *Ethnic and Racial Studies* attracts submissions from scholars in a diverse range of countries and fields of scholarship, and crosses disciplinary boundaries. It is now available in both printed and electronic forms. Since 2015 it has published 15 issues per year, three of which are dedicated to *Ethnic and Racial Studies Review* offering expert guidance to the latest research through the publication of book reviews, symposia and discussion pieces, including reviews of work in languages other than English.

The *Ethnic and Racial Studies* book series contains a wide range of the journal's special issues. These special issues are an important contribution to the work of the journal, where leading social science academics bring together articles on specific themes and issues that are linked to the broad intellectual concerns of *Ethnic and Racial Studies*. The series editors work closely with the guest editors of the special issues to ensure that they meet the highest quality standards possible. Through publishing these special issues as a series of books, we hope to allow a wider audience of both scholars and students from across the social science disciplines to engage with the work of *Ethnic and Racial Studies*.

Race and Ethnicity in Pandemic Times
Edited by John Solomos

Culture and Conflict in Palestine/Israel
Edited by Tamir Sorek

The Sexual Politics of Border Control
Edited by Billy Holzberg, Anouk Madörin and Michelle Pfeifer

For more information about this series, please visit: www.routledge.com/Ethnic-and-Racial-Studies/book-series/ERS

The Sexual Politics of Border Control

Edited by
Billy Holzberg, Anouk Madörin and Michelle Pfeifer

LONDON AND NEW YORK

First published 2022
by Routledge
2 Park Square, Milton Park, Abingdon, Oxon, OX14 4RN

and by Routledge
605 Third Avenue, New York, NY 10158

Routledge is an imprint of the Taylor & Francis Group, an informa business

Chapter 1 and 3–10 © 2022 Taylor & Francis
Chapter 2 © 2021 Ian Khara Ellasante. Originally published as Open Access.

With the exception of Chapter 2, no part of this book may be reprinted or reproduced or utilised in any form or by any electronic, mechanical, or other means, now known or hereafter invented, including photocopying and recording, or in any information storage or retrieval system, without permission in writing from the publishers. For details on the rights for Chapter 2, please see the chapter's Open Access footnote.

Trademark notice: Product or corporate names may be trademarks or registered trademarks, and are used only for identification and explanation without intent to infringe.

British Library Cataloguing-in-Publication Data
A catalogue record for this book is available from the British Library

ISBN13: 978-1-032-17087-9 (hbk)
ISBN13: 978-1-032-17088-6 (pbk)
ISBN13: 978-1-003-25175-0 (ebk)

DOI: 10.4324/9781003251750

Typeset in Myriad Pro
by codeMantra

Publisher's Note
The publisher accepts responsibility for any inconsistencies that may have arisen during the conversion of this book from journal articles to book chapters, namely the inclusion of journal terminology.

Disclaimer
Every effort has been made to contact copyright holders for their permission to reprint material in this book. The publishers would be grateful to hear from any copyright holder who is not here acknowledged and will undertake to rectify any errors or omissions in future editions of this book.

Contents

Citation Information	vii
Notes on Contributors	ix

1 The sexual politics of border control: an introduction
Billy Holzberg, Anouk Madörin and Michelle Pfeifer   1

2 Radical sovereignty, rhetorical borders, and the everyday
decolonial praxis of Indigenous peoplehood and
Two-Spirit reclamation   23
Ian Khara Ellasante

3 Blackness, biopolitics, borders: African immigration,
racialization, and the limits of American exceptionalism   43
Brenda N. Sanya

4 Borderlands of reproduction: bodies, borders, and assisted
reproductive technologies in Israel/Palestine   65
Gala Rexer

5 "We're dating after marriage": transformative effects of
performing intimacy in Vietnamese "marriage fraud"
arrangements   85
Grace Tran

6 Border panic over the pandemic: mediated anxieties about
migrant sex workers and queers during the AIDS crises in Turkey   105
Yener Bayramoğlu

7 Migration, sex work and trafficking: the racialized bordering
politics of sexual humanitarianism   123
*Nicola Mai, P.G. Macioti, Calum Bennachie, Anne E. Fehrenbacher,
Calogero Giametta, Heidi Hoefinger and Jennifer Musto*

CONTENTS

8 Predatory porn, sex work and solidarity at borders 145
Piro Rexhepi

9 Sexuality and borders in right wing times: a conversation 164
Alyosxa Tudor and Miriam Ticktin

10 Afterword – Entangled politics: borderscapes and sexuality 184
Radha S. Hegde

Index 189

Citation Information

The chapters in this book were originally published in the journal *Ethnic and Racial Studies*, volume 44, issue 9 (2021). When citing this material, please use the original page numbering for each article, as follows:

Chapter 1
The sexual politics of border control: an introduction
Billy Holzberg, Anouk Madörin and Michelle Pfeifer
Ethnic and Racial Studies, volume 44, issue 9 (2021) pp. 1485–1506

Chapter 2
Radical sovereignty, rhetorical borders, and the everyday decolonial praxis of Indigenous peoplehood and Two-Spirit reclamation
Ian Khara Ellasante
Ethnic and Racial Studies, volume 44, issue 9 (2021) pp. 1507–1526

Chapter 3
Blackness, biopolitics, borders: African immigration, racialization, and the limits of American exceptionalism
Brenda N. Sanya
Ethnic and Racial Studies, volume 44, issue 9 (2021) pp. 1527–1548

Chapter 4
Borderlands of reproduction: bodies, borders, and assisted reproductive technologies in Israel/Palestine
Gala Rexer
Ethnic and Racial Studies, volume 44, issue 9 (2021) pp. 1549–1568

Chapter 5
"We're dating after marriage": transformative effects of performing intimacy in Vietnamese "marriage fraud" arrangements
Grace Tran
Ethnic and Racial Studies, volume 44, issue 9 (2021) pp. 1569–1588

Chapter 6

Border panic over the pandemic: mediated anxieties about migrant sex workers and queers during the AIDS crises in Turkey
Yener Bayramoğlu
Ethnic and Racial Studies, volume 44, issue 9 (2021) pp. 1589–1606

Chapter 7

Migration, sex work and trafficking: the racialized bordering politics of sexual humanitarianism
Nicola Mai, P.G. Macioti, Calum Bennachie, Anne E. Fehrenbacher, Calogero Giametta, Heidi Hoefinger and Jennifer Musto
Ethnic and Racial Studies, volume 44, issue 9 (2021) pp. 1607–1628

Chapter 8

Predatory porn, sex work and solidarity at borders
Piro Rexhepi
Ethnic and Racial Studies, volume 44, issue 9 (2021) pp. 1629–1647

Chapter 9

Sexuality and borders in right wing times: a conversation
Alyosxa Tudor and Miriam Ticktin
Ethnic and Racial Studies, volume 44, issue 9 (2021) pp. 1648–1667

Chapter 10

Afterword – Entangled politics: borderscapes and sexuality
Radha S. Hegde
Ethnic and Racial Studies, volume 44, issue 9 (2021) pp. 1668–1671

For any permission-related enquiries please visit:
http://www.tandfonline.com/page/help/permissions

Notes on Contributors

Yener Bayramoğlu, Alice Salomon University of Applied Sciences, Berlin, Germany.

Calum Bennachie, Department of Criminology and Sociology, Kingston University, London, UK.

Ian Khara Ellasante, Program in Gender and Sexuality Studies, Bates College, Lewiston, USA.

Anne E. Fehrenbacher, Department of Criminology and Sociology, Kingston University, London, UK; Department of Psychiatry and Biobehavioral Sciences, Semel Institute, University of California, USA.

Calogero Giametta, Department of Sociology, LAMES, Aix-Marseille University, France.

Radha S. Hegde, Media, Culture and Communication, New York University, USA.

Heidi Hoefinger, Department of Criminology and Sociology, Kingston University, London, UK; Department of Political Science, John Jay College of Criminal Justice, City University of New York, USA.

Billy Holzberg, School of Education, Communication and Society, King's College London, UK.

P.G. Macioti, Department of Criminology and Sociology, Kingston University, London, UK; Faculty of Law, University of Technology Sydney, Australia.

Anouk Madörin, Department of English and American Studies, University of Potsdam, Germany.

Nicola Mai, School of Humanities and Social Sciences, University of Newcastle, Australia.

Jennifer Musto, Department of Criminology and Sociology, Kingston University, London, UK; Department of Women's and Gender Studies, Wellesley College, USA.

Michelle Pfeifer, Department of Media, Culture, and Communication, New York University, USA.

Gala Rexer, Department of Social Sciences, Humboldt-Universität zu Berlin, Germany.

Piro Rexhepi, Global Studies Department, Northampton Community College, USA.

Brenda N. Sanya, Educational Studies, Africana and Latin American Studies and the LGBTQ Studies programs, Colgate University, Hamilton, USA.

Miriam Ticktin, The New School for Social Research, USA.

Grace Tran, Centre for Criminology & Sociolegal Studies, University of Toronto, Canada.

Alyosxa Tudor, SOAS University of London, UK.

The sexual politics of border control: an introduction

Billy Holzberg ⓘ, Anouk Madörin and Michelle Pfeifer ⓘ

ABSTRACT
In this introductory article to the special issue, we ask what role sexuality plays in the reproduction and contestation of border regimes and think sexuality towards its various entanglements with border control. As borders have been understood as a method for reproducing racialized distinctions, we argue that sexuality is also a method of bordering and illustrate how sexuality works as a key strategy for the capture, containment and regulation of mobility and movement. Taking a transnational approach, we bring together queer scholarship on borders and migration with the rich archive of feminist, Black, Indigenous and critical border perspectives to suggest that these strategies need to be understood in close relation to the (I) intersecting dynamics of colonial histories of racialization, (II) national regimes of reproductive control and (III) the containment of contagion, disease and sexual deviance.

Thinking sexuality and borders

This special issue emerges out of a political moment in which we are witnessing the intensification of racialized border regimes and the surge of sexual and gendered nationalisms across the globe. This situation is exemplified, and further augmented, by the global circulation of SARS-CoV-2 and the intensification of border protections that rely on the household, the heteronormative nuclear family and gendered divisions of labour to safeguard the national body from contagion (Grewal et al. 2020). States tackle the pandemic through national frameworks despite warnings from the World Health Organization (2020) that generalized border controls do little to control the virus and might even accelerate its spread. This reaction highlights how the intensification of border regimes and racialised systems of segregation define our political present in which national protectionism has emerged as the preeminent strategy for dealing with wider economic, political and environmental destitution.

In 1984, Gayle Rubin (2013, 100) wrote that "it is precisely at times such as these, when we live with the possibility of unthinkable destruction, that people are likely to become dangerously crazy about sexuality." In "Thinking Sex," Rubin shows that while for some sexuality may seem an unimportant topic, "a frivolous diversion from the more critical problems of poverty, war, disease, racism, famine, or nuclear annihilation," the abjection of sexual behaviours, discourses and subjectivities deemed abnormal and unhealthy is more than collateral for political projects. It is, rather often, its fundamental logic and ultimate objective. While Rubin's focus lies on the stratification of sexuality and the ways in which erotic life is renegotiated into sex laws and mores, her insistence to recognize the centrality of sex to wider politics also is of value today as we see the corroboration of border regimes through sexual politics across a range of geopolitical contexts marked by racial capitalism and the legacies of colonialism.

Taking cue from Rubin, in this special issue we think sexuality towards its various entanglements with contemporary border regimes. We ask what role sexuality plays in the (re-)production and contestation of border regimes and scrutinize the sexual politics of border control from a transnational perspective. Rather than grounding our questions on identities, disciplines or particular geographies, we hone in on border and sexuality as analytics and conceptualize sexuality as a central frame through which cross-border movements are captured, framed and contained. In doing so, we build upon the work of Gloria E. Anzaldúa (1999) who parsed out the relationship between heteronormativity and the stretching of the border into various borderlands, subjectivities and temporalities. For Anzaldúa, sexual identities, behaviours and discourses are not given but shaped within borderlands; thereby constituting the border not as a simple divide but a cultural terrain that disciplines and produces the queer, the troublesome and the confines of the normative. Queer scholarship on migration and borders has further highlighted the centrality of sexuality in migration and border regimes (Manalansan IV 2006; Luibhéid 2008; Lewis and Naples 2014). Building upon those insights, this special issue brings together queer scholarship on borders and migration with the rich archive of feminist, Black, Indigenous and critical border perspectives that highlight how the heteronormativity of the border intersects with the larger dynamics of racial capitalism, imperialism and settler colonialism, reproductive inequalities and the containment of contagion, disease and virality.

This special issue illustrates that sexuality undergirds the formation of national boundaries, citizenship and geopolitical borders in ways that secure racial hierarchies, capital accumulation and Western hegemonies. Borders have been understood as a method for reproducing racialized distinctions of belonging, humanity, deservingness, labour, life and death (Tadiar 2008; Ticktin 2008; Neilson and Mezzadra 2013; Genova 2017; Yuval-Davis, Wemyss, and Cassidy 2019). We argue that *sexuality is also a method of bordering*. By this, we mean that the investment in the regulation and control of sexuality is a key strategy for the violent capture, containment and regulation of mobility and movement – and posit that this constitutive connection between bordering and sexuality demands more scholarly and political attention. Simultaneously, the border becomes understood, organized and contested through sexuality and sexual discourse. As such, our intervention sheds light on the centrality of intimacy and desire in the struggle against state violence. It is not least the desire for different sexual futures (Muñoz 2009; Rodriguez 2014) that can shape our political horizons today.

A transnational conversation

The special issue emerges out of the "Sexuality and Borders Symposium" convened in the spring of 2019 at the Department of Media, Culture, and Communication at New York University. Our goal was to bring together researchers from a wide array of disciplines and fields under the signs of sexuality and borders. We wanted to achieve this by leaving the terrain conceptually open to see what connections would be made in response to our call. The high volume of incisive submissions exceeded our expectations and the generative discussions at the conference took us from questions of sex work and borders, marriage migration, assistive reproduction technologies and queer asylum to debates around sexual border panics, contagion, anti-Blackness, settler colonialism and transnational kinship. This special issue brings together some of the contributions from the conference to continue these discussions beyond the spatial and temporal limits of the original conference.

There are many ways to sketch the trajectory of this project. Not least important was the sociality that brought the three of us, co-editors of this issue, together and the conversations that shaped this project. The ties of our queer friendship were always interwoven with knowledge production and our political commitments. In this way, the special issue is also an expression of the desire for collaboration against the individuation of research and writing and the necessity to think, write and argue together for more just futures. Working on the cultural politics of border control and the coloniality of surveillance technologies in Germany and Europe, all three of us encountered sexuality as a crucial parameter in our own work. From the moral panics around racialised "sex offenders" constructed as a threat to the nation that emerged after New Year's Eve in Cologne in 2015 (Holzberg and Raghavan 2020) to the colonial and slavocratic gaze of surveillance technologies (Madörin 2020) and the queer politics of refugee hunger strikes (Pfeifer 2018), sexuality figured as a prominent, if not always clearly articulated, force in the way borders are secured and contested in our own research context of German nationalism and the EUropean border regime.

A central aim of the conference and this special issue is to connect these insights and conversations to other geopolitical contexts and epistemological locations. Thinking sexuality and borders transnationally, this special issue starts with but extends beyond the EUropean context and includes contributions from and about different locales including histories of HIV in Turkey, the politics of reproduction in Palestine/Israel, settler colonialism and anti-Blackness in the United States, the sexual geographies of the Balkan and Southern Europe, the intimate politics of marriage migration between Vietnam and Canada and sex work in Australia, France, New Zealand and the United States. We acknowledge that this approach, while allowing for thinking sexuality transnationally and across a number of geopolitical contexts, also risks imposing a Eurocentric framework on other locales. Practicing a feminist politics of location remains in constructive tension with articulating a transnational conceptual language of sexuality and borders throughout this special issue.

Bringing different sites and locales together, this special issue is dedicated to developing a refined vocabulary for analysing the entanglement of sexual and border politics. Borrowing from transnational sexuality studies, we focus on the enactment and circulation of sexual discourses, practices and subjectivities in and across national contexts and analyse sexuality as a key site for the enactment of global hegemonies and national politics (Grewal and Kaplan 2001; Kim-Puri 2005; Hemmings 2007; Tudor 2017). As Alyosxa Tudor (2017, 20) reminds us, a transnational approach to the study of sexuality also has to focus on "analysing privilegings, contradictions and ambivalences in gendering, racialising and nationalising ascriptions of (non)belonging". The special issue takes the histories of European colonialism, imperialism and racial capitalism as a starting point to trace and understand the manifold geopolitical inscriptions of national borders through registers of the sexual. Based on the contributions for this issue as well as the insights derived from the conference, we suggest that these inscriptions are most evident and need to be understood in close relation to the (I) intersecting dynamics of colonial histories of racialization, (II) national regimes of reproductive control and (III) the containment of contagion, disease and sexual deviance.

Colonial histories of racialization

What emerges centrally from our conference and the contributions to this special issue is that the sexual politics of border control needs to be understood in close relation to the biopolitical histories of racialization. Michel Foucault's (2019) insight that sexuality is the preeminent site of biopolitics – as it is the point where the control of the body and the population meet – remains the starting point for many contributions to this special issue. While Foucault linked individual sexualities to the security and prosperity of the social body as nineteenth-century inventions, he paid little attention to the actual role of racialization and colonialism in his dissection of sexual discourses. In correcting this inattention to race, postcolonial scholars like Ann Stoler (1995, 2002) have shown that discourses of sexuality were integral to the making and maintenance of racial borders and imperial authority. Sexual discourses did not only define the distinctions of the white bourgeois self but mapped the moral parameters and borders of European nation states. Racial distinctions were essentially structured in sexual and gendered terms and sexuality at once classified colonial subjects into distinct (less than) human kinds while securing the boundaries of the metropole.

These colonial logics continue to structure border regimes today. A key case to think through the resonant sexual politics of the colonial past is the New Year's Eve of 2015 in Cologne. The "Night of Cologne" describes the sexual panic that unfolded around cases of mass sexual assault and rape of women during the New Year festivities at the Cologne cathedral by large groups of men – most of them framed as racialized men of Middle Eastern and North African descent. The "Shame of Cologne" (Sat1 2016) conjured the spectre of a dangerous Muslim patriarchal masculinity targeting German women, Western values and women's emancipation. Western media and German authorities deployed the term "taharrush" (harassment in Arabic), portraying collective sexual violence as a practice that originates from the Middle East and North Africa and as supposedly foreign to German and European culture (Abdelmonem et al. 2016). The Night of Cologne drew national and international attention and became read as the epitome for the failure of Germany's *Willkommenskultur* (welcome culture). Attributed to the Merkel administration and the many volunteers who came forward to help when Germany and other European states failed to provide immediate support in the early days of the so-called "refugee crisis" of 2015, this hospitality was swiftly replaced by a nationalist security discourse and the implementation of asylum restrictions. In this affective conjuncture, Cologne served as proof that asylum seekers were impossible to integrate, and sexual violence was understood as a result of open borders, a problem imported from outside of Europe (Dietze 2016; Boulila and Carri 2017; Tudor 2018; Hark and Villa 2020).

To make sense of these logics, we can draw on the work of Miriam Ticktin (2008) who has fittingly described sexual violence as the "language of border control" in the case of France. She discusses how in the late 2000s, French-Maghrebian teenagers accused of gang-raping young women of North

African origin in the outskirts of French cities became the focus of national media and political attention. "Les tournantes," as these mass sexual atrocities conducted by men from former French colonies were called, became a sudden focus in public political debates – after decades of public neglect against issues concerning sexual violence against women. Ticktin argues that the obsession regarding the protection of women from uncivilized Others must be understood in relation to the Orientalist frames through which they became intelligible as a matter of public concern. While other forms of gendered and sexual violence remained confined to the private sphere, forms of spectacularised sexual abuse became the focus of state action which often resulted in pushing affected women and their communities into even more precarious positions in French society.

What the cases of France and Germany highlight is how the racialization of sexuality is tied to the continued and renewed alliances between right-wing populist and carceral feminisms (Phipps 2020) where the protection and safety of women becomes pitted against struggles for the freedom of movement. In the wake of Cologne, parts of the feminist movement called for tighter border protections so that women would feel save again. In France, arguments for sexual emancipation have been used to outlaw practices like the wearing of the veil constructing the notion of a secular republic at threat from Muslim migration (Ticktin 2008; Korteweg and Yurdakul 2014). Sarah Farris (2017) has described these discourses as the rise of femonationalism in which feminist rhetoric around sexual rights and freedoms goes hand in hand with nationalist and protectionist discourses and border securitisation. Other scholars have drawn on Jasbir Puar's (2007) concept of homonationalism to analyse how discourses around gay rights and sexual diversity are increasingly central in securing the nation vis-à-vis presumably homophobic and intolerant migrant "Others." Here, scholars have often turned to the Netherlands where tolerance towards sexual minorities has become a measuring stick for immigrant integration into the nation-state (Jivraj and De Jong 2011; Bracke 2012; Mepschen 2020) and Israel where discourses of pinkwashing are crucial in justifying the ongoing occupation and securing ethnic hierarchies of citizenship (Maikey and Stelder 2015; Alqaisiya 2018).

For the study of sexuality and borders, colonial histories do not merely offer symbolic templates onto which the neocolonial present is represented and made legible, they rather inform and continue to shape the material parameters of contemporary border regimes. As Farris (2017) suggests, in the context of Europe, the "sexualization of racism" is directly linked to the increasing demand for gendered racialized labour. While migrant men are commonly framed as sexual threats, women are represented as agency-less victims who need to be integrated to fulfil increasing demands for care and reproductive labour. This form of "differential inclusion" (Neilson and Mezzadra 2013) sustains the international divisions of reproductive labour and capital accumulation (Parreñas 2000; Ehrenreich and Hochschild 2003). Marxist feminists have long insisted that capitalism inherently depends on seemingly non-capitalist milieux for its extension and primarily on women's bodies, most of all racialized women and those living in the Global South, have been targeted in processes of ongoing primitive accumulation (Mies 1998; Federici 2014, 2020; Bhattacharyya 2018). Discourses around sexual vulnerability, propriety and docility are key in the management and legitimization of the ongoing exploitation of care and reproductive migrant labour across Europe and beyond (Constable 1997; Näre 2014).

While borders are often presented as a defence against foreign sexual harm and violence, scholars have pointed out how border regimes actually tend to foster sexual violence (Rodriguez 2015; Freedman 2016; Tyszler 2019). Not only has the constant threat of deportation made it more difficult for (undocumented) migrants who have become victims of sexual violence to come forward, sexual violence also forms a key part of the larger systems of border violence. In the case of Australia and the US, Joseph Pugliese and Suvendrini Perera (2018) point out how rape and sexual abuse are a key part of the everyday violence enacted in immigrant detention prisons. They show how these forms of abuse need to be understood in relation to the distinct settler colonial histories of these contexts and the impunity with which violence has been enacted against other racialized Indigenous and enslaved people historically. Abolitionist perspectives on borders and prisons coming out of Black and Indigenous feminist theorizing are key to understanding and contesting the violence that gets enacted through the sexual politics of borders (Gilmore 2007; Davis 2011; Loyd, Mitchelson, and Burridge 2012; Paik 2020). Colonial constructions of the sexual are evident in the discursive, affective and material securitization of borders today and it is the legacies of settler colonialism (Driskill et al. 2011; Ellasante forthcoming) and the transatlantic slave trade (Sanya forthcoming) that have sedimented into contemporary border regimes such as in the US.

National regimes of reproductive control

This special issue further highlights how the sexual politics of border control need to be understood in close relation to (trans)national politics of reproduction. In the example of Cologne, the defence of the nation from racialized men was legitimized through the protection of the vulnerable white female body that has come to stand in as a figure for the nation itself. These logics can also be identified in other national contexts such as that of India, where the figuration of the normative Hindu woman as *Bharat Matha* (Mother India) in need of protection from outside intruders plays a key role in securing the nationalist project of the Hindu Right (Kapur 2013; Holzberg and Raghavan 2020). Feminist theory has provided a rich body of work and frameworks through which to understand such gendered analogies that tie the reproduction of the individual to that of national bodies. Mary Douglas (2013) suggests that the body as a bounded system can represent any boundaries that are perceived to be threatened or precarious. Bodily metaphors are put in the service of policing the thresholds of the bodies' openings, including the inside and outside of national bodies, making bodily control an expression of social control. Reading Douglas, Sara Ahmed (2013, 2–3) maintains that the national body is often perceived as soft and permeable, a feminized body prone to be "penetrated" or "invaded" by racialized others. The nation at risk not only bears the potential danger of being penetrated and feminized, but also of becoming less white or racially pure. This gendered imaginary works to augment the martial power of the state, including those of border control, framed as masculine power able to protect against this threat (Kim-Puri 2005).

The potency of such sexualized body metaphors shows how women have long been framed as the biological and cultural producers of the nation (Yuval-Davis 1997). As such, these body metaphors have dire political effects for the control of women and racialized migrant men. The role of idealized motherhood in securing the reproduction of the nation goes alongside the identification of migrant and other undesirable (potential) mothers as primary targets of border control (Anthias and Yuval-Davis 1989; Lentin 2004). Eithne Luibhéid (2013), for instance, has shown how the control of women's reproductive capabilities is directly inscribed into contemporary border controls. In her ethnography of border controls in Ireland, Luibhéid shows how pregnant women from the African continent were singled out as threats to the nation, suspected of trying to gain illegitimate citizenship through childbirth and kept from entry to the nation. In the US context, whistle-blower Dawn Wooten, a nurse working at Irwin County Detention Center (ICDC), a Georgia ICE immigration detention facility, revealed in September 2020 that forced hysterectomies were regularly performed on detained women in the ICE jail. In the same report penned by Project South (2020), Wooten also revealed a substantial lack of medical care regarding the protection from COVID-19 in the detention centre such as the systematic refusal of testing for detained persons and the continuation of deportations of detained persons who tested positive for COVID-19.

These practices demonstrate that border regimes principally target women's bodies and their reproductive capabilities and determine who is allowed to represent and reproduce the nation. Given their detrimental effect on racialized women in particular, eugenic policies such as those implemented in the ICE detention centre need to be understood in the context of ongoing state eugenics informed by the histories of colonialism, slavery and anti-Blackness. As Hortense Spillers (1987) has pointed out, the transatlantic slave trade relied on the ungendering of Black bodies and instituted sexual reproduction as a privilege encouraged for some subjects while denying it to others. Slave owners attempted to control the reproductive patterns of female slaves since the seventeenth century and it was after the termination of the Atlantic slave trade in 1807 when Caribbean and American planters adopted a "slave breeding" policy which included sexual and reproductive coercion to fill labour shortage and increase profits (Beckles 1995). Eugenic policies in the nineteenth century continued the control of women's reproduction and focused on the forced sterilization of Black and Native American women (Ordover 2003). These histories' ongoing legacies are tangible in the chilling accounts of women at ICDC referring to the doctor who has performed these forced hysterectomies as the "uterus collector" (Project South 2020, 19).

In response to their treatment in ICE detention, women at ICDC have provided testimonies and video messages from inside the jail that serve as a reminder that incarcerated and detained women continuously struggle and organize to resist these violent practices by making their claims public. In 2008, detained mothers in England's Yarl's Wood Immigration Removal Centre staged a naked protest to condemn the dehumanizing conditions under which they were held and protested in solidarity with a Burundian mother and her child who were destined for deportation. Imogen Tyler (2013) suggests that such maternal protests reveal the biopolitical grounds on which state immigration and border control function. The mothers contested the securitization of reproduction as a key principle targeting the bodies of non-citizen pregnant women and (potential) mothers. By stripping bare, the naked mothers staged the unconditional refusal of their disposability and refuted the biopolitical attention to their bodies as objects of criminalization and state control.

A focus on sexuality as reproduction also highlights how borders extend into the governmentality of national reproduction more generally (Rexer 2021). Far-right movements and parties in Europe are becoming increasingly invested in constructing the racist narrative of a "population swap" that would see the replacement of white citizens with racialized migrant populations (Kuhar and Paternotte 2017). Yet, also in more centrist, liberal and leftist spheres, discussions about decreasing fertility rates in European countries like Germany, Italy and France have been accompanied by racialized panics about migration and migrant fertility. Low fertility in East Asian countries such as South Korea has similarly sparked anxieties about the loss of ethnic homogeneity and resulted in debates and policies that further constrict migration for people from South East Asia and mainland China while easing it for those from Europe and Northern America (Huang and Wu 2018; Lankov 2020).

The containment of disease, contagion and deviant sexualities

In understanding the intersection of borders and sexuality we further need to pay close attention to the ways in which biopolitical regimes of border control have long operated through the threat of sexual and viral contagion. The COVID-19 pandemic has brought to the fore once again how border figures serve as a tool to manage the collective health of the nation and play a key role in their securitization especially in regard to sexually transmitted diseases and viruses such as HIV (Ahuja 2016; Bayramoğlu 2021). An instructive example in this regard is the detention of Haitian refugees at Guantanámo Bay between 1991 and 1994. In the early 1990s, thousands of Haitians fled persecution by the Cédras regime and were largely intercepted by the US Coast Guard at sea before reaching US shores and were subsequently detained at Guantanámo. At Guantánamo, the refugees were subject to asylum determination processes as well as health screenings that determined that of the 300 refugees considered bona fide many of them were HIV positive (Paik 2018). As it would have been a violation to return the refugees to Haiti under the Refugee Convention and an HIV ban forbid the entry of HIV positive aliens to the US at the time, the refugees were indefinitely detained at Guantánamo. While the United States mobilized a language of humanitarian intervention to justify this decision, it in fact put the refugees in a position of rightlessness (Paik 2016). This also serves as a reminder that military and medical interventions of humanitarianism are enactments of carceral control and containment that (re)produce racialized and sexualized distinctions of contagion and the human (Ticktin 2006; Ahuja 2016, 170–172).

Moreover, the offshore interception of refugees at sea effected a shifting of the border itself that marks a crucial moment in the history of detention, deterrence and the externalization of borders. Alison Mountz (2010, 144) has shown how migratory movements have been increasingly restricted and controlled through "altered geographies" created by interception, excision, detention or the ad-hoc creation of transit zones. As scholars have pointed out, contemporary border regimes are marked by simultaneous externalization, containment and deterrence that characterize borders as shifting geographies (Perera 2007; Casas-Cortes et al. 2015; Mitropoulos 2015). Still, there needs to be further attention and critical examination of how these shifting geographies also operate through discursive mobilization of contagion and the material and bodily control of sexuality as the examples of an extension to the outside (offshore detention) and the inside (the proliferation of immigration detention) bring into drastic relief.

The border control of disease and virality is linked to enshrining divisions between healthy and unhealthy sexuality or what with Rubin we might refer to as "good" and "bad" sexuality. Border regimes police boundaries of health and disease through the control and exclusion of sexual subjects associated with such contagion. Prime among those are migrant sex workers who have long been targeted by border officials as they are framed as bringing social, moral and physical decay into the body of the nation (Mai et al. forthcoming). Here too, the language of humanitarian intervention has become increasingly prominent over the last decades. Sex workers are no longer simply framed as sexual deviants but as victims of human trafficking and smuggling. As Andrijasevic and Mai (2016) note, the spectre of human trafficking has allowed governments across the globe to criminalize sex work without addressing larger causal or structural factors of inequality. It has also functioned as a key tool in justifying and naturalizing border securitization as a humanitarian endeavour.

Moreover, discourses and policies around trafficking and sex work need to be understood in relation to the securitization of the heteronormative foundations of the nation more generally. Kinship and love are increasingly governed through the border (d'Aoust 2013; Bissenbakker and Myong 2020). In her work on Taiwanese border controls, Mei-Hua Chen (2015) points out how moral panics about migrant sex workers from China has led to all female Chinese migrants to be suspected of sex work and to be engaging in "fake marriages" with Taiwanese spouses to secure citizenship. Congruently, the state has implemented "fake marriage" tests, including visits to couples' homes and bedrooms, to assess whether they adhere to a normative gendered and sexual conduct of marriage. We can see here how the border extends into the intimate sphere to reproduce proper norms of heteronormativity. As Bridget Anderson, Sharma, and Wright (2011, 7) argue, it is not only

> "hard workers" who are produced at the border but also "good wives" who do not challenge patriarchal families, "straight guys and gals" who adhere to correct sexual scripts [and] "good parents" whose parenting accords with the requirements to produce "good children".

While border controls police sexual subjectivities and practices, they also generate new forms of love migration and "strategic intimacies" that try to circumvent and make use of them (Tran 2021).

The heteronormative logic that underlies border practices such as marriage migration also directly impacts queer subjects. Based on the assumption that migrants and nations are and should be heterosexual, queer migrants have either been excluded from migration and asylum laws or been framed as direct threats to the nation seen, for instance, in the exclusion of lesbian and gay subjects from entry to the US until 1990 (Luibhéid 2002). Over the last years, we can see some changes to these patterns as countries like the US, the UK and South Africa have instituted special protections for gay, lesbian and trans asylum seekers persecuted in their countries of origin. In order to be recognized under those protections, however, asylum seekers have to prove their sexuality and/or gender identity alongside highly normative lines in which they do not only have to conform to stereotypical assumptions of gay, lesbian and trans identities but affirm spectacularised, orientalist depictions of homo- and transphobia in their countries of origin (Spruce 2014; Fassin and Salcedo 2015; Saleh 2020). The inclusion of sexual orientation and gender identity as recognized categories through which refugee protection becomes possible must be contextualized amidst the increasingly restrictive asylum granting process in countries in the Global North (Giametta 2020). Rather than necessarily challenging the heteronormative foundations of the nation, LGBT inclusion into asylum and laws often works to strengthen hetero- and homonormative imaginaries in which the inclusion of LGBT identities is seen as a sign of progressiveness vis-à-vis less civilized geopolitical contexts (Sabsay 2012). Queer and migration activism have long struggled against these logics of inclusion. For instance, Karma Chávez (2013, 6) has theorized the coalitional activist practice of what she terms queer migration politics "as [an] activism that seeks to challenge normative, inclusionary perspectives at the intersection of queer rights and justice and immigration rights and justice." Queer politics, therefore, enact solidarities and radical care amidst the continued racialised and sexualized violence of coloniality (Rexhepi forthcoming).

Contributions

While the colonial histories of the sexual politics of border control inform all the contributions for this issue, they are most clearly articulated in the papers focused on the US context which highlight how contemporary US border regimes need to be understood in close relationship to the ongoing legacies of settler colonialism and the transatlantic slave trade. Writing from within the field of Indigenous studies, in their paper "Radical Sovereignty, Rhetorical Borders, and the Everyday Decolonial Praxis of Indigenous Peoplehood and Two-Spirit Reclamation" Ian Khara Ellasante shows how the extension of frontiers in US settler colonial politics went hand in hand with the eradication of Indigenous systems of sexuality and gender. They extend the understanding of borders as immobile structures that control entry to outsiders and instead focus on how borders crossing communities are entangled with sexual dominance and hegemonic imposition. In an analysis of federal American Indian policies, Ellasante shows how the settler colonial imperative targeted the forceful acquisition of Indigenous lands along with the destruction of American Indian cultural systems including Indigenous kinship and gender models. Settlers attempted to annihilate and forcefully subject Indigenous peoplehood to heteropatriarchal norms and turn lands into Euro-Western private property. Pointing to the possibilities of resistance within the landscape of settler colonialism, a resistance embedded in the continuity of Indigenous peoplehood with its interdependent elements of land, language, sacred history, and ceremonial cycle, Ellasante suggests that the self-naming and re-naming of queer Indigenous identities are tantamount to everyday acts of decolonization in and against the border.

The ongoing legacies of settler colonialism and their relation to the trans-atlantic slave trade underlie Brenda Sanya's contribution "Blackness, Biopolitics, Borders: African Immigration, Racialization, and the Limits of American Exceptionalism." Sanya illustrates how anti-Blackness informs the biopolitical bordering logic of US exceptionalism. Conducting a critical media analysis of three mediatized encounters between Black immigrants to the United States, she centres the embodied experiences of Blackness in immigration discourses. Situating these mediatized encounters within an analytical framework that centres race, gender and sexuality as crucial for the history of immigration and citizenship policies in the United States, as exemplified by family reunification programmes and the reproduction of Black sexuality and kinship as aberrant, Sanya identifies the "border as a site for social reproduction." While African immigrants are seen both as the archetypical source of human capital, they are simultaneously positioned as a threat to the national cohesion of the American psyche, as such, laying bare not only the colonial legacies but the national regimes of reproductive control that underlie its bordering practices. Sanya provides a queer analysis to show how borders effect a racial sorting that puts Black immigration in a position of contradiction amidst continuous anti-Black state violence, surveillance and policing.

The racialized logics of reproductive control that Sanya's paper analyses are further addressed by Gala Rexer and Grace Tran's contributions to this issue. In her contribution, "Borderlands of Reproduction: Bodies, Borders, and Assisted Reproductive Technologies in Palestine/Israel," Rexer shows how reproductive politics in the context of Palestine/Israel are central for securing ethnic and racial borders in Palestine/Israel. Drawing on in-depth interviews with Palestinian women and medical staff in Israeli fertility clinics, Rexer provides an analysis of the spatial and bodily politics of assisted reproductive technologies. Attending to the multiple forms of border-making that are re-produced under conditions of settler colonialism, what Rexer calls "borderlands of reproduction," she analyses the resistant border-crossing practices of Palestinian women who underwent fertility treatment in Israeli fertility clinics. Politicizing what is constructed as a neutral medical non-space – imagined by Israeli fertility providers as a bio- and geopolitical context – Rexer draws out the multiplicity of material, symbolic, and linguistic borders that crisscross these borderlands of reproduction to show the entanglements of power, space and the body that Palestinian women have to navigate. Similarly to Sanya's analysis of the discourse of exceptionalism that places Black immigration into a space of contradiction, Rexer argues that

Palestinian women are included in fertility treatment as an exception to settler colonial discourses of reproduction.

Grace Tran's article "'We're Dating After Marriage' Transformative Effects of Performing Intimacy in Vietnamese 'Marriage Fraud' Arrangements" deals with the politics of belonging and reproduction in the context of the Canadian state's intent to control "fake marriage" migration in Canada. She examines the narratives of three Vietnamese women who participated in đám cưới giả ("fake wedding") with Canadian men to gain entry to the country. Analysing how these women make use of the state's highly stereotypical assumptions of heteronormative marriage, she develops the concept of "strategic intimacies" to examine how participants perform and navigate the classed, gendered and racialised ideals of love, marriage and the family that shape the Canadian border regime. Extending established work on love and marriage migration that mostly focuses on the confining effect of these policies, Tran traces their productive power by highlighting how the couples she interviewed fall in love after engaging in đám cưới giả. While these "strategic intimacies" are based on access to high economic capital and can expose women to further vulnerability and stigmatization, they question the state's efforts to control boundaries between proper and improper, real and fake intimacies. Similar to Rexer, Tran shows how racialised women navigate, circumvent and subvert the reproductive logics of contemporary border control.

The nationalist logics of sexual and viral contagion are articulated in Yener Bayramoğlu's and Nicola Mai's et al. contributions to this issue. In "Border Panic over the Pandemic: Mediated anxieties about migrant sex workers and queers during the AIDS crises in Turkey," Bayramoğlu shows how the arrival of AIDS/HIV in Turkey (1985–1995) created a border panic that entangled fears of migration and border crossings with sexual deviancy, contagion and virality. Providing a rich archival, media and discourse analysis, he shows how it were particularly queer men and migrant sex workers who served as contagious figures against which the nation could reterritorialize "Turkishness." While by the mid-eighties, Turkey's AIDS/HIV cases were still sparse, or, as authorities claimed, non-existent, the media was prolific in stoking fears about the virus and projected it on what was portrayed as the sexually tainted West that was conceived as a contagious outside. Looking at the first publicly mediated AIDS/HIV case in Turkey and the discourse surrounding migrant sex workers from the East Black Sea Region who were derogatorily referred to as "Nataşas," Bayramoğlu shows how queer and migrant bodies were denounced as the carriers of a foreign disease that would cross borders with the mobility of people. AIDS/HIV was thus conceived as a problem of circulation and pointed to the fragility and permeability of both geographical and sexual borders.

In their article "Migration, Sex Work and Trafficking: The Racialised Bordering Politics of Sexual Humanitarianism" Nicola Mai, P.G. Macioti, Calum Bennachie, Anne E. Fehrenbacher, Calogero Giametta, Heidi Hoefinger and Jennifer Musto further examine how migrant sex workers continue to be key targets of contemporary border controls. Based on extensive field-work and semi-structured interviews with migrant sex workers in France, Australia, New Zealand and the US, they develop a rich conceptual analysis of sexual humanitarianism. Showing how humanitarian and racialised forms of governance intertwine, they examine how migrant sex workers are constructed as particularly vulnerable. This construction of vulnerability, they argue, fuels the eradication of sex work out of a humanitarian rationale and augments the exploitability and deportability of marginalized migrant groups. Focusing in particular on the experiences of cis Asian and trans Latina women as over-represented targets of border controls across their four national settings, they show how racialised and sex-gendered criteria of victimhood are key for sexual humanitarian justifications and the deployment of anti-migration rhetoric. Through their intervention, Mai et al. complicate divisions between sexual securitization and humanitarianism and instead show how policies of biopolitical protection commonly rely on the control and further disenfranchisement of racially marginalized subjects.

Piro Rexhepi's contribution "Predatory Porn, Sex Work and Solidarity at Borders" engages with the possibilities of enacting solidarities and radical care amidst the continued racialised and sexualized violence of coloniality in Southern European borderlands. Taking us to the sexual geography of Salonika, Rexhepi examines the ways in which the economy of the refugee crisis investing in racialised securitization and surveillance not only generates profit but also desire. Specifically looking at what he calls "predatory porn" he shows how migrants in Salonika have to navigate the racial imaginaries that permeate the simultaneous desire for and dispossession of migrants. Rexhepi situates his reflections on Salonika as part of Euro-Atlantic enclosures, the legacies of colonialism and racial capitalism that mark not only forms of surveillance, extraction and precarity, but also inhere "moments and circumstances when sexual play generates new social and spatial relations." Thus, Rexhepi points to the forms of care, solidarity, intimacy, sex and friendship that are enacted in, and against this context to engage in decolonial praxis that attempts to queer knowledge production as an "otherwise" of extractive libidinal economies. As such, he challenges us to confront the forms of extraction inherent in academic modes of knowledge production by highlighting complexities and contradictions that decolonial praxis demands.

Thinking across the different themes raised by the articles for this special issue, in their conversation "Sexuality and Borders in Right Wing Times," Alyosxa Tudor and Miriam Ticktin identify sexuality as a key site where race

16 THE SEXUAL POLITICS OF BORDER CONTROL

and colonialism meet in our current times – both as a violent mode of capture and containment under postcolonial and pandemic conditions and as a mode for re-imagining different political horizons. They reflect on the intersections between sexuality and borders in times of COVID-19. Tudor and Ticktin argue that COVID-19 has brought into relief how national borders are framed as providing protection from sexualized contagion and invasion of "invasive others" heightening practices and technologies of surveillance and policing to distinguish between "healthy" and "deviant" subjects. At the same time, COVID-19 has also made visible our own entanglement with each other, between our bodies and those of non-humans providing possibilities for enabling expansive forms of relationality beyond the nuclear family and the nation-state as a response to the recognition of shared vulnerability and risk. They formulate a call for the need of transnational analysis of the gendered, racialised and sexualized ways vulnerabilities and risks unfold on highly unequal terrain, which dramatically reveal how neither the household nor the nation is a safe space, particularly for women, queer, trans and gender-nonconforming people, as well as border-crossers, migrants and refugees.

Finally, Radha Hegde reflects in her afterword to this special issue on the urgency of reflecting on the sexual politics of border politics today. Offering a closing to the special issue, she stresses the importance of confronting the entanglement of sexual politics with racialised border controls in the contemporary moment. While this special issue brings together an array of different cases across contexts and includes various theories and methods for analysing the sexual politics of borders, the urgency of further exploring the intersection of sexuality and borders consequently remains. Addressing the sexual politics of borders may include looking further into regimes of (feminized) labour and care and how they intersect with racialized border control (Gutiérrez-Rodríguez 2010). Analyses of how forms of sexual and gendered inequalities are enhanced by technological and media environments and how they particularly affect people unequally within surveillance regimes are also not included in this issue even though surveillance targets already precarious queer migrants, for instance in the context of love migration (Constable 2003; Brennan 2004). Further work might also address how the control of sexuality shapes borders within urban spaces by, for example, gentrifying neighbourhoods and making them a safe space for only some LGBTQ subjects (Hanhardt 2013). The pieces assembled in this issue, therefore, continue some pertinent discussions on sexuality and borders and, at the same time, call for and provide the contours for further research.

Conclusion

Based on the contributions of this special issue, we argue that sexuality needs to be understood as a method of bordering – a key locus for the securitization and contestation of contemporary border regimes. We posit that, as a key site of power, sexuality sits at the centre of biopolitical forms of governance focused on regulating the cultural and biological reproduction of the nation. Binary oppositions between sexual deviance and normalcy, perversity and purity, threat and protection, have long worked to secure racialized divisions and to legitimate border securitisations. These binaries have been crucially informed by biopolitical regimes of coloniality, the control of women's reproduction and the containment of disease and sexual deviance. Racialized border regimes, then, cannot be separated from the politics of sexuality as they are one of the key features of how contemporary biopolitics operate.

At the same time, the border plays a crucial role in policing and reproducing normative understandings of sexuality. Whether through the policing of properly gendered marriages, the uprooting of Indigenous sexual identities, or the containment of HIV-positive and migrant sex workers, this special issue points out how the border continues to be a prime site at which normative sexual identities, behaviours and discourses are regulated and produced. The sexual politics of borders then emerge as a key prism for critical scholarship and as a particularly potent site for renewed alliances between feminist, trans and queer and anti-racist and migrant (solidarity) activism. We can take cure here from Radha Hegde (2016, 38) and her reflections in the afterword for this special issue, who has argued that "[q]ueering the terrain of immigration radically denaturalized the stability and coherence of identity categories that have traditionally served as the basis for defining nationalism and citizenship." We thus need an insistence on feminist and sexual futures that extend action and care against and beyond contemporary border control.

Acknowledgment

We want to thank all the authors of this special issue and the participants of the "Sexuality and Borders" Symposium held at NYU in spring 2019 for their insightful contributions. A very special thank you goes to Clare Hemmings, Radha Hedge, Miriam Ticktin and Alyosxa Tudor for their generous support in bringing this issue to life as well as for their constructive feedback to this introduction. We also want to thank NYU's Department of Media, Culture and Communication, LSE's Department of Gender Studies and the DFG-funded Group "Minor Cosmopolitanism" at the University of Potsdam for their conference funding and assistance without which this work would not have been possible. We also would like to thank the editorial team at *Ethnic and Racial Studies*, especially Amanda Eastell-Bleakley, whose support and guidance throughout this process has been invaluable.

Disclosure statement

No potential conflict of interest was reported by the author(s).

ORCID

Billy Holzberg ⓘ http://orcid.org/0000-0003-1914-4760
Michelle Pfeifer ⓘ http://orcid.org/0000-0003-0317-2492

References

Abdelmonem, A., R. E. Bavelaar, E. N. Wynne-Hughes, and S. Galán. 2016. "The 'Taharrush' Connection: Xenophobia, Islamophobia, and Sexual Violence in Germany and Beyond." *Jadaliyya* 2016.

Ahmed, S. 2013. *The Cultural Politics of Emotion*. New York and London: Routledge.

Ahuja, N. 2016. *Bioinsecurities: Disease Interventions, Empire, and the Government of Species*. Durham: Duke UP.

Alqaisiya, W. 2018. "Decolonial Queering: The Politics of Being Queer in Palestine." *Journal of Palestine Studies* 47 (3): 29–44.

Anderson, B., N. Sharma, and C. Wright. 2011. "Editorial: Why No Borders?" *Refuge: Canada's Journal on Refugees* 26 (2): 5–18.

Andrijasevic, R., and N. Mai. 2016. "Editorial: Trafficking (in) Representations: Understanding the Recurring Appeal of Victimhood and Slavery in Neoliberal Times." *Anti-Trafficking Review* 7: 1–10.

Anthias, F., and N. Yuval-Davis. 1989. *Woman-Nation-State*. London: Palgrave Macmillan UK.

Anzaldúa, G. 1999. *Borderlands/La Frontera*. San Francisco: Aunt Lute Books.

Bayramoğlu, Y. 2021. "Border Panic over the Pandemic: Mediated Anxieties about Migrant sex Workers and Queers during the AIDS Crises in Turkey." *Ethnic and Racial Studies.* doi:10.1080/01419870.2021.1881141

Beckles, H. 1995. "Sex and Gender in the Historiography of Caribbean Slavery." In *Engendering History*, edited by V. Shepherd, B. Brereton, et al., 125–140. New York: Palgrave Macmillan.

Bhattacharyya, G. 2018. *Rethinking Racial Capitalism: Questions of Reproduction and Survival*. London: Rowman & Littlefield.

Bissenbakker, B., and L. Myong. 2020. "Governing Belonging Through Attachment: Marriage Migration and Transnational Adoption in Denmark." *Ethnic and Racial Studies* 1–20. doi:10.1080/01419870.2021.1876901

Boulila, S. C., and C. Carri. 2017. "On Cologne: Gender, Migration and Unacknowledged Racisms in Germany." *European Journal of Women's Studies* 24 (3): 286–293.

Bracke, S. 2012. "From 'Saving Women' to 'Saving Gays': Rescue Narratives and Their Dis/Continuities." *European Journal of Women's Studies* 19 (2): 237–252.

Brennan, D. 2004. *What's Love Got to Do with It? Transnational Desires and Sex Tourism in the Dominican Republic*. Durham: Duke University Press.

Casas-Cortes, M., S. Cobarrubias, N. De Genova, G. Garelli, G. Grappi, C. Heller, S. Hess, B. Kasparek, S. Mezzadra, et al. 2015. "New Keywords: Migration and Borders." *Cultural Studies* 29 (1): 55–87.

Chávez, K. 2013. *Queer Migration Politics: Activist Rhetoric and Coalitional Possibilities*. Chicago: University of Illinois Press.

Chen, M. H. 2015. "The 'Fake Marriage' Test in Taiwan: Gender, Sexuality, and Border Control." *Cross-Currents: East Asian History and Culture Review* 4 (2): 496–518.

Constable, N. 1997. "Sexuality and Discipline among Filipina Domestic Workers in Hong Kong." *American Ethnologist* 24 (3): 539–558.

Constable, N. 2003. *Romance on a Global Stage: Pen Pals, Virtual Ethnography, and "Mail Order" Brides*. Berkeley: University of California Press.

d'Aoust, A. M. 2013. "In the Name of Love: Marriage Migration, Governmentality, and Technologies of Love." *International Political Sociology* 7 (3): 258–274.

Davis, A. Y. 2011. *Are Prisons Obsolete?* New York: Seven Stories Press.

Dietze, G. 2016. "Das, Ereignis Köln'." *Femina politica: Zeitschrift für feministische Politik-Wissenschaft* 25 (1): 93–102.

Douglas, M. 2013. *Purity and Danger: An Analysis of Concepts of Pollution and Taboo*. London and New York: Routledge.

Driskill, Q.-L., C. Finley, B. J. Gilley, and S. L. Morgensen, eds. 2011. *Queer Indigenous Studies: Critical Interventions in Theory, Politics, and Literature*. Tucson: University of Arizona Press.

Ehrenreich, B., and A. R. Hochschild, eds. 2003. *Global Woman: Nannies, Maids and Sex Workers in the New Economy*. London: Granta Books.

Ellasante, I. K. forthcoming. "Radical Sovereignty, Rhetorical Borders, and the Everyday Decolonial Praxis of Indigenous Peoplehood and Two-Spirit Reclamation." *Ethnic and Racial Studies*.

Farris, S. R. 2017. *In the Name of Women's Rights: The Rise of Femonationalism*. Durham: Duke University Press.

Fassin, E., and M. Salcedo. 2015. "Becoming gay? Immigration Policies and the Truth of Sexual Identity." *Archives of Sexual Behavior* 44 (5): 1117–1125.

Federici, S. 2014. *Caliban and the Witch*. New York: Autonomedia.

Federici, S. 2020. *Revolution at Point Zero: Housework, Reproduction, and Feminist Struggle*. New York: PM press.

Foucault, M. 2019. *The History of Sexuality: 1: The Will to Knowledge*. London: Penguin UK.

Freedman, J. 2016. "Sexual and Gender-Based Violence Against Refugee Women: A Hidden Aspect of the Refugee 'Crisis'." *Reproductive Health Matters* 24 (47): 18–26.

Genova, N. De, ed. 2017. *The Borders of Europe: Autonomy of Migration, Tactics of Bordering*. Durham: Duke University Press.

Giametta, C. 2020. "New Asylum Protection Categories and Elusive Filtering Devices: The Case of 'Queer Asylum' in France and the UK." *Journal of Ethnic and Migration Studies* 46 (1): 142–157.

Gilmore, R. W. 2007. *Golden Gulag: Prisons, Surplus, Crisis, and Opposition in Globalizing California*. Berkeley: University of California Press.

Grewal, K., C. Hemmings, L. Sabsay, and A. Tudor. 2020. "Confronting 'The Household'." *Feminist Review* Blog. Accessed December 11, 2020. https://femrev.wordpress.com/2020/05/26/confronting-the-household/.

Grewal, I., and C. Kaplan. 2001. "Global Identities: Theorizing Transnational Studies of Sexuality." *GLQ: A Journal of Lesbian and Gay Studies* 7 (4): 663–679.

Gutiérrez-Rodríguez, E. 2010. *Migration, Domestic Work and Affect: A Decolonial Approach on Value and the Feminization of Labor*. Abingdon: Routledge.

Hanhardt, C. 2013. *Safe Space: Gay Neighborhood History and the Politics of Violence*. Durham: Duke University Press.

Hark, S., and P. I. Villa. 2020. *The Future of Difference: Beyond the Toxic Entanglement of Racism, Sexism and Feminism*. New York: Verso.

Hegde, R. S. 2016. *Mediating Migration*. Cambridge: Polity Press.

Hemmings, C. 2007. "What's in a Name? Bisexuality, Transnational Sexuality Studies and Western Colonial Legacies." *International Journal of Human Rights* 11 (1-2): 13–32.

Holzberg, B., and P. Raghavan. 2020. "Securing the Nation Through the Politics of Sexual Violence: Tracing Resonances Between Delhi and Cologne." *International Affairs* 96 (5): 1189–1208.

Huang, Y. L., and C. L. Wu. 2018. "New Feminist Biopolitics for Ultra-Low-Fertility East Asia." In *Making Kin Not Population: Reconceiving Generations*, edited by D. Haraway, and A. E. Clarke, 125–144. Chicago: Prickly Paradigm Press.

Jivraj, S., and A. De Jong. 2011. "The Dutch Homo-Emancipation Policy and its Silencing Effects on Queer Muslims." *Feminist Legal Studies* 19 (2): 143–158.

Kapur, R. 2013. "Gender, Sovereignty and the Rise of Sexual Security Regime in International Law and Postcolonial India." *Melbourne Journal of International Law* 14: 317–345.

Kim-Puri, H. J. 2005. "Conceptualizing Gender-Sexuality-State-Nation: An Introduction." *Gender & Society* 19 (2): 137–159.

Korteweg, A. C., and G. Yurdakul. 2014. *The Headscarf Debates: Conflicts of National Belonging*. Palo Alto: Stanford University Press.

Kuhar, R., and D. Paternotte, eds. 2017. *Anti-Gender Campaigns in Europe: Mobilizing Against Equality*. London: Rowman & Littlefield.

Lankov, A. 2020. "The Demographic Situation in South Korea: What is Next?" Vaildaclub. Accessed December 11, 2020. https://valdaiclub.com/a/highlights/the-demographic-situation-in-south-korea/.

Lentin, R. 2004. "Strangers and Strollers: Feminist Notes on Researching Migrant m/Others." *Women's Studies International Forum* 27 (4): 301–314.

Lewis, R. L., and N. A. Naples. 2014. "Introduction: Queer Migration, Asylum, and Displacement." *Sexualities* 17 (8): 911–918.

Loyd, J. M., M. Mitchelson, and A. Burridge. 2012. *Beyond Walls and Cages: Prisons, Borders, and Global Crisis*. Athens: The University of Georgia Press.

Luibhéid, E. 2002. *Entry Denied: Controlling Sexuality at the Border*. Minneapolis: University of Minnesota Press.

Luibhéid, E. 2008. "Queer/Migration: An Unruly Body of Scholarship." *GLQ: A Journal of Lesbian and Gay Studies* 14 (2-3): 169–190.

Luibhéid, E. 2013. *Pregnant on Arrival: Making the Illegal Immigrant*. Minneapolis: University of Minnesota Press.

Madörin, A. 2020. "'The View from Above' at Europe's Maritime Borders: Racial Securitization from Visuality to Postvisuality." *European Journal of Cultural Studies* 23 (5): 698–711.

Mai, N., P. G. Macioti, C. Benarchie, A. E. Fehrenbacher, C. Giametta, H. Hoefinger, and J. Musto. forthcoming. "Migration, Sex Work and Trafficking: The Racialised Bordering Politics of Sexual Humanitarianism." *Ethnic and Racial Studies*.

Maikey, H., and M. Stelder. 2015. "Dismantling the Pink Door in the Apartheid Wall: Towards a Decolonized Palestinian Queer Politics." In *The Global Trajectories of Queerness*, edited by A. Tellis, and S. Bala, 83–103. Leiden and Boston: Brill Rodopi.

Manalansan IV, M. F. 2006. "Queer Intersections: Sexuality and Gender in Migration Studies." *International Migration Review* 40 (1): 224–249.

Mepschen, P. 2020. "A Postprogressive Nation: Homophobia, Islam, and the New Social Question in the Netherlands." In *Public Discourses About Homosexuality and Religion in Europe and Beyond*, edited by M. Derks, 81–104. Cham: Palgrave Macmillan.

Mies, M. 1998. *Patriarchy and Accumulation on A World Scale: Women in the International Division of Labour*. London and New York: Zed Books.

Mitropoulos, A. 2015. "Archipelago of Risk: Uncertainty, Borders and Migration Detention Systems." *New Formations* 84: 163–183.

Mountz, A. 2010. *Seeking Asylum: Human Smuggling and Bureaucracy at the Border*. Minneapolis: University of Minnesota Press.

Muñoz, J. E. 2009. *Cruising Utopia: The Then and There of Queer Futurity*. New York: NYU Press.

Näre, L. 2014. "Moral Encounters: Drawing Boundaries of Class, Sexuality and Migrancy in Paid Domestic Work." *Ethnic and Racial Studies* 37 (2): 363–380.

Neilson, B., and S. Mezzadra. 2013. *Border as Method, or, the Multiplication of Labor*. Durham and London: Duke University Press.

Ordover, N. 2003. *American Eugenics: Race, Queer Anatomy, and the Science of Nationalism*. Minneapolis: University of Minnesota Press.

Paik, A. N. 2016. *Rightlessness: Testimony and Redress in U.S. Prison Camps Since World War II*. Chapel Hill: University of North Carolina Press.

Paik, A. N. 2018. "US Turned Away Thousands of Haitian Asylum-Seekers and Detained Hundreds More in the 90s." *The Conversation*, June 28.

Paik, A. N. 2020. *Bans, Walls, Radis, Sanctuary: Understanding Immigration for the Twenty-First Century*. Oakland: University of California Press.

Parreñas, R. S. 2000. "Migrant Filipina Domestic Workers and the International Division of Reproductive Labor." *Gender & Society* 14 (4): 560–580.

Perera, S. 2007. "A Pacific Zone? (In)Security, Sovereignty, and Stores of the Pacific Borderscape." In *Borderscapes: Hidden Geographies and Politics at Territory's Edge*, edited by P. K. Rajaram, and C. Grundy-Warr, 201–228. Minneapolis: University of Minnesota Press.

Pfeifer, M. 2018. "Becoming Flesh: Refugee Hunger Strike and Embodiments of Refusal in German Necropolitical Spaces." *Citizenship Studies* 22 (5): 459–474.

Phipps, A. 2020. *Me, Not You: The Trouble with Mainstream Feminism*. Manchester: Manchester University Press.

Project South. 2020. Re: Lack of Medical Care, Unsafe Work Practices, and Absence of Adequate Protection Against COVID-19 for Detained Immigrants and Employees Alike at the Irwin County Detention Center. Report, Atlanta, Georgia, September.

Puar, J. K. 2007. *Terrorist Assemblages: Homonationalism in Queer Times*. Durham: Duke University Press.

Pugliese, J., and S. Perera. 2018. "Sexual Violence and the Border: Colonial Genealogies of US and Australian Immigration Detention Regimes." *Social & Legal Studies*. Accessed December 8, 2020. https://journals.sagepub.com/doi/full/10.1177/0964663918767954.

Rexer, G. 2021. "Borderlands of Reproduction: Bodies, Borders, and Assisted Reproductive Technologies in Israel/Palestine." *Ethnic and Racial Studies*. doi:10.1080/01419870.2021.1887502

Rexhepi, P. forthcoming. "Predatory Porn, Sex Work and Solidarity at Borders." *Ethnic and Racial Studies*.

Rodriguez, J. M. 2014. *Sexual Futures, Queer Gestures, and Other Latina Longings*. New York: NYU Press.

Rodriguez, R. 2015. "'Not Counting Mexicans or Indians': The Many Tentacles of State Violence Against Black-Brown-Indigenous Communities." Accessed December 8, 2020. https://truthout.org/articles/not-counting-mexicans-or-indians-the-many-tentacles-of-state-violence-against-black-brown-indigenous-communities/.

Rubin, G. 2013. "Thinking Sex: Notes for Radical Theory." In *Social Perspectives in Lesbian and Gay Studies: A Reader*, edited by P. M. Nardi, and B. E. Schneider, 100–130. London: Routledge.

Sabsay, L. 2012. "The Emergence of the Other Sexual Citizen: Orientalism and the Modernisation of Sexuality." *Citizenship Studies* 16 (5-6): 605–623.

Saleh, F. 2020. "Queer/Humanitarian Visibility: The Emergence of the Figure of the Suffering Syrian gay Refugee." *Middle East Critique* 29 (1): 47–67.

Sanya, B. forthcoming. "Blackness, Biopolitics, Borders: African Immigration, Racialization, and the Limits of American Exceptionalism." *Ethnic and Racial Studies*.

Sat1. 2016. "Die Schande von Köln." *Akte*. Accessed July 10, 2019. https://www.sat1.de/tv/akte/video/2016-die-schande-von-koeln-clip.

Spillers, H. J. 1987. "Mama's Baby, Papa's Maybe: An American Grammar Book." *Diacritics* 17 (2): 65–81.

Spruce, E. 2014. "Kylie Concerts, Exotic Cocktails and Gossip: The Appearance of Sexuality Through 'Gay'Asylum in the UK." In *The Sage Handbook of Feminist Theory*, edited by M. Evans, C. Hemmings, M. Henry, H. Johnstone, S. Madhok, A. Plomien, and S. Wearing, 275–292. London: Sage.

Stoler, A. L. 1995. *Race and the Education of Desire: Foucault's History of Sexuality and the Colonial Order of Things*. Durham: Duke University Press.

Stoler, A. L. 2002. *Carnal Knowledge and Imperial Power: Race and the Intimate in Colonial Rule*. Berkeley: University of California Press.

Tadiar, N. 2008. "Introduction: Borders on Belonging." *The Scholar and Feminist Online* 6 (3).

Ticktin, M. 2006. "Where Ethics and Politics Meet: The Violence of Humanitarianism in France." *American Ethnologist* 33 (1): 33–49.

Ticktin, M. 2008. "Sexual Violence as the Language of Border Control: Where French Feminist and Anti-Immigrant Rhetoric Meet." *Signs: Journal of Women in Culture and Society* 33 (4): 863–889.

Tran, G. 2021. "'We're Dating after Marriage': Transformative Effects of Performing Intimacy in Vietnamese 'Marriage Fraud' Arrangements." *Ethnic and Racial Studies*. doi:10.1080/01419870.2021.1881142

Tudor, A. 2017. "Dimensions of Transnationalism." *Feminist Review* 117 (1): 20–40.

Tudor, A. 2018. "Cross-Fadings of Racialisation and Migratisation: The Postcolonial Turn in Western European Gender and Migration Studies." *Gender, Place and Culture* 25 (7): 1057–1072.

Tyler, I. 2013. "Naked Protest: The Maternal Politics of Citizenship and Revolt." *Citizenship Studies* 17 (2): 211–226.

Tyszler, E. 2019. "From Controlling Mobilities to Control Over Women's Bodies: Gendered Effects of EU Border Externalization in Morocco." *Comparative Migration Studies* 7 (1): 1–20.

WHO. 2020. "WHO Recommendations for International Traffic in Relation to COVID-19 Outbreak." Accessed December 4, 2020. https://www.who.int/news-room/articles-detail/updated-who-recommendations-for-international-traffic-in-relation-to-covid-19-outbreak.

Yuval-Davis, N. 1997. *Gender and Nation*. London: SAGE Press.

Yuval-Davis, N., G. Wemyss, and K. Cassidy. 2019. *Bordering*. Cambridge: Polity.

ⓐ OPEN ACCESS

Radical sovereignty, rhetorical borders, and the everyday decolonial praxis of Indigenous peoplehood and Two-Spirit reclamation

Ian Khara Ellasante ⓘ

ABSTRACT
As settler colonialism has forcibly constricted vast expanses of Indigenous lands, criss-crossing them with superimposed borders, it has sought to redraw the boundaries of Indigenous identity by imposing definitions and categories that invariably lead to Indigenous diminishment. Strategic and eliminatory categorization is essential to the settler-colonial imperative. This essay explores settler-colonial exercises of rhetorical imperialism that deploy language, connotation, and categorization to dismantle Indigenous cultural systems. The author discusses the political stake in who is designated Indigenous, the drive to remake Indigenous nations in the image of the settler-state, the enforcement of cis-heteropatriarchal capitalist norms, and assimilationist strategies aiming to disrupt Indigenous formations of gender and kinship. The author argues that Indigenous assertions of peoplehood as a definitional and unifying framework and *Two-Spirit* as a self-identifier are acts of resistance that they term "oppositional identification" and "contrast mechanisms." They are exercises of rhetorical and radical sovereignty, tantamount to everyday decolonization.

Settler colonialism plots borders and imbues them with meaning. These borders do more than delineate state lines, city limits, and reservation boundaries; more than span the continent to demarcate the domains of nation-states. These are the borders that safeguard national inheritance, designate capital, and proclaim private property; borders that, thus, declare alien, criminal, and trespasser. These are borders that began to take shape with the first European footprints pressed into Caribbean shores; when the invaders first cast their gazes about, seeking to lay claim. These borders have relentlessly

---

This is an Open Access article distributed under the terms of the Creative Commons Attribution-NonCommercial-NoDerivatives License (http://creativecommons.org/licenses/by-nc-nd/4.0/), which permits non-commercial re-use, distribution, and reproduction in any medium, provided the original work is properly cited, and is not altered, transformed, or built upon in any way.

unfurled throughout the Americas from 1492 onward. They have altered the countenance of the land by un-naming, renaming, and rewriting the narratives of Indigenous homelands; forcing drastic changes in the relationships between the people and the lands to which they have belonged for countless generations. Congressionally-imposed borders have apportioned communally-held Indigenous homelands into privately-held allotments; turning heritage into real estate, into slices of private property to which tribal members are required to apply capitalist heteropatriarchal rules of inheritance, into parcels of land that are then slivered and fractionated to the point of infeasibility among subsequent generations.

Similarly, the double-pronged settler-colonial imperative – to appropriate and annihilate – driven by its primary objective to acquire Indigenous peoples' lands, has attempted to fragment Indigenous cultural identity. It has drawn borders that are surveilled, guarded, and policed around what it means to be Indigenous – e.g. constrictive designations of in/authenticity and the "Anglo-American discourse on Indianness" (Wiget 1992). The settler-colonial imperative has stratified borders between rigid categories of race and gender. It has established hierarchical delineations between normative settler society and Indigenous social formations. While traversing these settler-imposed borders demands a degree of assimilation, many have been beckoned across by assurances of safety, security, and all manners of salvation; many have been forced to cross under demonstrated and active threat.

As settler colonialism has forcibly constricted vast expanses of Indigenous lands, criss-crossing them with superimposed borders, it has sought to compress and redraw the boundaries of Indigenous political and cultural identity by imposing definitions and categories that invariably lead to Indigenous diminishment. Strategic and eliminatory categorization has been crucial to the settler-colonial imperative, evident in designations of federally-certified Indigenousness and the enforcement of a cis-heteropatriarchal gender binary. In this essay, I explore settler-colonial exercises of rhetorical imperialism that deploy language, connotation, and categorization to dismantle Indigenous cultural systems. In this context, I discuss the political stake in who is designated *Indigenous* and the drive to remake Indigenous nations in the image of the settler-state, as well as the enforcement of cis-heteropatriarchal capitalist norms and federal assimilationist strategies that aim to disrupt Indigenous formations of gender and kinship. Conversely, I argue that Indigenous assertions of peoplehood as a definitional and unifying framework and *Two-Spirit* as a self-identifier are acts of resistance that I term oppositional identification. They are exercises of rhetorical and radical sovereignty that are tantamount to everyday decolonization.

Settler colonialism has as its implicit imperative the acquisition and transformation of Indigenous lands into private, productive, and appraisable property. On the North American continent, it has driven the violent dispossession of Indigenous lands, to which has been applied the brutally enforced labour of enslaved people of African descent, a combination which produces – in a "classically Lockean" (Wolfe 2013, 4) sense – settler private property. In the reckoning of this oppressive arithmetic, the settler-colonial imperative has mandated the elimination of all obstacles to the manifestation of its destiny to lay claim to the continent "from sea to shining sea."

In order to meet its ends, the settler-colonial imperative calls for an eliminatory accounting and categorizing, seeking always to diminish Indigenous peoples, especially the numbers of those who would make claims to their Indigenous peoplehood in respect to their connection and right to a particular land. Such practices of numerical termination are apparent in blood quantum regulations and the practices of "pencil genocide" (Coleman 2018) or "statistical genocide" (Lawrence 2004) that systematically manipulated racial designations and government documents. Patrick Wolfe (2006) outlines such a "logic of elimination" as a tendency of settler colonialism (388). The logic of elimination induces settler society to uproot any present-day and future-facing indicators of Indigenous permanence and, importantly, to fragment their collectivity, their peoplehood, reducing them from peoples to individuals. Settler colonialism is concerned with stripping away the collectivity of Indigenousness; thus, as Wolfe observes, "the tribe could disappear while its members stayed behind" (397). This is evident in policies that make Indigenous peoples into official private citizens of the nation-state, deculturalize[1] them in residential schools, and relocate them from tribal communities to isolate them in cities. Such strategies prove that settler colonialism is indeed not an event; it is a structure (Wolfe 2006, 390).

Rhetorical imperialism: re/defining the edges of Indigenous

Scott Richard Lyons (Ojibwe/Mdewakanton Dakota) (2000) defines rhetorical imperialism as "the ability of dominant powers to assert control of others by setting the terms of debate. These terms are often definitional – that is, they identify the parties discussed by describing them in certain ways" (452). Lyons goes on to point out that metaphors used to describe Indigenous people – like "wards" and "pupils" – in early U.S. Supreme Court cases are instances in which Indigenous people were "completely redefined by their interlocutors;" which then become entrenched in U.S. jurisprudence, leading to the paternalism that has marked U.S. relations with Indigenous peoples. Such rhetorical imperialism has transformed Indigenous peoples from "sovereigns" organized as "nations" who negotiate "treaties" to "wards" clustered in "tribes" who enter "agreements" (453). Thus, rhetorical imperialism is the use of language, connotation, and categorization in service of the settler-colonial imperative, as an implement of elimination.

Rhetorical imperialism is exercised to define and re/define the political borders around who is categorized as Indigenous, with U.S. federal recognition upheld as the hallmark of tribal legitimacy. Flora Price (2003) offers the similar concept of "situational (re-contextualized) identity": the notion that aspects of a people's cultural identity may be re-positioned, unacknowledged, or diminished by the dominating society for its own benefit, though to the detriment of the people (150). To illustrate the concept, Price highlights the case of the Mashpee Wampanoag who, not being a federally-recognized tribe at the time, brought a federal suit in 1976 for the possession of "Cape Cod's Indian Town," otherwise known as the 16,000 acres of Mashpee Township, which had become highly sought-after by retirees, vacationers, and luxury developers over the previous century. Over the course of the suit, as the crux shifted from rightful ownership of the land to the veracity of Mashpee claims of continuous tribal status, the Mashpee found themselves having "to prove that they had been themselves in the past … in order to be themselves in the present" (155). Thus, the pivotal question became whether or not a tribe known as "Mashpee Wampanoag" has continuously existed. The legal definition of "Indian tribe" in effect at the time – established by *Montoya v. United States* (1901) – states that a tribe is "a body of Indians of the same or similar race united in a community under one leadership or government and inhabiting a particular, though sometimes ill-defined, territory" (Clifford 1988, 334; qtd. in Price 2003, 156). By this definition, each of the critical constituents of race, governance, and territory were set to be interpreted, measured, and evaluated according to the agenda of the settler-state to ascertain their continuous presence. Based on this assessment, a jury determined that the Mashpee Wampanoag had only continuously existed as an "Indian tribe" in the eight years between March 31, 1834 to March 3, 1842, after which they were no longer a tribe. In considering the rhetorical imperialism enacted in this case and, in fact, in most settler-contrived characterizations of Indigenous identity, Price observes the following: "Alongside the Mashpee witnesses' narrative of their history and identity stood the American narrative of the history of Native Americans. In the historical narrative, Native Americans either died or changed; and if you changed, you were no longer an Indian and no longer a tribe" (158).

Who is Indigenous? Peoplehood, resistance, and rhetorical sovereignty

As the settler-state wields rhetorical imperialism to establish categories, re/define borders, un-name, and rename to suit its own ends, there are clear consequences – political, economic, social, and corporal sanctions – for daring to exist outside of the structures it has imposed. In the following section, I discuss notions of peoplehood: an Indigenously-defined concept that, among its many purposes, serves as a response to the question of "Who is Indigenous?"; a question too often asked and answered by the settler-colonial imperative and its eliminatory agenda. I argue that the assertion of Indigenous peoplehood as definitional is an act of oppositional identification and radical sovereignty that resists the rhetorical imperialism of settler-defined notions of nationhood. I argue that just as radical sovereignty is inherent in a people, it is an act of radical sovereignty to assert peoplehood.

Tom Holm (Creek/Cherokee), with coauthors J. Diane Pearson and Ben Chavis (Lumbee) (2003), advances a model of peoplehood designed to be both a "recognizable central core assumption" for the field of Indigenous studies and a framework for defining Indigenous cultural identity (11). The peoplehood matrix is comprised of four interrelated and interdependent elements – language, land or territory, sacred history, and ceremonial cycle – that are each alone important to Indigenous cultural, political, and historical identity. Yet, it is the perpetual interaction among these elements that is the vital crux of what the peoplehood model represents and that drive what it accomplishes, including its efficacy as a theory of Indigenous cultural identity. Peoplehood as a means to define Indigenous identity can expand to encompass the broad and often self-coalescent body of global Indigenousness just as easily as it can contract to pinpoint distinct communities with precision. Thus, the notion of Indigenousness itself – and not merely as it is defined "in contrast to and in contention with the colonial societies and states that have spread out from Europe and other centres of empire" (Alfred and Corntassel 2005, 597) – can be illustrated by the holistic peoplehood matrix.

A peoplehood is comprised of those who share a relationship in common with these elements and, within this shared relationship, describe their histories and origins, define their interactions with their environment, outline the timing and methods for their ceremonies, and structure their kinship networks (Holm 2000, 43). Peoplehood designates a community united for the purposes of surviving and thriving as a people (Lyons 2000, 454). The strong attachment a people maintain to their unique cultural identity and the distinctiveness of their particular relationships to these elements also remind a people that their culture is endangered by external assimilative and acculturating forces; that, in the face of settler colonialism, their persistence as a people will require their concerted effort.

I contend that the settler-colonial imperative induces two separate perspectives on the elements of Indigenous peoplehood and the cultural identity systems they delineate. First, there is the perspective of Indigenous peoples who see in them the interrelated expressions and reflections of themselves and their ancestors, the symbols of what they have held dear, what creates community and belonging among them, what necessarily sets them apart and has defined them as a distinct people. On the other side, there is the perspective of the settler-colonizer who sees in these elements what can be claimed and what must be either exploited or destroyed in order to facilitate this claim – and, therefore, the various institutions and systems that must be positioned and strategically engaged – from legislation, to education, to media that corroborates the settler-authored archive – in order to justify both the claim and the right to destroy. In relation to the peoplehood of Indigenous peoples, the settler-colonial imperative is thus to appropriate and annihilate.

Due to the force of the settler-colonial imperative, Indigenous peoples wield less political power than the dominating[2] society; yet, despite ongoing pressure to assimilate, peoplehood persists because the people manage effective separation from the dominating culture to maintain their differentiation. Therefore, a defining and imperative attribute of persistent peoplehood is Indigenous peoples' continuous resistance to assimilation and absorption by the dominating society. The peoples' perpetuation of this "oppositional process" (Spicer 1971, 797) is resistance as boundary maintenance that carves out a peoplehood, a cultural identity, distinct from that of the dominating or even surrounding peer societies. The act of resisting can be thought of as standing in wilful opposition. Since *oppose* shares a similar derivation as the term *opposite* ("late Middle English: via Old French from Latin *oppositus*, past participle of *opponere* 'set against'"), the act of opposing can also be conceptualized as actively contrasting, as intentionally positioning oneself on the opposite side relative to the other entity, as being persistently contradictory or at odds with the interests of another. Thus, in this sense, maintaining resistance and opposition requires an Indigenous people to be willing and able to continually change and shift in relative counterposition to settler society. The mechanisms of such resistance and opposition comprise manifold exercises and enactments that range from subtle to subversive, from involuntary to intentional, from covert to conspicuous. Below, I discuss a method of resistance that I term oppositional identification.

In too many contexts, Indigenousness is re/defined in the settler image by exercises of rhetorical imperialism. For example, the notion of peoplehood is more definitionally accurate and durable than nationhood[3], as peoplehood both precedes and outlasts nationhood (Holm 2000; Holm, Pearson, and Chavis 2003). Indigenous concepts of nationhood are, in fact, constructed and sustained from within the framework of Indigenous peoplehood (Lyons 2000, 454; Justice 2008, 151–152; Holm 2000, 44; Simpson 2017, 8–9; Andersen 2015, 11). However, rhetorical imperialism enacted as legislative and economic coercion (e.g. the Indian Reorganization Act of 1934, with its federally supervised self-governance and tribal constitutions modelled after the U.S. Constitution) aims to compel Indigenous peoples to reject a notion as "primitive" and "basic" as peoplehood (Holm 2000, 44) and commit themselves to organizing in the image of the settler-state; to view federal recognition as essential to legitimacy (Harjo 2019, 137); to build and construct nations and governance structures that mimic the very ones that have sought to dispossess and dehumanize them. It would induce them to establish coercive governance of private citizens and private property rather than structures that support and care for the people, their land, and their myriad resources as a collective network. Likewise, the settler logic of elimination demands the redefinition of peoples "from autonomous to derivative existence" and "away from cultural practices and community aspects of 'being Indigenous' towards a political-legal construction as [for instance] 'aboriginal' or 'Native American' ... " (Alfred and Corntassel 2005, 598–599). Such political-legal diminishment and redefinition of Indigenous identity aims to compel peoples to reproduce the very rhetorical designations by which their identities have been re/defined (Alfred and Corntassel 2005, 600).

Despite pressures to do otherwise, when Indigenous peoples identify themselves according to the holistic structures delineated by their peoplehood, rather than according to notions of private citizenship or allegiance to a nation-state, they are exercising oppositional identification. The settler-colonial imperative deploys rhetorical imperialism to re/define and modify what it means to be Indigenous; however, the people continuously engage in strategic choices related to their identity in order to defy erasure, maintain their distinct and collective selfhood, and resist. On the one hand, such acts of oppositional identification are part of a requisite boundary maintenance process in which the people must resist assimilation and subsumption by the dominating society. On the other hand, these are also acts of sovereignty. Lyons defines rhetorical sovereignty as "the inherent right and ability of peoples to determine their own communicative needs and desires ... to decide for themselves the goals, modes, styles, and languages of public discourse" (449–450). As a mechanism of resistance, oppositional identification is a vital assertion of rhetorical sovereignty. It is directly connected to the right of a people to determine their own name and is a means by which a people assert their own identity in resistance to settler-imposed definitions of who they are.

Radical sovereignty

There tend to be two ways of considering the concept of sovereignty[4] (Holm 2000; Lyons 2000, 456; Harjo 2019, 56). One type of sovereignty – that of empire-building and settler-nationhood – is concerned with the power not only to make laws, but to compel compliance with those laws; with who is permitted to govern and how much coercive authority they have to do so. The power imbuing this brand of sovereignty is legitimized based on its recognition by other sovereigns and political entities (Lyons 2000, 450). This is the type of political sovereignty held and exercised by nation-states like the United States and that, regarding Indigenous peoples, the nation-state has at first recognized, then undermined, and then meted out according to its own interests.

Despite at least two hundred years of sovereign-to-sovereign treaty-making between North American Indigenous peoples and European states, as the newly formed United States gained fiscal and military might, the settler-state began to erode Indigenous political sovereignty through legal maneuvering, economic coercion, and brute force (Lyons 2000, 451; Holm 2000, 42). After a series of U.S. Supreme Court cases, in particular those known as the Marshall Trilogy, Indigenous peoples were left with dejure sovereignty, a legally prescribed list of sovereign rights that must be either explicitly delineated or granted by the federal government (Holm 2000, 42; Lyons 2000, 451).

Conversely, there is another way to consider sovereignty: de facto sovereignty, which is inherent to peoplehood (Holm 2000, 43). This is a type of sovereignty that Indigenous peoples have always indisputably possessed and exercised, prior to and without permission from the settler-state. It comprises rhetorical sovereignty, or the right of a people to determine for themselves the manner in which they will be represented, both among themselves and to others; in other words, the right of a people to define themselves for themselves, rather than capitulate to settler-imposed definitions. As well, in contrast to state-regulated sovereignty, this can be conceptualized as radical sovereignty, which, as Laura Harjo (Mvskoke) (2019) observes, "does not have to wait for the nation-state to recognize it or deem it legitimate" (50). Harjo also interprets this as "este-cate sovereignty": "a type of action and freedom realized in everyday and vernacular spaces against the grain of the politics of settler colonial elimination ... a tool to find our way back to the ways in which community is already performing sovereignty and enacting energy and kinship governed by love for the community" (39). In considering practices of radical resurgence, Leanne Betasamosake Simpson (Michi Saagig Nishnaabeg) (2017) conceptualizes "radical" as "a thorough and comprehensive reform, and I use the term ... to channel the vitality of my Ancestors to create a present that is recognizable to them because it is fundamentally different than the one settler colonialism creates" (48). Thus, I contend that not only is peoplehood inherently imbued with radical sovereignty; the assertion of peoplehood as an Indigenous nation's unifying framework is itself an act of radical sovereignty.

Cis-heteropatriarchy administered and enforced

I have discussed the eliminatory exercises of rhetorical imperialism in re/defining the borders of Indigenousness and the peoples' resistance and oppositional identification in the assertion of peoplehood as radical sovereignty. I shift now to explore the ways in which rhetorical imperialism has been enacted in the imposition of cis-heteropatriarchy and its requisite binary conceptualization of gender. The application and enforcement of these categories as rigid borders necessarily changes the terms of identification by coercing a gender hierarchy and invisibilizing those whose genders will not be pared down to fit a strict dichotomy. I demonstrate such exercises of rhetorical imperialism in U.S. settler contexts in federal assimilationist strategies, residential school settings, and the homogenizing renaming of gender expansive roles. I then introduce the concept of rhetorical appropriation to consider the ways in which the settler-colonial imperative manipulates an imprint of Indigenousness to serve a queer settler agenda.

With the explicit goal of the expropriation of Indigenous lands, the U.S. government embarked upon an official campaign to assimilate Indigenous peoples. Cultivating a desire to accumulate personal wealth and private property was key to early plans to deculturalize Indigenous peoples with the hope of discouraging cultural practices like sharing and collective ownership. Ideally, they would learn to be contented agriculturalists who lived on private family farms and had little need for large tracts of communal lands for hunting. With a farm of one's own and as one begins to amass wealth, Thomas Jefferson noted, one would necessarily adopt a nuclear family model, followed by a cascade of corollaries including inheritance, accumulation, commerce, property law, and criminal law (Spring 2013, 9). The imposition of such settler-heteropatriarchal capitalist norms sought to demolish Indigenous cultural systems, in particular those related to gender and kinship, and reconstruct them in the image of the settler.

When, in his 1805 presidential inaugural address, Jefferson called for teaching Indigenous peoples "agriculture and the domestic arts; to encourage them to that industry which alone can enable them to maintain their place in existence … ", he was, in fact, calling for a complete overwrite of the gender-role structures of most North American Indigenous cultures in order to re/define them in terms legible by settler society (Justice, Rifkin, and Schneider 2010, 15). In an analysis of U.S. federal Indian policies as articulated in inaugural addresses, Bethany Schneider (in Justice, Rifkin, and Schneider 2010) observes of Jefferson's directive that the existence of Indigenous farming was "conveniently invisible" to settler observers, since such agricultural work was typically performed by women and was a foundation of their cultural authority. If men were to become farmers, rather than hunters, such a shift would disorder many gender systems and dispossess Indigenous women of their cultural standing and authority (Justice, Rifkin, and Schneider 2010, 15).

Thus it becomes clear that in Jefferson's notion of "enabl[ing] them to maintain their place in existence," his insistence that "agriculture and domestic arts" are to be conducted according to settler formations of gender is intended to shift the terms of Indigenous gender identification. This is a strategy of the settler-colonial imperative and an enactment of rhetorical imperialism. It is also clear, therefore, that his invoking the precarious prospect of their ongoing "existence" should they not undertake this drastic cultural shift is an ultimatum, meant to mark an insecure futurity for Indigenous peoples within the settler-state.

Similarly, in his 1821 inaugural address, James Monroe said of his Indian policy that " ... the right of soil should be secured to each individual and his posterity in competent portions ... ," rather than Indigenous peoples continuing to maintain "sovereignty over vast territories" (Justice, Rifkin, and Schneider 2010, 16). In addition to calls for the disruption of long-established Indigenous relationships to land, the insistence upon heteropatriarchal norms of inheritance and a nuclear family model is evident in the rhetoric of these presidential pronouncements.

These executive ultimatums, and others like them, are further codified by the 1887 Dawes Act, also known as the General Allotment Act, which fractured hunting territories and forced Indigenous men, many traditionally hunters, into the key agricultural roles most typically held by Indigenous women. It also sought to dismantle and reconstruct societies, which had functioned within more egalitarian structures, into legibly and hierarchically patriarchal cultures – deeply disrupting long-held social aspects of gender and essential patterns of kinship. Thus, rhetorical imperialism was codified by the state with the intent to demolish tribal collectivity and to coerce a cis-heteropatriarchal structure, framed by settler values and norms regarding private ownership, the nuclear family model[5], and patrilineal inheritance (Justice, Rifkin, and Schneider 2010, 20).

In these cases, the boundaries within which Indigenous people can "maintain their place in existence" are designated by a cis-heteropatriarchal binary, inconsistent with the gender and kinship systems that structured their relationships with each other and their lands, histories, and ceremonies. The imposition of these boundaries required the administration and enforcement of gender categories, ways of being classed and ranked as women or men – and, in particular, as racialized *Indian* women or men – as assigned by the settler-colonial imperative. Noteworthy in this binary construction is the erasure of Two-Spirit people. This is rhetorical imperialism, as the terms of identity are defined and described by settler authorities, with demonstrated penalties for noncompliance.

Among the apparatuses of the settler-colonial imperative, education has taken many forms, with the explicit goal to expropriate Indigenous lands by deculturalizing the people and establishing cis-heteropatriarchal binary norms among them. Most notorious among these is the deployment of residential schools, which required that Indigenous children be separated from their families, homelands, languages, histories, and ceremonies.

Settler authorities, as agents of both the church and state, amassed children from diverse Indigenous cultures in residential schools and systematically stripped them of their distinct cultural identities and, importantly, the varied gender conventions of their respective peoples. Indigenous children were separated according to their perceived sex and trained correspondingly, in one of two distinct genders, to emulate the gender norms of settler society. As Sarah Hunt/Tłaliłila'ogwa (Kwakwaka'wakw) (2015) points out, "at the same moment as Native children became 'Indians' through their institutionalization at residential schools, they were simultaneously gendered as Indian boys and girls as systems of race and gender were mutually articulated" (106). Residential schooling and the categorization that it enforced thus aspired to create a racialized and homogenized "Indianness," that was then bifurcated according to an Indian-inflected and settler-imposed cis-heteropatriachal binary. In this way, the settler-colonial imperative sought to fragment the collectivity and peoplehood of Indigenous peoples, by penalizing distinct tribal identities and replacing them with a brand of pan-Indianness encompassing an amalgamation of detribalized private individuals; an attempt to fulfil Richard Pratt's[6] mission to "kill the Indian and save the man."

The settler-colonial imperative employs rhetorical imperialism in the act of renaming: the erasure of an Indigenous name to replace it with one that better serves the settler agenda. Of Columbus's renaming of the Indigenous lands he encountered, Stephen Greenblatt (1991) writes, "The founding action of Christian imperialism is a christening. Such a christening entails the cancellation of the native name – the erasure of the alien, an exorcism, an appropriation, and a gift … [it is] the taking of a possession, the conferral of identity" (quoted in Miranda 2010, 260). Renaming and mis-naming manifests rhetorical imperialism wherever settlers have trod among Indigenous lands and cultures.

In the enforcement of a strict gender binary, not only did settler authorities systematically terrorize and condemn Two-Spirit individuals among Indigenous peoples, they also disregarded the vast range of tribally-specific terms for these roles. *Berdache* – a term with meanings that include "a boy kept for unnatural purposes," "male prostitute," and "passive homosexual partner" – was first used to refer to and condemn Indigenous gender-expansive people in an eighteenth century text titled *Jesuit Relations*. The word originated in Persia (bardaj) and extended to Arabia before spreading consecutively to the Italian, Spanish, and French languages by the sixteenth century (Jacobs, Thomas, and Lang 1997, 4). *Berdache* was later popularized by anthropologists and ethnographers to describe the "gender variance" they observed in North American Indigenous cultures. Rather than tribally-specific terms like *boté* or *badé* (Crow), *winkte* (Lakota), *'aqi* (Ventureno Chumash), *nádleeh* (Navajo), *kwidó* (Tewa), *tainna wa'ippe* (Shoshone), *dubuds* (Paiute), or *Ihamana* (Zuni), *berdache* sustained its prominence as the sole term for hundreds of designated roles in an exercise of rhetorical imperialism that necessarily imagined a static, homogenized, and settler-defined mode of Indigenous gender variance.

Rhetorical appropriation

By design, the settler-colonial strategies of erasure and replacement are often not a complete obliteration of Indigenousness. Instead, as Patrick Wolfe (2006) observes, "the process of replacement maintains the refractory imprint of the native counter-claim": an imprint necessary for settler society to articulate adequate differentiation and proclaim its independence from the mother country and, ultimately, to assert settler nationalism, so that "the native repressed continues to structure settler-colonial society" (389–390). Following this logic, the denotative work of the indelible imprint of Indigenousness in service of the settler-colonial imperative can be considered what I describe as rhetorical appropriation.

Rhetorical appropriation is manifested in the strategic retention, often with an anglicizing modification, of Indigenous place names (e.g. Tanasi in Cherokee becomes Tennessee; misiziibi in Ojibwe becomes Mississippi) or the misuse of Indigenous symbols as corporate branding, caricatures as team mascots, and depictions prominent in numerous official seals of cities and states. It is also apparent in the choice some non-Indigenous people have made to claim the identifier *Two-Spirit* for themselves. Any such displays of rhetorical appropriation are shorthand for Indigenous subjugation; meant to serve as evidence of a settler claim fulfilled.

One context in which rhetorical appropriation manifests is in the institutionalization of settler heteronormativity, as it was and continues to be formed and normed against Indigenous cultural patterns deemed abnormal, aberrational, abject. This is evident in the phenomena that Scott Lauria Morgensen (2010) terms "settler sexuality" and "settler homonationalism," (106) in which the imprint of Indigenous formations of kinship, gender, and sexuality is invoked to give significance and shape – even by way of contrast – to settler formations of both heteronormativity and, subsequently, homonormativity. Another context for rhetorical appropriation lies among the proclaimed historical roots of modern queer settler genders and sexualities, wherein Indigenous forms of gender and sexuality are appropriated as proof of a long-standing queer(ed) presence on these lands, a model for entrenched social acceptance of diverse genders and sexualities, and as Mark Rifkin (2011) observes, "a counter hegemonic symbol[7] of resistance to heterohomemaking" (8). Here, rhetorical appropriation manifests in the enfolding of Indigenous histories and systems of gender and sexuality into queer settler history in order to validate and affirm various forms of modern queer settler identities and expressions; despite the explicit and centuries-long operation of the settler-colonial imperative to stamp out such patterns of "deviance" from settler norms.

Two-Spirit: self-naming as resistance and reclamation

> Although naming ceremonies among North American Indians followed many traditions, varying according to tribe and often even by band or time period, what has never changed is an acknowledgment of the sense of power inherent in a name or in the person performing the act of naming, and the consequent right to produce self-names as utterances of empowerment.
>
> Deborah Miranda (Ohlone Costanoan Esselen) (2010, 260)

In 1990, at the third annual Native American/First Nations Gay and Lesbian Conference in Winnipeg, North American Indigenous LGBTQ+ and gender expansive people elected to use the term *Two-Spirit* to refer to themselves and their current and past roles (Jacobs, Thomas, and Lang 1997, 2). While the precise origins of the term are not clear, for many, the self-identifier indicates that an individual embodies multi-gendered spirits; underscoring a belief that, while each new life is at least imprinted by the combination of the energies that united to create it, in some people the diversely-gendered attributes of all these energies are more wholly manifested (Anguksuar/LaFortune 1997, 221). Other understandings of the term are that *Two-Spirit* marks one as both queer and Indigenous (Wilson 2018, 168); or "spiritually meaningful" in ways that are reflected "in all aspects of who we are" (Wilson 2008, 193). Capable of containing a vast diversity of Indigenous LGBTQ+ identities, adapting over time and space, *Two-Spirit* is suffused with many meanings by the Indigenous people and communities who have imbued it with their lived experiences and affirmed it with their stories. Still, as one Two-Spirit person observed, the term "is a placeholder until something comes along that more accurately fits the full continuum of who we are in a contemporary context" (Wilson 2018, 168).

As a self-identifier, *Two-Spirit* is an Indigenously defined, pan-tribally applicable term; a manifestation of self-naming as oppositional identification and rhetorical sovereignty, in that it supplants the oppressively inaccurate and homogenizing term *berdache*. *Two-Spirit* also rejects the settler imposition of a racialized and rigid gender divide that seeks to erase any beyond-the-binary conceptualizations of gender. The term challenges the settler-defined categories of lesbian, gay, bisexual, transgender, and queer, or LGBTQ; nomenclature that, despite its demarcations, invisibilizes a range of Indigenous genders and sexualities. By foregrounding Indigenous conceptualizations as the bases by which to define the identifier, *Two-Spirit* further distinguishes itself from LGBTQ (Driskill 2010, 73; Davis 2019, 66). The term is a "journey to a Sovereign Erotic," described by Two-Spirit poet and scholar Qwo-Li Driskill (Cherokee Descent) (2004) as "a return to and/or continuance of the complex realities of gender and sexuality that are ever-present in both the human and more-than-human world, but erased and hidden by colonial cultures" (56). *Two-Spirit* is grounded in the interdependent elements of Indigenous peoplehood and it emphasizes the significance of relationships with land, language, history, and ceremony. While *Two-Spirit* is not interchangeable with *LGBTQ*, many people make situational choices about when to don the pan-tribal designation alone, in combination with an LGBTQ-identifier, and/or with tribally-specific terms. As Jenny L. Davis (Chickasaw) (2019), a Two-Spirit poet and linguist, explains, "Two Spirit individuals frequently employ all of these terms more or less synonymously in order to highlight what they hold in common: gender and sexuality outside of a binary norm" (80). Whether applying *Two-Spirit* or tribally-specific names for their roles, these acts of reclamation are rhetorical sovereignty.

Two-Spirit people employ rhetorical sovereignty as a contrast mechanism by resisting ostensible accommodation in the subsuming hegemony of *LGBTQ* and instead asserting a multiply-marginalized identity as Indigenous and queer in a cis-heteronormative and white-supremacist settler society. The acts I term contrast mechanisms are exercises of conscious differentiation; practices and modes of expression that demonstrate a group's intentional distinction not only from settler society but also among the subcultures or other groups with whom they may otherwise be assumed to share similarities. The choice to assert a pan-tribal identifier like *Two-Spirit* is a means of strategically aligning with other Two-Spirit people, in strategic contrast to the homogeneity of LGBTQ designations.

As Beatrice Medicine (Standing Rock Lakota) (1997) has suggested, "The use of 'two-spirit' as a Pan-Indian term is not intended to be translated from English to Native languages … To do so changes the common meaning it has acquired by self-identified two-spirit Native Americans" (147). The use of the self-identifier in English, the enduring language of settler colonization in North America, undermines a primary instrument of the settler-colonial imperative. The English language has been deployed to control, regulate, categorize, and assimilate Indigenous peoples; therefore, the creation and use of an English-language self-identifier as a pan-tribal rejection of such rhetorical imperialism is inherently subversive. *Two-Spirit* is thus akin to what Cindy Patton (1990) describes as "dissident vernaculars": " … meanings created by and in communities [that] are upsetting to the dominant culture precisely because speaking in one's own fashion is a means of resistance, a strengthening of the subculture that has created the new meaning" (Patton 1990, 148; qtd. in Tafoya 1997, 194). The utility of *Two-Spirit* as resistance in this context is made especially meaningful because, though it is an English-language term, it not a term for non-Indigenous people to apply to themselves, regardless of the languages they speak.

Two-Spirit scholar Alex Wilson (Opaskwayak Cree) (2008) talked with other Two-Spirit people about their journeys of reclamation. Wilson describes "coming in" as the process in which Two-Spirit people affirm an interdependent identity "that integrates their sexuality, culture, gender and all other aspects of who they understand and know themselves to be," as contrasted by the mainstream notion of "coming out" which centres on declaring an independent identity (197). Coming in, therefore, expresses a Two-Spirit person's emerging understanding of their place in the peoplehood of their own community. One participant described their experience of coming in: "It has taken me a long time to see that I am valuable. Now that I see it and feel it, everything seems possible. I looked so many places … But here the answer was right within me and the answer is in our communities. We are our communities and they are us. Being two-spirited means I am always at home" (197).

Two-Spirit people, and other Indigenous queer and gender-expansive people who do not don the pan-tribal identifier, are substantially engaging with the elements of their peoplehood. They are learning and recounting the sacred histories of their roles among their communities; engaging in ceremonies for which their roles have been designated. They are gathering on their homelands throughout the continent to build, heal, and nurture relationships with Turtle Island. They are learning and speaking tribal languages, tribally-specific terms for their roles, and terms for other genders in their traditional systems. "Two-spirit identity is about circling back," Wilson (2008) writes, "to where we belong, reclaiming, reinventing, and redefining our beginnings, our roots, our communities, our support systems, and our collective and individual selves" (198).

Radical sovereignty and everyday Indigenous futurity

Like upholding peoplehood as the unifying framework of Indigenous nationhood rather than settler conceptions of nation, the assertion of Two-Spirit identity is an act of radical sovereignty, of everyday decolonization. Both evoke Harjo's (2019) notion of este-cate sovereignty, in that they are "a type of action and freedom realized in everyday and vernacular spaces against the grain of the politics of settler colonial elimination" (39). Both overwrite erasures, fill in silences, and counteract the settler colonial logic of elimination by radically multiplying, rather than subtracting or dividing, the everyday spaces of Indigenous agency and self-determination: the "intimate geographies" (Hunt and Holmes 2015, 157) within communities and homes, among friends and partners, and within the "the vernacular interstices" (Harjo 2019, 53).

Radical sovereignty is enacted everyday; as Sarah Hunt/Tłaliłila'ogwa (Kwakwaka'wakw) and Cindy Holmes (2015) observe, "Indigenous peoples' resistance to colonialism has unfolded in daily acts of embodying and living Indigeneity, honoring longstanding relationships with the land and with one another" (157). The everyday decolonization of foregrounding and enacting peoplehood and of asserting a Two-Spirit, queer Indigenous identity are practices of Indigenous futurity. Laura Harjo (Mvskoke) (2019) describes the concept of Indigenous futurity as "the enactment of theories and practices that activate our ancestors' unrealized possibilities, the act of living out the futures we wish for in a contemporary moment, and the creation of the conditions for these futures" (5). Practiced both in the daily present and in the time to come, Indigenous futurity involves generative dialogue "with the unactivated possibilities of our past, present, and future relatives," actuates those potentialities, and continues "an archive of knowledge and possibilities" (Harjo 2019, 30, 216).

Indigenous futurity as a praxis of radical sovereignty evokes the seven-generations structure that Two-Spirit scholar Kai Pyle (Métis/Nishnaabe) (2018) notes is reflected in *aanikoobijigan* (Ojibwe) and *âniskotâpân* (Plains Cree), terms that each indicate great-grandparents and great-grandchildren and the seven generations between them (576). Pyle theorizes the concept of "trans*temporal kinship" to consider the "ability of transgender and Two-Spirit Indigenous people to establish kin relations across time, with both ancestors and descendants" (575–576). Similarly, Leanne Betasamosake Simpson (Michi Saagig Nishnaabeg) (2017) reflects on *kobade*, a Nishnaabeg word to refer to great-grandparents and great-grandchildren and the significance of being "a link in the chain between generations, between nations, between states of being, between individuals" (8). In each of these frameworks, the practice of Indigenous futurity is countering the settler-authored "terminal narratives" of Indigenous peoples that depict only their diminishment and disappearance (Wilcox 2009, 11–15).

In order to facilitate its primary objective – the acquisition of Indigenous lands and resources – the settler-colonial imperative has necessarily sought the diminishment of Indigenousness by disrupting Indigenous cultural systems, dismantling distinct and collective cultural identity, and demonizing Indigenous conceptualizations of gender, sexuality, and kinship. Nevertheless, Indigenous peoples have never simply acquiesced, using the means that are available to them to overtly or covertly defy these attempts. Often this has meant working within enforced assimilation and under the demonstrated threat of violence and loss. It has meant transforming settler-colonial institutions into sites of resistance. In this requisite opposition, Indigenous communities have long co-opted many of the instruments that have been used to subjugate and dehumanize them, including language, to change the narrative.

Just as rhetorical imperialism, with its eliminatory re/definitions and categories, has real and tangible consequences for Indigenous peoples, exercises of rhetorical sovereignty continue to be an effective challenge to the subtractive logics of settler colonialism. Settler schemes for the function of Indigenous nationhood explicitly erode sovereignty and self-determination; settler definitions of who gets to be Indigenous are blatantly eliminatory. Settler-imposed cis-heteropatriarchy and its accompanying gender binary, when mapped onto Indigenous cultures, marginalizes and erases particularly those whose genders cannot fit a rigid binary construction. However, Indigenous radical sovereignty responds to counter and unravel these oppressions: by upholding peoplehood as a unifying framework that predates and outlasts settler conceptions of nation, by self-naming and asserting an identifier like *Two-Spirit* to overwrite histories of erasure and condemnation. Such acts are the everyday praxis of decolonization.

Notes

1. Deculturization is defined by Joel Spring (2013) as "the educational process of destroying a people's culture and replacing it with a new culture" (9).
2. The pursuit of settler colonialism's inherent objectives is yet underway as its ramifications continue to unfold. I use the present participle *dominating* to connote the active and ongoing work of colonizing, settling, dominating, and subjugating and to indicate that settler colonialism is a necessarily dynamic structure that must be vigorously and systematically maintained.
3. Chris Andersen (Métis) (2015) notes that it is necessary differentiate the notion of Indigenous nationhood from that of settler nationhood by stripping the term of its "western teleology and apparently natural links to modern state building" (17).
4. Indigenous scholars note the necessity of both types of sovereignty, as evidenced by the case of the Mashpee Wampanoag. For example, Lyons (2000) calls for "an understanding of the twin pillars of sovereignty: the power to self-govern and the affirmation of peoplehood" (456). Laura Harjo (Mvskoke) (2019) observes that while "formal tribal sovereignty" is essential "to block the dispossession of Mvskoke land, gain fair access to health, education, and housing, and ensure the security of one's body, I still insist that tribes and Indigenous communities have always enacted and continue to enact a form of estecate sovereignty bound up in local community knowledge and practice" (50).
5. For an extended discussion of Jeffersonian assimilationist tactics, the marginalization of Indigenous modes of kinship, and formation of the nuclear family as a settler strategy of Indigenous diminishment, see Rifkin 2011, 45–77, wherein the author observes that " … the coalescence in the United States over the course of the nineteenth century of the ideal of the nuclear, sentimental family can be understood partially as an effect of the emergence of an imperial hegemony that helped legitimize the exertion of settler state authority over indigenous peoples and territory" (47).
6. Richard Pratt founded the Carlisle Indian Industrial School in 1879.

7. For example, Rifkin (2011) argues that the novel *Stone Butch Blues* (1993), by Leslie Feinberg, "positions native peoples as a tool for raising the consciousness of non-natives about the presence and need to include gender and sexual minorities, presenting indigenous polities as a pedagogical and imaginative resource for reconfiguring non-native publics ... " (42).

Acknowledgements

For their invaluable feedback on this article, I thank the three anonymous reviewers for *Ethnic and Racial Studies*. And to Hilary, I offer my gratitude always.

Disclosure statement

No potential conflict of interest was reported by the author(s).

ORCID

Ian Khara Ellasante (iD) http://orcid.org/0000-0002-7899-061X

References

Alfred, Taiaiake, and Jeff Corntassel. 2005. "Being Indigenous: Resurgences Against Contemporary Colonialism." *Government and Opposition* 40 (4): 597–614.

Andersen, Chris. 2015. "Peoplehood and the Nation Form: Tools for Thinking Juridically about Métis History." Paper presented at the Reconciliation and the Métis Conference, Ottawa, ON.

Anguksuar/LaFortune, Richard. 1997. "A Postcolonial Colonial Perspective on Western [Mis]Conceptions of the Cosmos and the Restoration of Indigenous Taxonomies." In *Two-Spirit People: Native American Gender Identity, Sexuality, and Spirituality*, edited by Sue-Ellen Jacobs, Wesley Thomas, and Sabine Lang, 217–222. Urbana: University of Illinois Press.

Clifford, James. 1988. *The Predicament of Culture: Twentieth Century Ethnography, Literature and Art*. Cambridge: Harvard University Press.

Coleman, Arrica L. 2018. "From the 'Pocahontas Exception' to a 'Historical Wrong': The Hidden Cost of Formal Recognition for American Indian Tribes." *TIME Magazine*.

Davis, Jenny L. 2019. "Refusing (Mis)Recognition: Navigating Multiple Marginalization in the U.S. Two Spirit Movement." *Review of International American Studies* 12 (1): 65–86.

Driskill, Qwo-Li. 2004. "Stolen from Our Bodies: First Nations Two-Spirits/Queers and the Journey to a Sovereign Erotic." *Studies in American Indian Literatures* 16 (2): 50–64.

Driskill, Qwo-Li. 2010. "Doubleweaving Two-Spirit Critiques: Building Alliances Between Native and Queer Studies." *GLQ: A Journal of Lesbian and Gay Studies* 16 (1-2): 69–92.

Greenblatt, Stephen. 1991. *Marvelous Possessions: The Wonder of the New World*. Chicago: University of Chicago Press.

Harjo, Laura. 2019. *Spiral to the Stars: Mvskoke Tools of Futurity*. Tucson: University of Arizona Press.

Holm, Tom. 2000. "Sovereignty and Peoplehood." *Red Ink* 8 (2): 41–44.

Holm, Tom, J. Diane Pearson, and Ben Chavis. 2003. "Peoplehood: A New Model for the Extension of Sovereignty in American Indian Studies." *Wicazo Sa Review* 18 (1): 7–24.

Hunt, Sarah/Tłaliłila'ogwa. 2015. "Embodying Self-Determination: Beyond the Gender Binary." In *Determinants of Indigenous Peoples' Health in Canada: Beyond the Social*, edited by Margo Greenwood, Sarah de Leeuw, Nicole Marie Lindsay, and Charlotte Reading, 104–119. Toronto: Canadian Scholars' Press.

Hunt, Sarah, and Cindy Holmes. 2015. "Everyday Decolonization: Living a Decolonizing Queer Politics." *Journal of Lesbian Studies* 19 (2): 154–172.

Jacobs, Sue-Ellen, Wesley Thomas, and Sabine Lang. 1997. *Two-Spirit People: Native American Gender Identity, Sexuality, and Spirituality*. Urbana: University of Illinois Press.

Justice, Daniel Heath. 2008. "'Go Away Water!' Kinship Criticism and the Decolonization Imperative." In *Reasoning Together: The Native Critics Collective*, edited by Janice Acoose, et al., 147–168. Norman: University of Oklahoma Press.

Justice, Daniel Heath, Mark Rifkin, and Bethany Schneider. 2010. "Introduction." *GLQ: A Journal of Lesbian and Gay Studies* 16 (1-2): 5–39.

Lawrence, Bonita. 2004. *"Real" Indians and Others: Mixed-Blood Urban Native People and Indigenous Nationhood*. Lincoln: University of Nebraska Press.

Lyons, Scott Richard. 2000. "Rhetorical Sovereignty: What Do American Indians Want from Writing?" *College Composition and Communication* 51 (3): 447–468.

Medicine, Beatrice. 1997. "Changing Native American Sex Roles in an Urban Context." In *Two-spirit People: Native American Gender Identity, Sexuality, and Spirituality*, edited by Sue-Ellen Jacobs, Wesley Thomas, and Sabine Lang, 145–255. Urbana: University of Illinois Press.

Miranda, Deborah A. 2010. "Extermination of the Joyas: Gendercide in Spanish California." *GLQ: A Journal of Lesbian and Gay Studies* 16 (1-2): 253–284.

Morgensen, Scott Lauria. 2010. "Settler Homonationalism: Theorizing Settler Colonialism within Queer Modernities." *GLQ: A Journal of Lesbian and Gay Studies* 16 (1-2): 105–131.

Patton, Cindy. 1990. *Inventing AIDS*. New York: Routledge.

Price, Flora. 2003. "Forgotten Spaces And Resident Places: New Mexico Black Towns & Communities (1897-1930)." PhD diss., University of New Mexico.

Pyle, Kai. 2018. "Naming and Claiming: Recovering Ojibwe and Plains Cree Two-Spirit Language." *TSQ: Transgender Studies Quarterly* 5 (4): 574–588.

Rifkin, Mark. 2011. *When Did Indians Become Straight? Kinship, the History of Sexuality, and Native Sovereignty*. New York: Oxford University Press.

Simpson, Leanne Betasamosake. 2017. *As We Have Always Done: Indigenous Freedom through Radical Resistance*. Minneapolis: University of Minnesota Press.

Spicer, Edward. 1971. "Persistent Cultural Systems: A Comparative Study of Identity Systems That Can Adapt to Contrasting Environments." *Science* 174 (4011): 795–800.

Spring, Joel H. 2013. *Deculturalization and the Struggle for Equality: A Brief History of the Education of Dominated Cultures in the United States*. 7th ed. Boston: McGraw-Hill.

Tafoya, Terry. 1997. "M. Dragonfly: Two-Spirit and the Tafoya Principle of Uncertainty." In *Two-spirit People: Native American Gender Identity, Sexuality, and Spirituality*, edited by Sue-Ellen Jacobs, Wesley Thomas, and Sabine Lang, 192–200. Urbana: University of Illinois Press.

Wiget, Andrew. 1992. "Identity, Voice, and Authority: Artist-Audience Relations in Native American Literature." *World Literature Today* 66 (2): 258–263.

Wilcox, Michael V. 2009. *The Pueblo Revolt and the Mythology of Conquest: An Indigenous Archaeology of Contact*. Berkeley: University of California Press.

Wilson, Alex. 2008. "N'tacimowin Inna Nah': Our Coming In Stories." *Canadian Woman Studies* 26 (3-4): 193–199.

Wilson, Alex. 2018. "Skirting the Issues: Indigenous Myths, Misses, and Misogyny." In *Keetsahnak: Our Missing and Murdered Indigenous Sisters*, edited by Kim Anderson, Maria Campbell, and Christi Belcourt, 161–174. Edmonton: University of Alberta Press.

Wolfe, Patrick. 2006. "Settler Colonialism and the Elimination of the Native." *Journal of Genocide Research* 8 (4): 387–409.

Wolfe, Patrick. 2013. "The Settler Complex: An Introduction." *American Indian Culture and Research Journal* 37 (2): 1–22.

Blackness, biopolitics, borders: African immigration, racialization, and the limits of American exceptionalism

Brenda N. Sanya ⓘ

ABSTRACT
Centreing the corporeal experiences and material significance of bodies lays bare the border as a site for social reproduction. Utilizing critical discourse analyses on three mediatized encounters – Abdi Nor Iftin, Amadou Diallo, and Ahmed Mohammed – between African immigrancy to the United States and that nation-state's surveillance of bodies discloses a key contradiction within those encounters: a mésalliance that positions Africans as an archetype of human capital and simultaneously a critical threat to the national psyche. This essay argues that African immigrants expose this contradiction, raising questions on Blackness, sexuality, identity, immigration, anti-colonialism, and the afterlife of slavery. This dynamic not only reveals how contingent U.S. citizenship can be, while also "calling the bluff" of its exceptionalism and the underlying social contract of global neoliberalism, but also grounds Blackness transnationally as a way to avoid reproducing the racialized "sorting" that occurs before, during, and after face-to-face encounters.

Introduction

Abdi Nor Iftin won the lottery!

| Abdi: | I put my confirmation number. I put my date of birth, and then clicked Submit. There was a few seconds of silence. But then, "You have been randomly selected." |
| Ira Glass (Host): | Everybody went nuts, lifted him up in the air in his chair. But Abdi didn't believe it. He […] started entering his information into the computer again and again. (Glass 2020) |

"Abdi and the Golden Ticket" (Glass 2015), a podcast episode of *This American Life*, lyrically sketches the life of a young Somali refugee from his childhood in Mogadishu, Somalia through his attempts to claim his diversity visa "lottery winnings". Iftin's story particularly captured U.S. and British media attention because it could be narrated alongside global events linked to the War on Terror that left him profiled and in a state of precarity as a refugee living in the Eastleigh district of Nairobi, Kenya.

Between Iftin winning the lottery and his embassy interview, a Somalia-based militant group, al-Shabaab (which, by Iftin's admission, had unsuccessfully tried to recruit him), launched an internationally covered attack at the Westgate Shopping Mall in Nairobi, Kenya that wounded and killed dozens of people. Kenya, a partner to the U.S. in the so-called global War on Terror, responded to the attacks by arresting Somalis and detaining them in "concentration camps" (Sperber 2015). While he was not caught in that initial sweep, Iftin spent months dodging the Kenyan police as he tried to secure the documentation he needed for a diversity visa, including a formal police clearance letter after "being a refugee became a crime".

While the narration of Abdi's lottery win is thrilling – with heroic, relatable figures, villains (al-Shabaab), stereotypically unreasonable and corrupt actors (Kenyan police), and "a giant soccer stadium that Kenyan authorities and police were using as a makeshift jail to hold hundreds of refugees" (Glass 2020) – missing throughout are analyses of the structural forces at play: why Somalia has been a nation at war for decades, the role of the United States in that civil war, the War on Terror's violent consequences for Kenya and Kenya's proxy role in it (Sanya et al. 2018), and the systemic violence and abuse (not simply individual corruption) of Kenyan security forces on Somalis (Simpson 2013; see also Patel 2015). While listeners, myself included, are compelled to root for Abdi's quest for "This American Life" built upon exceptional American dreams nurtured in Africa, these were not "freedom dreams" (Kelley 2002) rooted in African American political, social, and intellectual histories as written against structural racism and societal representations of Black people. Rather, they were dreams whose reality could only produce "freedom with violence" built upon "a unique structure of state violence and social emancipation" (Reddy 2011, 37). Dreams narrated without any interrogation of a colonial history of the present that normalizes the profiling of ethnic Somalis as unlawful actors crossing into Kenya as cattle rustling or terrorism.

In a follow-up podcast episode released five years later, we hear Abdi pledging allegiance as he is sworn in as a U.S. citizen (Glass 2020). This happened in Portland, Maine, where an embattled mayor in the state's second-largest city who referred to elderly Black people as "antique farm equipment" (Pescaro 2019) and the governor had "blamed [B]lacks and Hispanics for his state's heroin epidemic and endorsed racial profiling" (Graham 2016). Condemning the heroin epidemic, the governor explained that "the traffickers [...] come up here, they sell their heroin, and they go back home [...] half the time they impregnate a young, white girl before they leave" (Sharp

2016). Although the second episode addressed the Muslim ban, it still centred U.S. exceptionalism rather than the antiblack political climate, including the recent ban which featured six African nations (Knox 2020). This was the climate, emerging from a long-intertwined history of race and sexuality, wherein "as racialized social boundaries were increasingly policed" (Somerville 2000, 2), that greeted Abdi Nor Iftin upon his arrival.

This essay offers that missing interrogation of this Black American life by examining how the U.S. immigration system multiplies the inequities of racial capitalism (Robinson 1983), in particular, by situating African immigrants simultaneously as "iconic vessel[s] of human capital" (Murphy 2017, 117) and racializing them as threats to the national psyche. Using critical discourse analyses of news and popular culture reporting on three incidents involving African immigrants, this essay examines how Black bodies are made to carry a contradiction between the legitimate status of the desirable and exceptional immigrant and the illegitimate status of being Black in a society still characterized by the "continuities of slavery and freedom" (Hartman 1997, 13).

Race, sexuality, and the cornerstones of US immigration: analytical lens

Blackness is "antithetical to the heteronormative" (Weheliye 2014, 96) and "eccentric to the normative" (Ferguson 2004, 26; see also Abdur-Rahman 2012; Callier 2018; Holland 2012). That is, ideologies and ideological state apparatuses (Althusser 1971) that collude to disqualify Black people from access to full legal, political, economic, educational, and social participation, exploit heteronormativity (by default or deliberately) by not only excluding persons who do not appear to "fit" (or who refuse to "fit") that norm, but also by framing them as outsiders or deviant (Ferguson 2004). Sexuality is central to citizenship – in part because sexuality is a constitutive part of identity and racial difference – and thus, informs how we understand racialized gender and how norms order difference. As Abdur-Rahman argues of race in the U.S. context:

> Circuits of desire are particularly meaningful in the African American context because desirability, both in social and political contexts and in cultural production, is a crucial part of ascribing individual and communal value to Blackness. Moreover, desirability in the realm of the social is a key factor in determining who gets recognized in the body of the citizenry and who may thereby access the entitlements of citizenship and the resources of the state. (2012, 15)

Thinking about race, gender, and sexuality constitutively within a transnational framework allows for an exploration of how citizenship is unevenly produced and reproduced (cf. Nuñez 2016, 479). In the United States, family reunification has and continues to be a cornerstone of U.S. immigration policy, which has contributed to racialized patterns in immigration.

Notably, congressional records from U.S. House of Representatives from the debate on the *Family Unity and Employment Opportunity Immigration Act of 1990* reflect how citizenship has been *produced* in the United States. Making a plea for an increase of visas for highly skilled labourers, while maintaining provisions for family reunification visas, Congressman Glenn M. Anderson impressed upon Congress the need to "distinguish between illegal and legal immigration". The congressman from California's 35th district argued that while the nation needed to reduce the number of "illegal" immigrants, there also was a need to increase the number of legal immigrants because the United States was under "economic attack by nations like Japan [and] must use all possible advantages of the brainpower and expertise that immigrants offer us" (101 Cong. Rec. E3098, 1990). Anderson's speech focused on economic concerns and reiterated the "cornerstones" of U.S. immigration policy: family reunification and labour.

These distinct cornerstones invoked by Anderson are the most commonly used rationales for immigration and are linked together, given that the ability to access one of them typically leads to immigration applications in the other. If one is accessible and the other is an option, then an applicant will rely on the other. Family reunification relies upon and reifies a normative social ordering that excludes subaltern social groups whose family structures cannot be understood within the visa categories defined by the state (Hong and Ferguson 2011; Luibhéid 2008; Somerville 2005). Thus, the increase of immigration through education or skilled labour significantly shifted the notion that immigration was a process to reunite families. This disentanglement of citizenship from familial links ostensibly created a space for single people, and people without normative or biological familial links, to enter the country on the condition they were desirably employable.

Yet, understood within the context of the violent history of displacement and enslavement in the United States, family reunification as the cornerstone of immigration policy (101 Cong. Rec. E3098, 1990) and normative sexuality (birth and marriage) as central to the production of citizenship is a biopolitical tool which reifies the racial logics that produce differential statuses between racialized social groups. Following Kitossa, I read these rationales within the framework of "sexual racism, [and] a variety of population control mechanisms, including criminalization, mass imprisonment, segregation, sterilization and toxic exposure" (Kitossa, n.d., 2). Throughout the history of the U.S., Black sexuality, norms, families, and citizenship have been surveilled, policed and understood as aberrant within the United States (Callier 2018; Cohen 1997; Ferguson 2004; Somerville 2000). Sexuality "as the dense transfer point for relations of power" (Foucault 1978, 103) has been central to the regulation of Black bodies as evidenced in the "history of rape, lynching, and other forms of physical and mental terrorism" and in contemporary social stratification where Black people, "marginal group […] lacking power and privilege although engaged in heterosexual behaviour, have often found themselves defined as outside the norms and values of dominant society" (Cohen 1997, 454). The power relations embedded in these histories of race and sexuality in the making of citizenship rely upon antiblack tropes, and "an *idea* of the Black body [that] has been and continues to be projected across actual physical bodies; it chronicles how the misrecognition of individuated bodies as 'the black body' creates similar experiences" (Young 2010, 4 author's emphasis). It is within this history, the history of the classification of citizens, a history of scrutiny of Black bodies and Black lives, a history in which "negotiations of the colour line […] shaped and were shaped by the emergence of notions of sexual identity and the corresponding epistemological uncertainties surrounding them" (Somerville 2000, 3) that I seek to explore the enticements of the American Dream in the cases of Abdi Nor Iftin, Amadou Diallo, and Ahmed Mohammed.

Beyond the allure of the American dream, the entanglements between race, and sexuality are inextricably sutured to citizenship. The normative ideologies that defined families placed boundaries that excluded Black people who were "constitute[d] as nonnormative and then punishe[d] them for this deviance" (Hong and Ferguson 2011, 13). This absence of normative familial connections functions similarly to exclusionary (anti-immigrant) laws (Ngai 2004, 26–27). The production of citizenship, which is over determined by family reunification visa category (like many U.S. policies and institutions), thereby remains elusive and unavailable to people of African descent, given that the transatlantic slave trade deracinated Africans for enslavement, thereby eliminating any possibility of reunification. Equally, once European nations began practicing direct and indirect colonialism, immigration quotas assigned to African nations were under the authority of the European colony, thereby determining who had the opportunity to emigrate.

In the lives of Black immigrants, we routinely see "the historical and geographical immanence of this construction of the human [and] the real, tangible differences between bodies that matter in face-to-face encounters" (Saldanha 2006, 14). It is at the border where the relationship between politics, history, and thought – in collaboration with institutional regulation and the utility of race (Roberts 2011) – serves to activate a biopolitical logic, namely, an "excessive defense that ruinously turns on the same body that continues to activate and strengthen it" (Esposito 2008, 148). Thus, while African immigrants can initially benefit from their high academic achievement during immigration procedures – procedures designed to calculate "the differential life worth of racialized bodies in terms of their contribution to future economic productivity" (Murphy 2017, 11–12) – those advantages can quickly disappear at the border between "legal" immigrant status and the lived realities of Black citizenship. Moreover, successfully meeting requirements for documentation and/or being considered economically productive inadequately protects against what can happen when the machinery of the surveillance state encounters Black bodies in situ, "in face-to-face encounters" (Saldanha 2006, 14).

While Black people living in the U.S. have historically distinct and geographically varied pathways that led them to precarious lives in America, Black life is predicated on "common differences" (Mohanty 2003, 244) that produce a precarious everyday existence. As such, immigrants of colour – and particularly African immigrants – must persuade the immigration system of their exceptional desirability and national commitment, while simultaneously dealing with the U.S. system of race-sorting that labels Black people as threats to be neutralized. This was true for Abdi, as it was for 14-year-old Ahmed Mohamed, the son of Sudanese immigrants who was arrested for bringing a digital clock to school. Black immigrants and citizens alike must navigate what it means to live in a society that, in the same breath, both welcomes and terrorizes in the name of civilization – where, as Chandan Reddy puts it, "the military of a Western nation-state [...] codes its own terror as civilization" (2011, 240).

Amadou, Abdi, and Ahmed: antiblackness, biopolitics, and contradiction

Before Iftin's lyrically described "American Life" carried him from Somalia via Nairobi and finally to Maine, before Ahmed Mohamed carried his clock and his dreams of NASA into a classroom in Texas, there was Amadou Diallo more than two decades earlier. However, unlike Iftin's story, Mohamed and Diallo's stories more clearly exhibit connections to that longer lineage, the "afterlife-of-slavery" (Hartman 1997) that would order the lives of these Africans.

On 4 February 1999, when four plainclothes New York Police Department (NYPD) officers shot and killed Guinean immigrant Amadou Diallo in the vestibule of his apartment building, news reports of yet another case of arbitrary force and police violence in New York sparked protests led by organizations that had long fought for the civil rights and liberties of African Americans. This killing, before the digital era of social media intensification, became a flashpoint for a series of political campaigns that also led to the disbanding of New York's infamous Street Crime Unit (SCU), which had terrorized low-income communities since the 1970s under the motto, "We Own the Night". While the SCU officers who shot Diallo were acquitted of murder, the case remains exemplary for the themes of this essay.

Several striking details emerged from the very first reports of Diallo's killing: (1) the four officers were already under investigation and had been assigned to desk duty; (2) the officers did not communicate over their radios before approaching Diallo; (3) the shooting scene investigators found no weapon on or near Diallo; and (4), an anonymous police officer stated, "It looks like one guy may have panicked and the rest followed suit" (Cooper 1999). The *New York Times* referred neither to Diallo's nor to the officers' race in a description of Diallo provided by friends and family: "Mr. Diallo [was] a shy, hard-working man with a ready smile, a devout Muslim who did not smoke or drink" (Cooper 1999).

As the protests spread and persisted, media reports and the public decried the killing of Diallo – with extensive reporting in *The Village Voice* and *The New York Daily News* – while national news covered the case systematically and extensively. Ten days after the killing, several political leaders attended Diallo's funeral at an East Harlem mosque, but the news coverage was not accompanied by a photograph of Diallo or the more than 2000 mourners inside and outside the mosque. Instead, the article's photo was captioned, "Accompanied by escorts, former Nation of Islam spokesman Khallid Abdul Muhammad, centre foreground, arrives at the Islamic Center of New York on Friday for a memorial service for Amadou Diallo" (Grunwald 1999). While this caption accurately accounted for the reality that "throughout the 20th-century Muslim life was most synonymous with Blackness" (Ali 2017, 111), it became clear throughout the news coverage that Diallo was being positioned as somehow not a part of the existing patterns of racial profiling cases that brutalized African American communities and families.

At first glance, the picture captured how African American, Caribbean, and Puerto Rican organizers and activists in New York City, including the Nation of Islam, claimed Diallo as their own – a Black victim of police violence, and it documented a recognized relationship between Blackness and state violence. Read more closely, however, the picture and text function as a sorting tool (deployed consciously or not) for asserting ethnic distinctions. For example, a piece in *The Washington Post* only mentioned Diallo's race once while instead focusing on his piety, painting him as a hardworking victim in New York City who "loved Allah, and [...] America too" (Grunwald 1999). Also nestled in this pre-9/11 story is Diallo's love for learning math and computer science.

While "the Black community's anger with the police has risen to its highest levels since several white officers were accused of abusing a Haitian immigrant named Abner Louima with a toilet plunger in 1997" (Grunwald 1999), the article bracketed Diallo as somehow outside of the long history of racist policing, as if he weren't part of the same Black community. Perhaps more importantly, the case (linked only to Louima's) was presented as an aberration, not an endemic part of policing. While the article's photo inescapably revealed the connections between Diallo and the African American and Caribbean organizers who came to mourn his death, the photo's caption worked to elide those connections (or, at least, to make them appear illegible).

The reader is left with the impression that the family's mourning and the community's response to the persistent, systemic killing of Black people somehow can't exist in the same space. Juxtaposing the ski masks worn by the Nation of Islam mourners and the clothing of Diallo's grieving mother, this creative choreography of the funeral posthumously shifted focus away from the terms that framed how Diallo lived and died (his Blackness) vis-à-vis his relationship to both U.S. immigration officials (initially) and the SCU officers who eventually executed him.

A year later, a *BBC* (2000) report addressed race without ever describing Diallo as Black, while a *Los Angeles Times* (Goldman 2000) article used the word *black* only in reference to a gun described in an officer's testimony. Atypically – especially given how citizen documentation of police brutality and killings have been increasingly publicized since 1999 – one of the acquitted SCU officers "admitted that Diallo really didn't closely resemble the description of the man they were pursuing" (Goldman 2000). While the officer's confession was significant, Goldman's framing seemed to implicitly accept the idea that if Diallo had "resembled" the man being pursued, then his murder would be justified, somehow understandable (Sanya 2017).

Over the years, Diallo's execution has been studied and analyzed by scholars of race, police brutality, and summary executions, and immigration scholars with focuses on racial profiling, the criminalization of Blackness, and unconscious bias (Carbado and Rock 2016; Pratt-Harris et al. 2016). Reading the case as an entry into understanding Black heterogeneity and assimilation, Jemima Pierre insightfully considered the descriptions of the unassuming, ordinary, shy, hardworking Diallo:

> I cannot help but wonder if, at some point, Diallo's "Africanness" came to be used to underscore the heinousness of the crime. More specifically, could his immigrant status have allowed him to be implicitly understood as "innocent" in contrast to the African American often assumed to be guilty of criminality. (Pierre 2004, 142)

I concur that the response to Diallo's killing prompts haunting questions about antiblackness and Black immigration. The invocation of "Africanness" as innocence (contrasting with African Americans as guilty) represents a key part of the sorting discourses of ethnic distinction underlined above. The fact that Africanness can be mobilized by an antiblack society as a sympathetic trait (while it simultaneously maintains its geopolitical exploitation of Africa under circulating tropes of Africa's savagery) is not contradictory, but ideologically congruent. This is the central paradox disclosed by this essay. These seemingly contradictory ideas function as a system, a "bureau-cratic administration of Black death-making"(Kitossa, n.d., 2), that celebrates African immigrants as the highest educated population in the United States, while failing to address that "Black immigrants, similar to African Americans, have the highest unemployment rates of any foreign born popu-lation […] and face tremendous amounts of discrimination in the workplace and wage theft" (see also Mason and Austin 2011; Tometi 2016).

Moreover, Diallo's status as an immigrant became a theme in his killers' murder trials. Lawyers for one of the SCU officers sought to justify the shoot-ing by claiming that a "fraudulent asylum application might have caused Mr. Diallo to react nervously to the police". Diallo's attorney denied any such frau-dulence and maintained that any perceived nervousness in Diallo arose from a credible fear rooted in his experiences in Guinea that led him to seek asylum in the first place. Nevertheless, a *New York Times* article invoked exceptional-ism to deny this claim: "There is no indication that Mr. Diallo, who came from a well-educated and relatively well-off Guinean family, feared persecution in Guinea" (Waldman 1999). While this pivots away from police brutality and racial profiling, this "foreigner meme" (Dery 2001) also bends the "positive" of Diallo's educational achievement toward a "negative" of criminality: Diallo becomes sly, cunning, or trying to scam the system, despite his reported love of learning (Razack 2000).

Contrived media suspicion toward Diallo's asylum claim fuelled a nativist argument that his undocumented presence in the U.S. justified his execution. It was never addressed that the police knew nothing about Diallo's immigra-tion status when they shot him, or that the punishment for such demon-strated fraudulence is not summary execution (much less within the jurisdiction of the SCU). In other words, Diallo's immigration status was inves-tigated and invoked only *after* his execution to justify this extrajudicial killing. If, instead, we would look for unusual (and documented) "nervousness", then we might instead ask how and why "one guy may have panicked and the rest followed suit" (Cooper 1999). Consequently, the assumed criminality and "illegality" of immigrants invoked by lawyers to justify the SCU officers' actions continues to be a widespread practice when victims are Black. This discloses just how starkly the materiality of bodies matters in face-to-face encounters, because the only "body of evidence" the SCU had was Diallo's Black body.

If Amadou Diallo's killing illustrates the consequences of not "visibly" or "persuasively enough" demonstrating bona fides of legal and valid immigra-tion in face-to-face encounters, having to secure that validity incriminates the processes of gathering the proof of that immigration as well, even in cases for DV lottery winners. That is, winning the DV lottery alone is not enough; lottery winners must still apply, collect evidence (based on their location and a variety of logistical and legal hurdles), and then pass a visa interview. The case of Abdi Nor Iftin exemplifies these hurdles.

What is at stake here is nothing more than the desire by a human being, fleeing unlivable circumstances in his place of origin, to find a new, safe home elsewhere – a process much more easily accomplished by certain kinds of bodies than others. As certain bodies pass "seamlessly" through the sieve of a border (ultimately, as a kind of social reproduction of citizenship), other bodies get caught in (sometimes multiple) meshes. The implication is that those who pass seamlessly through do so because their "humanness" is assumed, and that more "foreign" bodies must go to more extraordinary lengths to secure the equivalent recognition; hence, Iftin had to navigate the Kenyan documentary landscape to provide evidence that the U.S. system would accept.

For Black people, valid and recognized documentation can prove insufficient, exposing them to suspicion, annulment of their rights, and terrorization. In a notorious example from Texas, 14-year-old Ahmed Mohamed (a U.S. citizen and son of a Sudanese-born immigrant) was taken into custody, not permitted to see his parents, and transported to a juvenile detention facility after bringing a homemade clock to school that was construed by a teacher, the principal, and the police as a bomb. After Mohamed was released to his parents, the police subsequently admitted that the clock could not have been a bomb, and no charges were pressed. While the national virality of the story understandably (and, I would argue, accurately) imputed anti-Muslim sentiment to Mohamed's accusers, the most telling aspect of the creatively crafted depiction of the event is the persistence of conspiracy theories that Ahmed purposefully and maliciously perpetrated a hoax, that he intentionally brought a fake bomb to school.

In the end, what blew up was the story, not the clock, but the volatility of the situation illustrates a precarity and fragility for Mohamed's social position. In the persistence of the conspiracy theories, documentation (and disregard for it) plays a key role. For example, despite documented testimony from his teachers that Ahmed was widely known to be an electronics enthusiast, the conspiratorial imagination shifted attention to that familiar defamation often levelled against Black and Brown youth: the *disciplinary problem*. The documentation of Mohamed's disciplinary conduct – a suspension for blowing soap bubbles in his school's bathroom and an overturned suspension for reacting to anti-Muslim bullying – function as "mediators" that "shape the significance of the signs inscribed on them and their relations with the objects they refer to" (Hull 2012, 253): the claim that Mohamed would deliberately fabricate a bomb threat. His family understood the entanglements that produced the terror Ahmed encountered; the first phone call they made when they brought Ahmed home from the police station was to their local chapter of the National Association for the Advancement of Colored People (NAACP) (Contrera 2016).

In a practical sense, this sudden and tacit annulment of Mohamed's citizenship – not only as legal recognition by the state but also socially in school, society, and the body politic generally – echoes the fragility of the Black immigrant experience, which can similarly (with the stroke of a pen) revoke one's rights in this country, up to and including summary deportation. Such "colonianormativity" (Mendoza 2015, 92) – which relies upon a system that dislocates, dispossesses, and profits from racialized groups – shows that what appear to be fractures of imperial ideology about education and exceptionalism (i.e. an apparent contradiction that Mohamed's ingenuity would be used to frame him as a terrorist) is again actually a coherent ideology that discloses how some people are allowed to innovate and excel in service of wider profit margins, while others are not. This is not only the central paradox of this essay, but it also comes together in some of the "uses" to which the U.S. media put Mohamed (at least until his family, unable to endure the ongoing abuse and pressure they were receiving, emigrated to Qatar). For instance, comedian Dean Obeidallah's (2017) tongue-in-cheek article was titled, "Ahmed Mohamed Is the Muslim Hero America's Been Waiting For", and Seemangal (2015) referenced a globally viral image of Mohamed in handcuffs while wearing a NASA sweatshirt to insist, "Ahmed, and the NASA logo, have catapulted the topic of STEM education in America back into the spotlight. And now, children will be inspired to study STEM thanks to Ahmed's continued interest in it beyond all odds". The effusiveness in both articles aptly illustrates the innocence of Africanness – the simultaneous status of "iconic vessel[s] of human capital" (Murphy 2017, 117) and the perceived threat to the national psyche (as crypto-terrorists) – while channelling this iconicity as a triumph of and for STEM education, assimilation, and exceptionalism. The fact that Mohamed briefly relocated to Qatar adds a perfect commentary on such effusiveness.

Both Iftin and Mohamed's interactions with the state occurred in an era when the Movement for Black Lives had a loud political presence. Viewing Diallo's case post-9/11, we would understand that the analyzed news reports and consider the consequences of profiling where the entanglements between citizenship, race, and sexuality have been introduced into the political discussion of Islamophobia and antiblackness. Diallo's case explicitly states what is implicit in Mohamed's experience. Taken together, these cases beg the question: How must we view religion in relationship with sexuality, race, and citizenship? In all three cases there is ample evidence that the surveillance of Blackness, dark matters, (Browne 2015) looms large in their lives. It is Diallo's Blackness that puts him in the crosshairs of the state. In Mohamed, we see a confluence between antiblackness and Islamophobia playing out within the larger systemic pathologization and criminalization of Black youth in schools. Kenya's War on Terror policies directly impacted Iftin's, and the broadening of the Muslim Ban with a sharp focus on African nations certainly can have consequences in family reunification (see Hornak 2017).

Deviance and American exceptionalism

Ideologically, it is entirely congruent that American exceptionalism means that Diallo, Mohamed, and Iftin could be framed as laudable (as desirable, the trope of the model minority) *and* deviant (Ferguson 2004). Despite an initial valorization – which "admitted" the inclusion of Diallo in the reporting of his killing, and Iftin at the border, and documented Mohamed's ingenuity – the "racial coordinates of imperialism" (Dawson and Schueller 2007, 2) decentre the laudable for deviance. Such transformations are not limited to Blackness, of course, but the speed, suddenness, and extremity (e.g. 41 bullets in Diallo's body, or the instantaneous transformation of a long-naturalized Sudanese family into a clandestine terror cell) with which they occur are unique to Black people's lives. The response-emotion from Diallo's case – "It looks like one guy may have panicked and the rest followed suit" (Cooper 1999) – seems just as applicable to Mohamed's.

This deviance attributed to immigrants has been studied by queer theorists (Cohen 1997; Gopinath 2005; Hong and Ferguson 2011; Manalansan IV 2003), who address "how racial, gender, class, and geopolitical hierarchies constitutively interconnect with normative heterosexuality to produce a range of subalternized social groups and unvalued family forms" (Luibhéid 2008, 296), and thus who is and who is not deemed a desirable immigrant. Hong and Ferguson further asserted that the "African immigrant can only be seen as deviant" (2011, 20) as a call to apply history to current institutional centres of power.

While education created a pathway to gain immigration documentation, and thereby produce citizenship, this alternative genealogy for citizenship bypasses the earlier notion of kinship in the architecture of citizenship law (which excluded people of African descent). As such, the African immigrant presents as a queer subject, one who "inhabits social (and sometimes sexual) margins, throwing into crisis and into relief our most precious and pervasive ideations of the normative, along with the ideological, economic, and political apparatuses in which the violences of normativity operate" (Abdur-Rahman 2012, 6).

It is in this way that queer theory[1] – "as a scholarly conceptual or theoretical approach, as a political perspective and a form of self-identification or assemblage of practices of the self" (Browne and Nash 2010, 3) – methodologically operates as a frame that connects education and the law, as well as racial slavery's temporality, to articulate how the law preserves multiple historical moments for the production of future repercussions connected to those moments (without necessarily reproducing them contemporarily). Thus, while slavery (and its racialized/gendered hierarchies) is constantly renewed in the law through exclusionary forms of structural racism central to and constitutive of settler-colonial states, it also contextualizes contemporary institutional relations as transmissions of that history shifted into the contemporary moment.

Hence, the social reproduction of citizenship at the U.S. border relies upon the historical interdependence of theories of race and sexuality for racial sorting that can be traced throughout all U.S. immigration and citizenship law (Somerville 2000). This sorting produced Diallo, Iftin, and Mohamed as liminal citizens with distinct histories and experiences peppered by moments in which their lives were held up as exceptional, dislocated from the larger and longer history that confers legal and/or social status. That is, they were (first) sorted at the border by the social and political mechanisms that feature federal immigration policy orientations (reinforced by public discourse and social norms), demanding Black exceptionalism precisely at the very moment when such exceptionalism is rendered irrelevant by antiblackness. Blackness, understood relationally, includes:

> subjects normatively defined as black, the relations among blacks, whites, and others, and the practices that produce racial difference. Blackness marks a social relationship of dominance and abjection and potentially one of redress and emancipation; it is a contested figure at the very center of social struggle. (Hartman 1997, 56–57)

If Diallo's life was marked by a governmentality born of the War on Drugs, Mohamed's "clock-making prowess" and Iftin's "successful crossing" are marked by that history layered on a governmentality born of the War on Terror as well, with neither ever fully addressed openly. That these African immigrants were framed as exceptional is part of that (internal and external border) sorting upon which economies thrive.

African immigrants are encouraged to assimilate, but that encouragement is not toward the group whose lived experiences with racism, surveillance, and extrajudicial force mirrors (without being identical to) their own. If we trace discourses of race in the earliest iterations of U.S. citizenship and immigration law, along with the ensuing amendments and precedent decisions, it is clear that the constantly shifting and sometimes elusive legal definition of citizenship has been adjudicated based on social constructions of phenotype with implications for who gets what rights and when. Or, as Leigh Patel wrote:

> Black Americans and Native Americans encounter, more than any other populations, simultaneous conferral and denial of U.S. citizenship. [...] The United States' Voting Rights Act of 1964 guaranteed the right to vote for all Black

Americans, but it is renewable every 25 years, meaning also that it is fundamentally temporary. (Patel 2017, 64)

—and also, I would argue, always up for debate.

Consequently, the norms of middle-class, male-dominated, and family-centric communities are restricted to certain people who are the product of certain conditions. Hortense Spillers (1987) documented and theorized how Black families in the United States are defined by and against family normativity, even as Black families were systemically destroyed by centuries of slavery. For example, Spillers explained that gender identities are subject to familial arrangements under forced labour systems where violence and torture are ever-present realities or threats for enslaved Black women. Spillers' explanation of how Blackness is produced through practices of un-gendering reorients our thinking. That is, even though un-gendering emerges from violence, it has become central in queering the reproductive systems of citizenship that order institutions excluding Black people.

In this context, "the customary lexis of sexuality, including 'reproduction,' 'motherhood,' 'pleasure,' and 'desire' are thrown into unrelieved crisis" (Spillers 1987, 458). Understanding race in the United States, therefore, binds sexuality to a racial identity "conceived, regulated, and disciplined through sexuality – through sexual practices, violations, and norms" (Abdur-Rahman 2012, 2), an identity that restricts human beings to two distinct sex/gender categories (male/man and female/woman) with performances and performativity rooted in racialized power imbalances. These ideologies fuse Blackness and queerness, thereby interpellating Black people's "positionality *vis-à-vis* the normative" (Halperin 1995, 65) as outsiders, as noncitizens, and even as non-human subjects (Spillers 1987; Walcott 2014; Wynter 2003).

While these imperial constructs have a global reach, each local context has specific implications through norms, laws, and policies. Spillers (1987) demonstrated that Black subjectivity and state policies are traceable to a system of power and the ownership of property, but Black immigrant subjectivity can also be restricted by/to colonial patriarchal framings, albeit with different pressures, violence, and outcomes. Although globalization can shift the sense of what is local, Black people living in the U.S. have specific, varied, and fraught relationships with a nation-state driven by global Eurocentric settler-colonial and transatlantic slavery histories. These realities rely on a discourse about race that is "colonial [in] origin and character, but [...] has proven to be more durable and stable than the colonialism in whose matrix it was established" (Quijano 2000, 215).

That racialized bodies entering new geographical spaces experience embodied subjectivities that are tied to language or culture (Butler 1993) parallels how settler-colonialism conjures up "the native into existence and perpetuates his existence" (Fanon 1963, 36) for the settler-colonial project. This highlights how both spectacular and quotidian instantiations of colonial violence place the (generated) subject in a state of contradiction (McKittrick 2006). Similarly to Foucault (1980),[2] Amina Mama (1995) argued that Black subjectivity should be traced through struggles of power and circulations of knowledge, while Abdur-Rahman astutely positioned sexuality as "a crucial component of racial difference" (2012, 6) with concomitant implications for (desirable) citizenship. While these subjectivities of Black people living in the United States are disciplined and curtailed based on a specific social Blackness (regardless of one's attachment to the state or time of migration), they are also produced by "diverse cultural referents available to many Black people" (Mama 1995, 52). Mama explained:

> Racial oppression itself is inadequately conceptualized as monolithic, total, and homogeneous in its effects. The nuances and intricate set of social etiquette and behavior, of betrayal and collusion, of inversion and resistance that constitute racism as a social process are barely touched upon. (1995, 48)

Not to settle into neat categories of race or space, and remembering that the relationship between race, bodies, and space is volatile, underlying questions emerge: What happens as a person enters a new geographic location, loaded with numerous historically contingent discourses? As persons who come to the United States from a nation where race bears on national and identity politics in culturally and historically contingent ways, how are their subjectivities (at the nexus of legal subjectivity,[3] Black subjectivity, gendered subjectivity, and numerous other sites of production) shifted? While skin is not the only marker of race, one cannot separate the social from the phenotypical, because the body not only masks the ways that society imposes upon it, but also obscures how the body constructs the social and all of its concepts, capacities, commitments, and communities.

Debates on immigration have largely been predicated on the experiences of "visible" immigrants depicted as threatening, on "controlling unauthorized immigration" (Luibhéid 2008) by any means, on the policing of persons whose racialized bodies are read as foreign, unauthorized, and (in popular and political rhetoric) "illegal", and above all, on the relationship of bodies to the state. Missing from this is an emphasis on those embodied experiences of Blackness that not only provide insights into the intimate encounters of immigrants, but also hold rich insight into the links between movement, emplacement, identity, and citizenship, in particular, the queer experiences brought into being (Fanon 1963) at the border (when not rendered already invisible by exclusion in the visa office) by colonianormativity (Mendoza 2015).

Like any immigrant group in the U.S., Black immigrants often discover upon arrival the ubiquitous challenges of U.S. immigration, including anti-immigrant discourses, low wages, and demands to forswear prior national loyalties and identities. Additionally, they encounter pervasive racism and antiblack bias across numerous forms of American life. Similar to U.S.-born Black people, Black immigrants can be targeted at any moment by state surveillance, state violence, or informal (but sanctioned) reprisals, whether cisgendered or not, even as such targeting tacitly discloses the queerness and contradiction of (citizen or immigrant) Blackness. Such embodied experiences point to shifting subjectivities, and how knowledge creation and transformation is a hegemonic project that always responds to actors' desires and needs, as well as institutional demands, as the ground that informs and strengthens modernity (Mignolo 2007). Migration and geography have always been determining factors in African American identities (Griffin 1996). Migration and place, then, have remained central arguments in authenticity debates (whether within the U.S. or concerning the African continent). Overarchingly, however, empire sets "the parameters and limits of thought and practice, sanctioning and prescribing normal and /or deviant behaviours" (Hardt and Negri 2000, 23) in such subjectivities and debates, whether locally (in citizenship) or globally (in settler-colonialism).

While the experiences of Black immigrants are rarely visible in popular discourse – and then, frequently framed as exceptional stories of triumphant assimilation (Iftin) or imputed crypto-terrorism (Diallo, Mohamed) – nonetheless, these experiences provide key insights on not only national frontiers (and what kinds of bodies cross easily or not), but also on the queering of bodies as suitable (or not) for national identity. Keeping these experiences and locations of Blackness within global and local contexts, one turns to the immigrant as a figure of hybridity – but one not only (or not simply) "based not on the exoticism of multiculturalism or the diversity of cultures, [...] on the inscription and articulation of culture's hybridity" (Bhabha 1994, 38), but also in the way that Black immigrant experiences hinge on that paradoxical simultaneity of valorization and terror highlighted in this essay and drawn by McKittrick (2006) as a state of contradiction. Connecting to the afterlife of slavery, this contradiction also echoes and evokes a kind of double consciousness (DuBois 1903/2009).

Conclusion

Crossing the border, Black immigrants are met with the enforcement of US racial taxonomies: an introduction to "uneven devaluation of racialized life" (Hong and Ferguson 2011, 11) where their lives are ordered by the *idea* of Blackness, the *abstraction to* bodies (Young 2010). Within the context of the U.S. settler-colonial state, this desire for immigrants to present themselves as desirable, worthy, and productive citizens, along with its systems of difference and exclusion, is part of a "history of the present" (Foucault 1977, 31), which is always already racialized. A queer analysis allows us to "denaturalize" (Somerville 2007) assumptions about how citizenship, for African immigrants, is produced; and brings into sharper focus the type of citizenship that is produced within the longer history of Black citizenship in the U.S. These systems of difference and exclusion rely upon positioning Blackness vis-à-vis the construction of whiteness-as-a-condition-of-citizenship. As such, when seeking to meet immigration requirements, applicants reiterate "discourses already operating in culture, discourses saturated with history and ripe with the potential for appropriation ... they rely upon certain discursive expectations to gain recognition as subjects" (West 2013, 28).

The hopeful narrativization of Abdi's path to U.S. citizenship, not the historical or geopolitical context that produced his lived experiences, serves as a reinforcement of American exceptionalism. Unstated, however, is that when a Black immigrant encounters the sentiment "Be American", this is rarely (if ever) a directive to be an African American. Rather, such jingoism calls less for assimilation and more for the (self)policing of the borders of language, dominant culture, and a settler-colonial history. Arguably an "agreement" or a command faced by documented U.S. immigrants, for Black immigrants, the impossibility of this agreement is immediately (or tragically, as for Diallo and Mohamed) self-evident. More broadly, what does this central contradiction say about "This American Life" (or, more capaciously, for "being American") for all immigrants, for the social project of the United States, and the queered possibilities of identity at (and across) borders? What possibilities for gender become visible in the erotics of crossing, passing, and trans-gressing? And ultimately, how does this queer our understanding of Blackness – which produces citizens disentangled from family reunification, birthright citizenship, and acknowledged categories of bodies – and continue to reproduce or challenge structures of power?

The media narratives of Abdi Nor Iftin, Amadou Diallo, and Ahmed Mohammed, immigrants who manage to enter the US and attempt to cleave to the American dream. Yet, the long history of race in the making of American citizenship renders them ineligible in pursuit of the American dream because of their Blackness. Blackness, biopolitics, and borders are sites to understand the lived realities of Black citizens and immigrants, and collectively, they bring into sharp focus the precarity and fragility of Black life and the volatility of Black space in general. Black immigrant life in a new geographic location has historically been met with contingent discourses and social practices that threaten Black survival and Black humanity itself, notwithstanding any challenges to structures of power, specifically, the corporeal experiences and material significance of Black bodies as an afterlife of slavery as revealed in African immigrancy to the U.S. and the subsequent state surveillance of such bodies. In the end, the interpellation of Blackness,

Notes

1. I invoke the queer in its radical political potential, not only challenging hetero-normativity (Ferguson, 2004), but also encouraging the fluidity and movement of peoples' sexual lives (Cohen, 1997). "Queer" describes a critical relationship to existing sexual and social norms, recognizing particular political, economic, and social geographies and communities that transcend space and time; it is "a regulatory ideal, an elusive construct, a dangerous component of hegemony" (Abdur-Rahman 2012, 5; cf. Cohen 1997; Cobb et al. 2005).
2. Foucault (1980) argued that the subject is the result of social processes, and that subjectivity is produced by a system of knowledge that controls the subject's identity.
3. Legal scholar Anja Louis provided a current definition of legal subjectivity as "the ability to bear rights and responsibilities, basic equality before the law, respect and self-determination" (2005, 12).

Disclosure statement

No potential conflict of interest was reported by the author(s).

ORCID

Brenda N. Sanya http://orcid.org/0000-0003-0270-4012

References

Abdur-Rahman, A. 2012. *Against the Closet: Black Political Longing and the Erotics of Race*. Durham, NC: Duke University Press.

Ali, A. I. 2017. "The Impossibility of Muslim Citizenship." *Diaspora, Indigenous, and Minority Education* 11 (3): 110–116. doi:10.1080/15595692.2017.1325355.

Althusser, L. 1971. "Ideology and Ideological State Apparatuses (Notes Towards an Investigation)." In *Lenin and Philosophy and Other Essays*, edited by L. Althusser, 127–186. New York, NY: New Left Books.

BBC News. 2000. "Officers Cleared of Diallo Murder." *British Broadcasting Corporation News*, February 26. http://news.bbc.co.uk/2/hi/americas/657454.stm.

Bhabha, H. K. 1994. *The Location of Culture*. New York, NY: Routledge.

Browne, S. 2015. *Dark Matters: On the Surveillance of Blackness*. Durham, NC: Duke Univeristy Press.

Browne, K., and C. J. Nash. 2010. "Queer Methods and Methodologies: An Introduction." In *Queer Methods and Methodologies: Intersecting Queer Theories and Social Science Research*, edited by K. Browne, and C. J. Nash, 1–24. New York, NY: Ashgate.

Butler, J. 1993. *Bodies that Matter: On the Discursive Limits of Sex*. New York, NY: Routledge.

Callier, D. M. 2018. "Still, Nobody Mean More: Engaging Black Feminist Pedagogies on Questions of the Citizen and Human in Anti-Blackqueer Times." *Curriculum Inquiry* 48 (1): 16–34. doi:10.1080/03626784.2017.1409594.

Carbado, D. W., and P. Rock. 2016. "What Exposes African Americans to Police Violence?" *Harvard Civil Rights-Civil Liberties Law Review* 51: 159–187.

Cobb, M., D. L. Eng, R. A. Ferguson, E. Freeman, G. Gopinath, J. Halberstam, J. R. Jakobsen, J. O. Lee, M. F. Manalansan IV, and J. E. Muñoz. 2005. "What's Queer about Queer Studies now?" *Social Text* 23 (3): 1–15.

Cohen, C. 1997. "Punks, Bulldaggers, and Welfare Queens: The Radical Potential of Queer Politics." *GLQ: A Journal of Lesbian and Gay Studies* 3: 437–465. doi:10. 1215/10642684-3-4-437.

Contrera, J. 2016. "A Year Ago, Ahmed Mohamed Became 'Clock Boy.' Now, He Can't Escape that Moment." *The Washington Post*. August 2. https://www. washingtonpost.com/lifestyle/style/a-year-ago-ahmed-mohamed-became-clock-boy-now-he-cant-escape-that-moment/2016/08/02/2b8650be-484b-11e6-bdb9-701687974517_story.html.

Cooper, M. 1999. "Officers in Bronx Fire 41 Shots, and an Unarmed Man Is Killed." *New York Times*. February 5. https://www.nytimes.com/1999/02/05/nyregion/officers-in-bronx-fire-41-shots-and-an-unarmed-man-is-killed.html.

Dawson, A., and M. J. Schueller. 2007. "Exceptional State: Contemporary U.S. Culture and the New Imperialism." In *New Americanists*. Durham, NC: Duke Univeristy Press.

Dery, L. V. 2001. "Amadou Diallo and the Foreigner Meme: Interpreting the Application of Federal Court Interpreter Laws." *Florida Law Review* 53: 230–291.

DuBois, W. E. B. 2009. *The Souls of Black Folk*. New York, NY: Oxford University Press. (Original work published 1903).

Esposito, R. 2008. *Bios: Biopolitics and Philosophy*. Minneapolis, MN: University of Minnesota Press.

Fanon, F. 1963. *The Wretched of the Earth*. New York, NY: Grove Press. doi:10.2307/20048263.

Ferguson, R. A. 2004. *Aberrations in Black: Toward a Queer of Color Critique*. Minneapolis, MN: University of Minnesota Press.

Foucault, M. 1977. *Discipline and Punish: The Birth of the Prison*. New York, NY: Vintage.

Foucault, M. 1978. *The History of Sexuality. Volume 1: An Introduction: Vol. I*. New York, NY: Random House.

Foucault, M. 1980. "Power/Knowledge: Selected Interviews and Other Writings, 1972–1977." In *New York (Vol. 23)*. New York, NY: Pantheon Books.

Glass, I. 2015. "Abdi and the GoldenTicket 2015." *This American Life*. July. https://www. thisamericanlife.org/560/abdi-and-the-golden-ticket.

Glass, I. 2020. "Abdi the American 2020." *This American Life*. February. https://shortcut. thisamericanlife.org/#/clipping/693?_k=oh82eu.

Goldman, J. 2000. "NYPD Officer Says He Mistook Wallet for Gun." *Los Angeles Times*. February 15. https://www.latimes.com/archives/la-xpm-2000-feb-15-mn-64450-story.html.

Gopinath, G. 2005. *Impossible Desires: Queer Diasporas and South Asian Public Cultures*. Durham, NC: Duke University Press.

Graham, D. A. 2016. "Maine's Governor Insists the Problem Isn't His Racism—It's Being Called a Racist." *The Atlantic*. August 30. https://www.theatlantic.com/politics/archive/2016/08/paul-lepage-resign-racism/498020/.

Griffin, F. J. 1996. *"Who Set You Flowin'?": The African-American Migration Narrative*. Oxford: Oxford University Press.

Grunwald, M. 1999. "Immigrant Killed by Police Mourned." *Washington Post*, A3. February 13.

Halperin, D. M. 1995. *Saint Foucault: Towards a Gay Hagiography*. Oxford: Oxford University Press.

Hardt, M., and A. Negri. 2000. *Empire*. Cambridge: Harvard University Press.

Hartman, S. V. 1997. *Scenes of Subjection: Terror, Slavery, and Self-Making in Nineteenth-Century America*. Oxford: Oxford University Press.

Holland, S. P. 2012. *The Erotic Life of Racism*. Durham, NC: Duke University Press.

Hong, G. K., and R. A. Ferguson. 2011. *Strange Affinities: The Gender and Sexual Politics of Comparative Racialization*. Durham, NC: Duke University Press.

Hornak, L. 2017. "The Story of Two Brothers, One Green Card and Trump's Ban." *The World*. February 14. https://www.pri.org/stories/2017-02-14/story-two-brothers-one-green-card-and-trumps-ban.

Hull, M. S. 2012. "Documents and Bureaucracy." *Annual Review of Anthropology* 41 (1): 251–267. doi:10.1146/annurev.anthro.012809.104953.

Kelley, R. D. G. 2002. *Freedom Dreams: The Black Radical Imagination*. Boston, MA: Beacon Press.

Kitossa, T. n.d. "Anti-Black Sexual Racism: Linking White Police Violence, COVID-19, and Popular Culture." *Antipode: A Radical Journal of Geography*, 1–13.

Knox, L. 2020. *Civil Rights Groups Condemn Trump's Travel-Ban Expansion to Six African Countries*. February 27. https://www.nbcnews.com/news/nbcblk/civil-rights-groups-condemn-trump-s-travel-ban-expansion-six-n1142231.

Louis, A. 2005. *Women and the Law: Carmen de Burgos, an Early Feminist*. Woodbridge: Tamesis.

Luibhéid, E. 2008. "Sexuality, Migration, and the Shifting Line Between Legal and Illegal Status." *GLQ: A Journal of Lesbian and Gay Studies* 14 (2–3): 289–315. doi:10.1215/10642684-2007-034.

Mama, A. 1995. *Beyond the Masks: Race, Gender and Subjectivity*. New York: Routledge.

Manalansan IV, M. F. 2003. *Global Divas: Filipino Gay Men in the Diaspora*. Durham, NC: Duke University Press.

Mason, P. L., and A. Austin. 2011. *The Low Wages of Black Immigrants: Wage Penalties for U.S.-Born and Foreign-Born Black Workers*. http://www.epi.org/publication/the_low_wages_of_black_immigrants/.

McKittrick, K. 2006. "Demonic Grounds: Black Women and the Cartographies of Struggle." In *Annals of the Association of American Geographers*, Vol. 97, Issue 2. Minneapolis, MN: University of Minnesota Press.

Mendoza, V. R. 2015. *Metroimperial Intimacies: Fantasy, Racial-Sexual Governance, and the Philippines in U.S. Imperialism, 1899–1913*. Durham, NC: Duke University Press.

Mignolo, W. D. 2007. "Introduction: Coloniality of Power and De-colonial Thinking." *Cultural Studies* 21 (2–3): 155–167. doi:10.1080/09502380601162498.

Mohanty, C. T. 2003. "'Under Western Eyes' Revisited: Feminist Solidarity Through Anticapitalist Struggles." *Signs: Journal of Women in Culture and Society* 28 (2): 499–535.

Murphy, M. 2017. *The Economization of Life*. Durham, NC: Duke University Press.

Ngai, M. M. 2004. *Impossible Subjects: Illegal Aliens and the Making of Modern America: Illegal Aliens and the Making of Modern America*. Princeton: Princeton University Press.

Nuñez, D. C. 2016. "Mapping Citizenship: Status, Membership, and the Path in Between." *Utah Law Review, No. 3*. https://dc.law.utah.edu/ulr/vol2016/iss3/2.

Obeidallah, D. 2017. "Ahmed Mohamed Is the Muslim Hero America Has Been Waiting For." *The Daily Beast*. April 14. https://www.thedailybeast.com/ahmed-mohamed-is-the-muslim-hero-americas-been-waiting-for.

Patel, S. 2015. "The road to Garissa." *The New Inquiry*. https://thenewinquiry.com/the-road-to-garissa/.

Patel, L. 2017. "The Ink of Citizenship." *Curriculum Inquiry* 47 (1): 62–68.

Pescaro, M. 2019. "Maine Mayor Resigns after His Racist Text Message Is Leaked." *NBC Boston*. March 8. https://www.nbcboston.com/news/local/lewiston-maine-mayor-shane-bouchard-resigns-after-his-racist-text-message-is-leaked/1379/.

Pierre, J. 2004. "Black Immigrants in the United States and the 'Cultural Narratives' of Ethnicity." *Identities* 11 (2): 141–170. doi:10.1080/10702890490451929.

Pratt-Harris, N. C., M. M. Sinclair, C. B. Bragg, N. R. Williams, K. N. Ture, B. D. Smith, I. Marshall Jr, and L. Brown. 2016. "Police-Involved Homicide of Unarmed Black Males: Observations by Black Scholars in the Midst of the April 2015 Baltimore Uprising." *Journal of Human Behavior in the Social Environment* 26 (3–4): 377–389. doi:10.1080/10911359.2015.1132853.

Quijano, A. 2000. "Coloniality of Power and Eurocentrism in Latin America." *International Sociology* 15 (2): 215–232. doi:10.1177/0268580900015002005.

Razack, S. 2000. "'Simple Logic': Race, the Identity Documents Rule and the Story of a Nation Besieged and Betrayed." *Journal of Law and Social Policy* 15: 181–209. http://heinonlinebackup.com/hol-cgi-bin/get_pdf.cgi?handle=hein.journals/jlsp15&section=9.

Reddy, C. 2011. *Freedom with Violence: Race, Sexuality, and the US State*. Durham, NC: Duke University Press.

Roberts, D. 2011. *Fatal Invention: How Science, Politics, and Big Business Re-create Race in the Twenty-First Century*. New York, NY: The New Press.

Robinson, C. J. 1983. *Black Marxism: The Making of the Black Radical Tradition*. Chapel Hill: Univ of North Carolina Press.

Saldanha, A. 2006. "Reontologising Race: The Machinic Geography of Phenotype." *Environment and Planning: Society and Space* 24 (1): 9–24. doi:10.1068/d61j.

Sanya, B. N. 2017. *DISSERTATON States of Discretion: Black Migrating Bodies and Citizenship in the United States*. University of Illinois at Urbana-Champaign. http://hdl.handle.net/2142/97582.

Sanya, B. N., K. Desai, D. M. Callier, and C. McCarthy. 2018. "Desirable and Disposable: Educative Practices and the Making of (Non) citizens." *Curriculum Inquiry* 48 (1): 1–15. doi:10.1080/03626784.2017.1421308.

Seemangal, R. 2015. "NASA Is the Unlikeliest 'Design Firm' in History." *The New York Observer*. September. https://observer.com/2015/09/nasa-is-the-unlikeliest-design-firm-in-human-history/.

Sharp, D. 2016. "Maine Governor: Out-of-State Drug Dealers Getting 'Young White' Girls Pregnant." *CBS Boston*. January 8. https://boston.cbslocal.com/2016/01/08/maine-governor-paul-lepage-drug-dealers-young-white-girls-pregnant/.

Simpson, G. 2013. *"You Are All Terrorists": Kenyan Police Abuse of Refugees in Nairobi*. Report states United States. https://www.hrw.org/sites/default/files/reports/kenya0513_ForUpload_0_0.pdf

Somerville, S. B. 2000. *Queering the Color Line: Race and the Invention of Homosexuality in American Culture*. Durham, NC: Duke University Press.

Somerville, S. B. 2005. "Sexual Aliens and the Racialized State: A Queer Reading of the 1952 US Immigration and Nationality Act." In *Queer Migrations: Sexuality, US*

Citizenship, and Border Crossings, edited by E. Luibhéid, and L. Cantú Jr, 75–91. Minneapolis, MN: University of Minnesota Press.

Somerville, S. B. (2007). "Queer." In *Keywords for American Cultural Studies*, edited by B. Burgett & G. Hendler, 187–191. New York, NY: New York University Press.

Sperber, A. 2015. "Little Mogadishu, Under Siege." *Foreign Policy*. April 14. https://foreignpolicy.com/2015/04/14/kenya-shabab-somalia-garissa-kenyatta/.

Spillers, H. J. 1987. "Mama's Baby, Papa's Maybe: An American Grammar Book." *Diacritics* 17 (2): 65–81. doi:10.2307/464747.

Tometi, O. 2016. "The Difficult Bridge Facing Black Immigrants." *EBONY Magazine*. March. http://www.ebony.com/news-views/black-immigrants-challenges#axzz4Ho as971H.

Walcott, R. 2014. "The Problem of the Human: Black Ontologies and 'the Coloniality of Our Being'." In *Postcoloniality-Decoloniality-Black Critique: Joints and Fissures*, edited by S. Broeck, and C. Junker, 93–105. Frankfurt: Campus Verlag.

Waldman, A. 1999. "His Lawyer Says Diallo Lied on Request for Political Asylum." *New York Times*. March 17. http://www.nytimes.com/1999/03/17/nyregion/his-lawyer-says-diallo-lied-on-request-for-political-asylum.html.

Weheliye, A. G. 2014. *Habeas Viscus: Racializing Assemblages, Biopolitics, and Black Feminist Theories of the Human*. Durham, NC: Duke University Press.

West, I. 2013. *Transforming Citizenships: Transgender Articulations of the Law*. New York, NY: New York University Press.

Wynter, S. 2003. "Unsettling the Coloniality of Being/Power/Truth/Freedom: Towards the Human, after Man, Its Overrepresentation—An Argument." *CR: The New Centennial Review* 3 (3): 257–337.

Young, H. 2010. *Embodying Black Experience: Stillness, Critical Memory, and the Black Body*. Ann Arbor, MI: The University of Michigan Press.

Borderlands of reproduction: bodies, borders, and assisted reproductive technologies in Israel/Palestine

Gala Rexer ⓘ

ABSTRACT

This article focuses on the intersection of bodies, borders, and assisted reproductive technologies (ART) in Israel/Palestine. By turning to Palestinian women's experiences in Israeli hospitals, the case of sperm smuggling in the West Bank, and Israeli medical staff's perception of the fertility clinic, this article examines reproductive border-crossings. Israel's fertility economy is thriving and the country is among the most liberal states worldwide regarding the regulation, implementation, and subsidization of ART. However, Israel's pronatalism is best described as selective and stratified. As a function of settler colonialism, it mainly targets Jewish citizens of Israel, which results in a politicization of Palestinian and Israeli bodies and populations. Drawing on fifty in-depth interviews with Palestinian women and medical staff in Israeli fertility clinics conducted in Israel/Palestine between 2016 and 2019, this article provides a spatial analysis of assisted reproduction, drawing out continuities between past and present technologies of power in medical space.

Introduction

Within current gendered geopolitical power structures, reproduction has to be understood as a focal point in the imagination, production, and management of borders. In nationalist, (settler) colonial, and capitalist population politics, reproductive concerns intersect with race, class, sexuality, and gender (Clarke and Haraway 2018). Reproduction is even more bound up in border politics when access to reproductive technologies is state-regulated, as has been in most countries since the emergence of technologies such as in-vitro fertilization (IVF) in the late 1970s.[1] Reproductive politics take centre stage in post Trump's North America, in the UK in times of Brexit, or in European states' growing right-wing movements (Franklin and Ginsburg 2019). These developments give rise to questions concerning the relationship between the individual body and nation-states' border anxieties. Touching upon intimate, everyday decision making as well as broader discourses around population politics, these questions are central to the production of culture (Ginsburg and Rapp 1995) and bio- and necropolitical in scope (Foucault 2008; Mbembe 2003).

In Israel/Palestine, the question of reproduction has and continues to be central to settler state-building, evident in pronatalist attitudes and various population policies since the establishment of the state of Israel in 1948 (Vertommen 2017a). Israel's fertility economy is thriving and, as has been discussed extensively, the country is among the most liberal states worldwide regarding the regulation, implementation, and subsidization of assisted reproductive technologies (ART) (Birenbaum-Carmeli 2016; Lipkin and Samama 2010; Sperling and Simon 2010). At the same time, Israel's pronatalism and technological progress in the realm of ART has been described as selective and stratified. Palestinian citizens of Israel make up 20% of the Israeli population and should hence de jure derive benefit from Israel's repro-economy. However, as a function of settler colonialism, Israel's pronatalism mainly targets Jewish citizens of Israel, which results in a politicization of Palestinian and Israeli bodies and populations – both within and beyond the Green Line (Ivry 2010; Kanaaneh 2002; Nahman 2013; Portugese 1998; Puar 2017; Vertommen 2017a; Weiss 2002). Legal definitions of practices such as surrogacy or egg donation illustrate the state's ideological stance: Israeli law does not allow surrogacy for gay couples, and cross-religious egg donation and surrogacy are prohibited if either the intended mother, the egg donor, or the surrogate is Jewish (Birenbaum-Carmeli and Montebruno 2019; Teman 2018). These specifications suggest that Israeli reproductive policies work to reproduce heteronormativity as well as narrowly Jewish cultural, religious, and political notions of kinship, motherhood, and citizenship (Mitra, Schicktanz, and Patel 2018).

A large body of scholarly work has focused on transnational reproduction economies and cross-border practices of assisted reproduction, or "reproflows" (Inhorn and Gürtin 2011; Merleau-Ponty, Vertommen, and Pucéat 2018; Mitra, Schicktanz, and Patel 2018; Nahman 2013, 2016). While these studies focus on transnational or comparative analyses of the transfer of knowledge, bodies, and body parts across state borders, this article focuses on the intersection of bodies, spatial regimes, and assisted reproductive technologies within the "de-bordered" borders of Israel/Palestine (Tawil-Souri 2012).[2] By attending to the ongoing (un)making of borders in the Israeli-Palestinian situation, and foregrounding how Palestinian women undergoing fertility treatment in Israeli medical institutions perform border-crossings, this article highlights the spatial dimension of the body politics of assisted reproduction.

Attending to spatial questions is crucial to understanding the historical and current developments in Israel/Palestine (Parsons and Salter 2008;

Tawil-Souri 2011, 2012). Space is, after all, "a focal point for power, but space is also part of a rivalry between the one who controls it and others who are trying to reclaim it and to resist this dominance" (Sowa 2014, 1). Bringing a spatial lens to an analysis of assisted reproduction draws out important historical continuities between past and present technologies of power. Questions of land and demography shaped the conflict between Zionist settlers and indigenous Palestinians from early on (Masalha 2012). The Zionist slogan of "a land without people for a people without land" thus illustrates how borders, bodies, and reproduction were always entangled in the case of Israel/Palestine.

Bringing a spatial lens to reproduction also underscores the experience of Palestinian women living, and trying to get pregnant, in Israel/Palestine. Fragmented across Israel, the West Bank, East Jerusalem, and Gaza, Palestinian women's access to (reproductive) health is embedded in equally fragmented jurisdictions, structured and constrained by a variety of borders. The 1.6 million Palestinian citizens of Israel enjoy the same access and subsidies to reproductive medicine as Jewish-Israelis. However, most fertility clinics are located in Jewish-Israeli majority areas and, as I will show in this article, clinical encounters are often shaped by linguistic and affective boundaries that sharpen institutional racism (Zu'bi 2018). Roughly 3 million Palestinians live in the West Bank and about 2 million in Gaza. These populations are subject to Israel's permit regime, which controls all passage between Palestinian territories and Israel. If Palestinians require a health service that is not available in either the West Bank or Gaza, they have to go through a complicated and deliberately opaque process of issuing a permit to enter or pass through Israeli territory (Berda 2017; Majadle 2020). Of these 5 million Palestinians, 337,000 live in occupied East Jerusalem and hold the status of so-called permanent residents (their ID card is usually referred to as "Jerusalem ID"). Permanent residents are allowed to live and work in Israel, receive social benefits, hold an Israeli health insurance, and are thus entitled to receive fertility treatment in Israeli hospitals. However, their residency status is fragile and can be revoked at any time. In order to ensure that their children obtain residency status, East Jerusalem residents must give birth in an Israeli hospital. A spatial emphasis is thus key in order to understand issues faced by Palestinian women who desire to get pregnant in Israeli fertility clinics (Birenbaum-Carmeli and Kochman-Haimov 2010; Shalhoub-Kevorkian 2015a).

Drawing on these approaches and insights, this article focuses on the complicated intersection of bodies, borders, and ART in Israel/Palestine. The empirical material presented here is part of a larger research project on the body politics of assisted reproduction in Israel/Palestine, which I have been conducting since 2016. It constitutes the general material corpus the article is based on; however, only those materials decidedly speaking to the categories of space and borders were included in the analysis presented here. The material encompasses 20 in-depth semi-structured interviews with medical staff in Israeli fertility clinics, 20 interviews with Palestinian women (Palestinian citizens of Israel and residents of East Jerusalem) going through fertility treatment in Israeli medical institutions, seven interviews with Palestinian women living in the West Bank who got pregnant by using their imprisoned husbands' sperm in IVF processes, and three interviews with medical staff of West Bank fertility centres, facilitating the process of sperm smuggling. Most interviews with medical staff were conducted in English, while roughly two-thirds of the interviews with Palestinian women were conducted together with an Arabic interpreter and subsequently translated and transcribed to English.

This article examines three critical spaces of assisted reproduction in Israel/Palestine. I begin with the space of the Israeli fertility clinic, illustrating how medical staff describe and imagine the fertility clinic as what I call a *utopian non-place* and, by doing so, construct its borders against an outside, which is not able to penetrate the medical sphere. To challenge this narrative, I turn to several routes of medical exchange between Israeli medical institutions and the West Bank. These circuits emphasize how the borders of the ostensibly neutral medical space are in fact porous. Finally, I turn to those who travel these routes and navigate the borderlands of reproduction: Palestinian women striving to get pregnant. Attending to reproductive technologies from a spatial perspective provides theoretical insights into how space and borders are constructed in Israel/Palestine, and how they enable or curtail access to reproduction in material, symbolic, and linguistic ways. Ultimately, this article underscores how every body and every cell is a matter of political concern under settler colonialism (Gutkowski 2020).

The Israeli fertility clinic: a *utopian non-place*?

Medical staff in Israeli public and private hospitals and fertility clinics described their working environment as a very particular space: depleted of the so-called conflict and thus ostensibly apolitical. In what follows, I outline how staff frame the fertility clinic a *utopian non-place*. Drawing from anthropologist Marc Augé's notion of a "non-place" (Augé 1995), I highlight how medical staff's own understanding of the Israeli fertility clinic works to unmake political borders.

Irit,[3] a Jewish-Israeli obstetrician-gynecologist working in the IVF unit of a hospital in Jerusalem referred to her unit as a "weird capsule" and continued: "even if, you know, Intifada could happen, and we are close to all these terroristic sites, where terrible things happen, but in this room, it's like an extra-territorial room, okay?". Similarly, Lena, a Jewish-Israeli senior physician in the same hospital underlined that there is something strange about this situation, stating that she might be a little naive in framing the hospital like that, "but I think when it comes to health and medicine, you know, it's outside, maybe I'm naive, but I feel that in a hospital we are just a no man's land". Two nurses and a medical assistant I interviewed in the same unit referred to their shared medical space as "neutral" in a similar way. What all these descriptions have in common is a clear demarcation of an inside/outside boundary. In the outside world "terrible things happen", but they are not able to penetrate the inside of the medical space. Existing political tensions are acknowledged, for example, by the mention, almost in passing, of the prospect of (another) Intifada breaking out on the hospital's doorstep. Reference to "all these terroristic sites" further stresses the spatial aspect. While it is not clear which places exactly Irit is referring to, her remark suggests that nearby Palestinian places of residency in East Jerusalem or sites of previous clashes between Palestinians and the Israeli military are meant. Furthermore, the description of the fertility clinic as a "capsule" or "extra-territorial room" intensifies its perceived spatial insularity. Such descriptions evoke Augé's notion of non-places as not actually places but spaces "which cannot be defined as relational, or historical, or concerned with identity" (Augé 1995, 78). Augé defines non-places as interstitial spaces, surrendering people to the fleeting, the temporary, and the ephemeral. All of these characteristics are present in the descriptions of the IVF unit of the Jerusalem hospital: demarcated from an imagined outside, and thus not in any relation to what happens there. The history and presence of the social world outside does not penetrate its borders, resulting in a space described as "weird" or at least so peculiar one has to be "naive" to believe in its existence.

The Zionist project in Palestine was informed by various references to the concept of *terra nullius,* interpreting the land as empty and therefore as a space for settler colonial development (Lentin 2016; Vertommen 2017b). The association of a "no man's land" echoes the notion of *terra nullius.* This is reinforced by similar remarks, describing multiculturalism as the guiding principle of the fertility clinic, and the belief in Israeli medical space as universal. In a place that belongs to no one and is structured by universal notions of equality, "a person entering the space of a non-place is relieved of his [*sic*] usual determinants" (Augé 1995, 103). These descriptions add up to an understanding of the fertility clinic as a space in which identity seems to be dissolved and suggest a continuation of the Zionist ideal of bringing Western, liberal values of equality, technology, and health to a previously empty and uncultured land.

Salam, a Palestinian senior physician who works in a larger public hospital in the Tel Aviv area described the specificity of the fertility clinic in similar terms by referring to the uniqueness of staff dynamics: "It's a utopia in hospitals, in Israel, relatively, it's a utopia, it's not perfect, but it's a utopia [...]. And the dynamics between the staff members and the colleagues is very different than anything outside the hospitals". Framing the Israeli fertility clinic as "utopian" only functions in a narrative in which outside relations are perceived as not related to what happens inside the clinic. Salam's description of the fertility clinic as utopia conjures a vision of an alternative future which has seemingly already arrived within the hospital walls.

This narrative of the fertility clinic as a *utopian non-place* was put forward by Jewish-Israeli and Palestinian (Christian and Muslim) medical staff alike. As is often noted, making up 17% of Israel's physicians, jobs in the health-service sector have become comparatively accessible for Palestinian citizens of Israel (Keshet and Popper-Giveon 2017). Yet, following Palestinian physician and scholar Osama Tanous, their inclusion furthers the notion of medical space as a neutral site of coexistence by presenting Israeli hospitals as "political and cultural junction where everyone is equal since everyone – from Jewish settlers to Palestinian activists – receives nationalized health care there" (Tanous 2020, 38). This normalcy is praised in Israeli health news, furthering an understanding of Israeli medical space as advanced and Western vis-à-vis the Palestinian health system (Birenbaum-Carmeli 2014). In framing Israeli hospitals and infrastructure in such way, media, public discourse, as well as medical staff disregard the settler colonial history and present which simultaneously shape the Israeli health sector and enable its construction as *utopian*.

Within the narrative of a *utopian non-place*, the fertility clinic is non-relational, ahistorical, and unconcerned with identity. Even if political questions, Palestinian-Israeli history, or current social relations and power structures in Israeli society are clearly known, named, and acknowledged, they are eclipsed by an understanding of the medical sphere as universal and neutral. The perceived neutrality of Israeli medical space enables the existence and visibility of Palestinians physicians within its infrastructure, as it ostensibly relieves people from their usual social determinants and transforms them as neutral themselves (Shalev 2016). This may, in part, be attributed to an understanding of medicine as a "culture of no culture" (Taylor 2003). However, in the case of reproductive medicine in Israel/Palestine, the narrative of the clinic in terms of *terra nullius* reveals how medical space is national/settler space, and always determined by territorial politics. The construction of the fertility clinic as a *utopian non-place* thus serves a settler colonial function: it marks the clinic as promoting Western ideals of medicine as universal, yet by excluding what happens outside of the clinic, the narrative masks why what happens inside has to be described as *utopian* or *extra-territorial* in the first place.

Porous borders: bodies, sperm/egg cells, and "future terrorists" on medical routes of exchange

While the perception of the fertility clinic indicates a space with clear borders, different and closed off from the outside, medical staff referred to several routes of medical exchange, linking this ostensibly sealed space to other

THE SEXUAL POLITICS OF BORDER CONTROL

spaces and bodies. This concerns border-crossings which illustrate that categories other than the medical do in fact shape what happens in the clinic, as well as more tangible border-crossings, embodied by Palestinian women who have to cross actual borders, from the West Bank into Israel or East Jerusalem, in order to receive treatment.

Ziva is a social worker who offers Arabic translation services for East Jerusalemites and West Bankers seeking treatment in the IVF unit of a Jerusalem hospital. When discussing her experience in the IVF unit, she first referred to the fertility clinic in the grammar of the *utopian non-place*, but then proceeded to recount how medical staff voice fears and anger related to their Palestinian patients:

> when outside something happens, you know, in Gaza or in the West Bank, we are trying that this hospital will be an island, that nothing touches it, but it's here. So you can hear, sometimes, the staff, they are not so understanding and they're saying, like, "how do they have the guts to come here and ask for help when after a few hours they will throw stones at us? They have the Chutzpah to come here and ask?" But after you take these words aside, and sit with a woman that cries, that wants children, you forget it [...]. When a woman comes inside, we are closing the door for everything outside. But it's not clear, we can't, we can't and sometimes … you can hear, you know, under, behind the door that, you know, we're helping them to have, erm, future terrorists.

Ziva still acknowledged the universal and humanist approach to medicine, and reproductive medicine more specifically, by noting that they will close the door "for everything outside" when they sit with a woman. Yet, she also recognized that it is not always possible to disentangle affect, politics, and medical neutrality in such situations. Her reference to the (re)production of "future terrorists", talked about behind closed doors, clearly speaks to the ways in which reproductive medicine and politics are intertwined in Israel/Palestine (Yurdakul et al. 2019). In order to maintain the hospital as a *utopian non-place*, the permeation by politics has to be discussed behind closed doors. This illustrates how a settler colonial understanding of Palestinian bodies affectively structures space in the fertility clinic, yet needs to be masked in order to construct the Israeli state and its institutions as indebted to equality.

Ziva's account reveals the spatial, juridical, and administrative separation Palestinian citizens and residents experience in Israel and East Jerusalem, and non-citizens of the West Bank experience towards Israel: that of an "inclusive exclusion". Ariella Azoulay and Adi Ophir describe how the effort to simultaneously separate and rule Palestinians leads to this paradoxical situation: "The fantasy of once and for all separating inside from outside, 'security threats' from peaceful citizens, while nonetheless paradoxically containing and ruling the excluded" (Azoulay and Ophir 2013, 97). The ambiguity of this situation comes to the fore in Ziva's reflection, where Palestinians are described as outside threats yet, when they enter the clinic, they still need to be treated according to a humanistic approach. "What is kept apart is considered 'outside', and is included as such" (Azoulay and Ophir 2013, 97), the indigenous Palestinian population is included as the Other in order to demarcate and manage their otherness. This structure of including while excluding enables the construction of the Israeli fertility clinic as impermeable by politics.

Both modes of separation, spatial and juridical/administrative, appear in how Eran, a Jewish-Israeli head of an IVF centre in a hospital in Tel Aviv, talked about the Israeli fertility economy and its Other(s), exemplified by various border-crossings between the West Bank and Israel:

> There are several IVF units in the Palestinian Authority and they work there, but we almost never see Palestinian Authority patients [...], they have no reason to come here I think, if you don't have financial coverage, the rates there are cheaper. We sometimes see Israeli Arabs who go and get their service over there, because they have no regulation, it's a wild, a wild west, a real wild west country, and we ... get back their complications, their quadruplets, gestations of the very severe, of hyperstimulation cases, very flawed things that we, we learned here not to do any more.

By noting that West Bank residents have no reason to receive treatment in Israel, Eran glosses over the administrative and bureaucratic effort it takes to receive a permit to enter Israel. As non-citizens, West Bankers are not entitled to Israeli state subsidies for fertility treatment, yet the proper development of their own healthcare system has been prevented by Israel since the occupation of the West Bank in 1967 (Majadle 2020). The effect the occupation has on the Palestinian economy and health services reflects in limited access to technological resources in fertility clinics in the West Bank, which most Palestinian women (citizens and residents of Israel and West Bankers alike) recounted in our interviews. However, Eran continues, "Israeli Arabs" (Palestinians with Israeli citizenship) who are entitled to fertility treatment in Israel might approach West Bank clinics for treatments "over there". The reason for this, he suggests, is to receive treatments that are not subsidized or readily available in Israel, such as non-medical sex selection. While this might be true for some, many Palestinian women with citizenship I interviewed had also tried regular IVF treatment in the West Bank. Among the reasons to do so were cultural or linguistic barriers, or referral to a specific doctor known to their family or friends.

Fertility treatment in the West Bank – and in turn the West Bank as a whole – is depicted in Orientalist terms (Said 1978). Medical knowledge and hygiene played a crucial role in the Zionist movement and the Israeli nation building project. The depiction of Mizrahi Jews[4] and Palestinian Arabs as unhygienic enabled the Jewish Westernization project in Palestine to cast itself as superior and rational, which in turn further legitimized its settler colonial ambitions (Hirsch 2009). Eran elicits the colonial afterlife of Zionist medical knowledge by pointing out that "very flawed" things are happening in this "wild west country", and thus produces an Israeli self-conception as modern and more developed. In his description of routes of medical exchange between the West Bank and Israel, the narrative of Palestinians and the West Bank as the spatial and bodily Other is allegedly corroborated by the reason for their border-crossing: the advanced Israeli repro-economy. Yet the borders they have to cross are simultaneously the reason for their othering.

The bodies and movements of Palestinian patients challenge the supposed impermeability of Israeli medical neutrality. As Helga Tawil-Souri outlines, the constant shifting and blurring of Israel's borders is embedded in a rationale of "defensible borders" reflecting Israel's fear of threats to its existence. As a result, she argues "Israel's borders then are not easily mapped along any (geographic/territorial) boundary, but on Palestinian mobilities and flows" (Tawil-Souri 2012, 173). The following passage, in which Irit described her Palestinian patients in Jerusalem, illustrates just this:

> The patients are Palestinian oriented, they are Israeli, they carry this new identity card, but still, I mean, I would say the political orientation is Palestinian. Now, many are married across the border, some women are married to Arab men that live in the Occupied Territories and sometimes we encounter many difficulties because we cannot bring the husband into Israel because of all kinds of political restraints. So sometimes the women, or a family member, can go to the checkpoint and just hand a sperm sample to be brought to Israel. But as I said, mostly our couples come from East Jerusalem, and even if they are separated across the borders, we can write a letter to the Israeli army and they get a permission to come to Israel, or, you know, to freeze sperm […], so it's kind of crazy.

Irit addressed how the fragmentation of Palestinian citizens of Israel, residents of East Jerusalem, or West Bankers affects their everyday life and intimate decision-making. She described how, if a person with a Jerusalem ID is married to a West Bank resident and they want to have children by using ART, bodies and body parts have to literally cross borders: a sperm sample has to traverse the checkpoint controlling and surveilling Palestinians' movement and access to Israel, frozen and parcelled, or the West Bank partner has to cross the border him- or herself to receive treatment in an Israeli hospital. Her difficulties in naming her patients "Palestinians", granting them an identity other than Israeli, and her description of their fragmented relationships speak to the ways in which Israel's borders are defined through Palestinians' identities and mobilities. "So it's kind of crazy": it is only through the rights, needs, and movements of Palestinians from which she is able to perceive the actually existing borders they have to cross.

In all three accounts of border-crossing (the encroaching of the political onto the *utopian non-place*, border-crossings between the West Bank and Israel and the associated othering along those lines, and fragmented relationships and their cross-border reproduction), we can see how the Israeli "politics of fear" (Shalhoub-Kevorkian 2015b) are incorporated into governance, surveillance, assimilation, and rejection of Palestinians. What makes the symbolic borders of the fertility clinic, as well as the actual borders between Israel, East Jerusalem, and the West Bank visible, are Palestinian bodies, egg cells or sperm, and the associated meaning they receive from a settler colonial perspective. In medical staff's narratives of Palestinians' border-crossings on their way to get pregnant, we can see how, from a hegemonic Israeli perspective, these borders are, in-fact, "de-bordered", as they map onto the Palestinian body and its parts. Yet ultimately, Palestinian women who want to get pregnant and have to turn to fertility treatment in Israeli hospitals, are the ones experiencing the tangible effects of these borders and the spatial structure of the Israeli fertility clinic.

Repro-politics: navigating the borderlands of reproduction

For Palestinian women with Israeli citizenship or residency status and for West Bankers seeking treatment in Israel, the symbolic and material borders structuring access to the fertility clinic vary. However, in order to defragment Palestinian women's practices of trying to conceive across Israel/Palestine (Salamanca et al. 2012), I draw from Chicana theorist Gloria Anzaldúa's notion of the borderland. I do so in order to show how these different experiences are expressions of yet the same bio- and necropolitical management of bodies: while Jewish-Israelis are encouraged to breed and multiply, Palestinians – citizens, residents, and occupied subjects alike – are spatially, symbolically, and linguistically deprived from resources and easy access to fertility treatment (Lentin 2016).

In the following section, I argue that Palestinians receiving fertility treatment in Israeli hospitals, or Palestinians involved in practices of smuggling sperm out of Israeli prisons and into fertility clinics in the West Bank or Gaza, exemplify a crossing or passing over into the borderlands of reproduction. This is, to borrow Anzaldúa's framing, a "third country – a border culture". Due to their "included exclusion" in Israeli society or Israel/Palestine as a whole, Palestinians seeking treatment must navigate these borderlands, yet by doing so, constantly "grate against" the borders erected to control, manage, and surveil their (reproductive) movement (Anzaldúa 1987, 25)

Since 2012, Palestinian political prisoners, their wives and families, NGOs, and fertility clinics work together in what can be termed a communal practice of biopolitical resistance: they manage to smuggle a sperm sample of the imprisoned husband out of the Israeli prison and into a fertility clinic in the

West Bank or Gaza (Hamdan 2019; Vertommen 2017a). This exceptional practice illustrates how Palestinians cross, contest, and unmake borders, and exemplifies how reproductive resistance is linked to the spatial dimension of the Israeli occupation and settler colonialism. By banning conjugal visits for Palestinian political prisoners from the West Bank and Gaza, the Israeli Prison Service (IPS) actively controls Palestinian prisoners' reproduction, while Israeli prisoners with equally long sentences do enjoy those rights (Vertommen 2017a).[5] In order to resist these restrictions and to be able to have a family, long-term Palestinian political prisoners smuggle sperm samples out of Israeli prisons and into cooperating fertility clinics. There, the sample will be immediately cryopreserved in order to enable subsequent IVF cycles for their wives to get pregnant.

With the financial and medical support of Palestinian doctors and clinics, religiously approved by an official fatwa in April 2013, and publicly promoted by media and the clinics themselves, IVF with smuggled sperm is deeply embedded in social structures of the West Bank. According to the spokesperson of the Razan Fertility Center in Nablus, as of 2019, 65 children have been born by approximately 50 women (some of whom had twins or triplets, or used the same sperm sample again), both in the West Bank and in Gaza. Reflecting on the Israeli "politics of fear" (Shalhoub-Kevorkian 2015b), Sameer, a gynecologist working in a fertility clinic in Ramallah, asked a simple question about why Palestinian prisoners are denied conjugal visits, pointing to the political relevance Palestinian bodies and their reproduction have under settler colonialism: "it will not affect Israel and it will not affect the security of Israel if they give permission for the prisoner to sleep with his wife in the prison for a few hours".

While conceiving with smuggled sperm constitutes an opportunity to have offspring in the equally pronatalist Palestinian society, the women involved in practices of sperm smuggling are well aware of the political dimension of this border-crossing practice. Farida, a 54-year-old woman, lives in a village close to Ramallah together with her daughter-in-law, who got pregnant by undergoing IVF with her husband's smuggled sperm. For Farida, her family's way of conceiving was clearly political: "in the prisons, there are men behind the metal, but we are smarter than them and we defied them, by having children with prisoners". To frame sperm smuggling as defiance of the Israeli military only works because of the hegemonic Israeli interpellation of both the Palestinian and the Israeli population in political terms. It is not only that in the practice of sperm smuggling the supposedly most solid and impermeable border, the border of the prison, is crossed by sperm cells. This border-crossing also contributes numerically, but even more so, symbolically, to the growth of the Palestinian population in the West Bank and in Gaza.

Sperm smuggling entails bodies and body parts crossing various borders. Sperm cells move from the prison, across the Green Line, into the fertility clinic, while, at the same time, changing physical condition, as the sample is being frozen. The sperm is injected into the membrane of an egg cell, which is then placed into a woman's womb. While Palestinian women acknowledge and embrace the political potential of sperm smuggling, they simultaneously normalize both, the artificiality and the political implications of this practice. By deploying several practices to embed sperm smuggling in their every day, they are trying to live what resembles a regular family life. After our interview, Farida proudly showed me a photo collage she had made: it shows her son Rafaat holding her grandson Ahmed. Yet, the two of them have only ever seen each other a few times, through the glass partition of the prison. The borders that had to be overcome for Ahmed to exist and which still separate them day to day, are visually unmade in what looks like a regular family portrait (Figure 1).

The practice of sperm smuggling can be interpreted as an embodied form of resistance against the occupation and an unmaking of the processes of bordering that structure West Bank residents' everyday lives. However, there are less spectacular and more ambivalent ways of navigating the borderlands of reproduction by Palestinians who use ART in Israeli medical institutions. These illustrate how the notion of the fertility clinic as neutral and apolitical is not only challenged by the presence of Palestinian bodies, but how the settler colonial structuring of this space affects Palestinian women's abilities to get pregnant.

Reem, a 41-year-old resident of East Jerusalem, reflected on her experience of undergoing fertility treatment in an Israeli hospital:

> For example, having the medical services, but it is compulsive of course. You know, when you live under occupation, it is a struggle, even when you go there [to the fertility clinic], you feel that there is a gap, especially when you remember, for example a week ago, or a few weeks ago, they arrested my brother, they arrested my neighbor, or they bomb Gaza, yes ... there's a struggle.

For Reem, being a resident of East Jerusalem entitles her to an Israeli health insurance, which in turn enables her to undergo fertility treatment in an Israeli hospital. However, as she described, her embeddedness in the Israeli health care system feels compulsive – she didn't choose to live in an Israeli state. She feels this strongly when entering a fertility clinic, which she described as a "gap" opening up when she remembers the effect settler colonialism has on her immediate surroundings and life. What Israeli medical staff describes as a "no-man's land", a *utopian non-place*, is perceived as the exact opposite by many Palestinian women I have interviewed: they were constantly reminded of their status as the Other, their "included exclusion" as Palestinians in Israel/Palestine.

Celine, a 34-year-old woman from Bethlehem, has been treated at a Jerusalem hospital for many years: her three children were conceived there,

Figure 1. Photo of a photo collage made by Farida. It shows her son Rafaat and her grandson Ahmed, who has been conceived by sperm his father had smuggled out of prison. Source: Photo taken by the author.

and at the time I met her, she was undergoing another IVF cycle. Celine receives her fertility treatment in an Israeli hospital because her husband suffers from a serious genetic illness causing infertility. His illness was discovered upon birth and has had to be treated in a specialized hospital ever since. The couple told me that it cannot be treated in West Bank medical institutions due to their lack of specialized knowledge and equipment. Celine's husband has a health related permit to enter Israel which has to be renewed every three months, and Celine is registered to accompany her spouse to the hospital. They use this permit to enable Celine's fertility treatment, because, as she said, the treatment in an Israeli clinic has proven to be "more specific, more scheduled [...] everything is in order" in contrast to clinics in Hebron or Ramallah. This means that they have to pay for the treatment by themselves (approximately 30.000 NIS/8700$ per IVF cycle), since as non-Israeli citizens they are not entitled to state subsidies.

Celine's case profoundly illustrates how Palestinians are made dependent on and forced to navigate Israeli medical institutions across borders. Due to the ongoing occupation of the West Bank, it is vital for Celine's husband to get specialized treatment in an Israeli hospital, and Celine confirmed that IVF works better in Israeli clinics. Even if this medical space might not always feel welcoming, as in the case of Reem, the effect the occupation has on health care in the West Bank is felt by women who tried to get pregnant in both settings. Several studies have addressed the restricting effects the occupation has on Palestinian women's pregnancy, childbirth, and reproductive health in the West Bank and East Jerusalem (Hamayel, Hammoudeh, and Welchman 2017; Shalhoub-Kevorkian 2015a). I asked Celine if she had had difficult experiences crossing checkpoints so frequently in order to become pregnant or in the early stages of her pregnancies. She said "sometimes, not always [...], depending on the political situation at that time, if everything is stable, they are happy to help and let us pass". This illustrates the arbitrariness of having to navigate the borderlands of reproduction: Celine's passage depends not only on her husband's permission to enter Israel, but also on the checkpoint soldiers, whose disposition and opinion of the political situation can vary day to day.

I interviewed Celine twice, once right before the egg retrieval, and a second time right after the fertilized eggs had been transferred into her uterus. Our second interview took place in the day care unit of the hospital in Jerusalem, located in its windowless basement, closed off by an automatic door and only accessible for patients, spouses, and their visitors. The beds in the day care unit were separated by curtains only, so one could hear people talking in the next segment; from time to time, a nurse would come in to check on Celine, she would begin to talk in Hebrew, so Celine had to ask "in English please". This language barrier, which Celine patiently and politely overcame every time, constitutes yet another border which was felt by women from East Jerusalem and the West Bank, and sometimes Palestinians with Israeli citizenship. Women who are not fluent in Hebrew rely on their husbands or other family members to accompany them to their appointments in the fertility clinic, or hope that the physician or a nurse speaks some Arabic or English.

This linguistic border also constitutes a barrier to becoming pregnant. As Maysam, a woman in her early twenties and a resident of East Jerusalem noted:

> I would take the wrong medications which would affect me, and I would stop the treatment. That's a problem for me. Like, I would stop taking medications just because I don't understand them, which makes it complicated. I don't understand the words.

In these narratives, the self-congratulatory neutrality of Israeli medical space appears fragile. However, in order to get pregnant, Palestinian women have to act according to the narrative of the *utopian non-place*: overcome their feelings of otherness, try to get by in a different language, and hope they will get a pass at the checkpoint.

Reem's, Celine's, and Maysam's narratives of Israeli medical space can seem less related to the political situation, considering the accessibility of fertility treatment for residents and citizens of Israel, and even for West Bankers if they have the financial means to pay for their treatment. However, I argue that this is the function of the fertility clinic as a *utopian non-place*: it is presented as neutral and universal, while its spatial, affective, and linguistic structure only allows Palestinians to be included as an exception. While Palestinian women's experiences in the fertility clinic might look less extreme than other manifestations of dispossession, surveillance, and control towards Palestinians, they reveal how space and power materialize on multi-scalar levels and attest to the strategic role borders play in the fabrication of social worlds (Mezzadra and Neilson 2013). From the checkpoint Celine has to cross, Reem's affective reaction to her inclusion into Israeli medical space, to Maysam, who won't get pregnant because she is unable to follow her doctor's instructions: the spatiality of settler colonialism illustrates how the "borderland is a vague and undetermined place created by the emotional residue of an unnatural boundary" (Anzaldúa 1987, 25). Palestinian women are able to enter the borderlands of reproduction, yet the outcomes of their reproductive choices are determined by a variety of borders and a structuring of space as universal and neutral, which mutes any reference to their experiences. It is thus imperative to not only examine Israeli-Palestinian questions writ large, but to attune to the more nuanced entanglements of politics, space, and technology, which construct the "intimate frontiers" (Stoler 2010), and porous borders of the Israeli fertility clinic.

Bodies, borders, and assisted reproductive technologies in Israel/Palestine

This article has analyzed how space is fundamental to different narratives, processes, and practices related to assisted reproduction in Israel/Palestine. The hegemonic Israeli understanding of the fertility clinic as a *utopian non-place* is challenged by medical routes that lead in and out of the clinic, and across several material and symbolic borders. The borders structuring spaces of fertility are (un)made across Palestinians' bodies and body parts. Throughout these transactions, an Orientalist self-perception of Israeli (reproductive) medicine as neutral and universal produces Palestinians and the West Bank as spatial and racial Others. The narrative of the fertility clinic is rooted in a settler colonial framing of demographic questions and references to the hospital as a "no man's land", which presents the clinic as a space in which identity dissolves. This suggests a continuation of the Zionist ideal of bringing Western, liberal values of equality and health to a previously empty and uncultured land.

The situation of Palestinian citizens of Israel, residents of East Jerusalem, or West Bankers who use ART in Israeli medical institutions reveals how the narrative of the Israeli fertility clinic as a *utopian non-place* masks its settler colonial structure. On the one hand, access to and availability of technologies of reproduction are regulated by the Israeli fertility economy, which includes Palestinian women as *patients only*. On the other hand, Palestinian women's pregnancies' outcome is influenced in various ways by Israel's surveillance and control of Palestinian's everyday lives through a multilevel socio-technological security regime – from the bedroom to the hospital and back (Shalhoub-Kevorkian 2015b; Stoler 2016). Finally, the case of sperm smuggling constitutes an example of how borders, such as the Green Line, but also the border of the prison, are challenged by Palestinian families through a communal practice of reproductive resistance.

Bringing a spatial lens to an analysis of assisted reproduction in a settler colonial context furthers an understanding of how power is produced and contested in the ostensibly neutral space of medicine. A spatial lens exposes how geopolitical, symbolic, affective, and linguistic borders overlap and (dis)connect in unpredictable and nuanced ways (Mezzadra and Neilson 2013). The hegemonic Israeli self-perception of medical space as neutral parallels the *terra nullius* doctrine of (settler) colonial movements then and now (Veracini 2016): space described as belonging to no one. However, the encroaching of the political onto the *utopian non-place*, fragmented intimate relationships and their cross-border reproductive practices, the case of sperm smuggling, and Palestinian women's experiences in the Israeli fertility clinic attest to the continued spatiality of settler colonial power.

Notes

1. Sophie Lewis argues that pregnancy had already been "techno-fixed" before that. Safer, i.e. medically supported pregnancies were mostly a privilege of the (white) upper classes and in that sense, technologies such as surrogacy ultimately constituted a mere continuation of that "gestational fix" (Lewis 2019). However, in this article, I am concerned with technologies specifically aiming at enhancing or enabling pregnancies (for all sorts of reasons, usually subsumed under the term infertility, but also in cases of sex selection), such as in vitro fertilization, intracytoplasmic sperm injection, intrauterine insemination, third-party donation of eggs and sperm, freezing and storage of sperm, embryos, oocytes, and ovarian tissue.

2. Helga Tawil-Souri describes the state of Israel as "de-bordered" for two reasons. On the one hand, Israel was founded as a nation-state of the Jewish people worldwide, not simply for its Israeli citizens, Jewish or not. On the other hand, Israel's external and internal borders continue to be contested.
3. Most names of interview partners have been changed and institutions have been reduced to a generic description, except for some of the names and institutions involved in the sperm smuggling case upon participants' request for visibility.
4. The term Mizrahi refers to Jewish people from Middle Eastern and North-African descent.
5. The most well-known case in this context is Yigal Amir, convicted of the murder of then-Prime Minister Yitzhak Rabin.

Acknowledgements

I would like to express sincere thanks to Najla Fawwaz and Mary Khadija for their Arabic-English translations and thoughtful suggestions. I also thank Sophia Goodfriend, Michelle Pfeifer, Gökçe Yurdakul, Morgana Karch, Yoav Koko, Ruth Patir and Moritz Gansen for their valuable feedback and comments on earlier versions of this article. Four anonymous reviewers from *Ethnic and Racial Studies* have helped me hone my arguments further. Many thanks to the organizers and participants of the *Sexuality and Borders Symposium* at NYU in 2019 for their feedback and for making this Special Issue happen.

Disclosure statement

No potential conflict of interest was reported by the author(s).

Funding

This research was supported by the Caroline von Humboldt Program (Humboldt-Universität zu Berlin) and a doctoral fellowship by the Heinrich Böll Foundation.

ORCID

Gala Rexer ⓘ http://orcid.org/0000-0002-6447-1878

References

Anzaldúa, G. E. 1987. *Borderlands/La Frontera: The New Mestiza*. San Francisco: Aunt Lute.
Augé, M. 1995. *Non-places: Introduction to an Anthropology of Supermodernity*. London: Verso.
Azoulay, A., and A. Ophir. 2013. *The One-State Condition: Occupation and Democracy in Israel/Palestine*. Stanford: Stanford University Press.
Berda, Y. 2017. *Living Emergency: Israel's Permit Regime in the Occupied West Bank*. Stanford: Stanford University Press.

Birenbaum-Carmeli, D. 2014. "Health Journalism in the Service of Power: 'Moral Complacency' and the Hebrew Media in the Gaza–Israel Conflict." *Sociology of Health & Illness* 36 (4): 613–628.

Birenbaum-Carmeli, D. 2016. "Thirty-five Years of Assisted Reproductive Technologies in Israel." *Reproductive Biomedicine & Society Online* 2: 16–23. doi:10.1016/j.rbms.2016.05.004.

Birenbaum-Carmeli, D., and R. Kochman-Haimov. 2010. "Fertility Treatments Under Semi/Occupation: The Case of East Jerusalem." *F, V & V IN OBGYN*, 35–42.

Birenbaum-Carmeli, D., and P. Montebruno. 2019. "Incidence of Surrogacy in the USA and Israel and Implications on Women's Health: a Quantitative Comparison." *Journal of Assisted Reproduction and Genetics* 36: 2459–2469.

Clarke, A. E., and D. J. Haraway. 2018. *Making Kin Not Population*. Chicago: Prickly Paradigm Press.

Foucault, M. 2008. *The Birth of Biopolitics: Lectures at the College de France, 1978–79*. Basingstoke: Palgrave Macmillan.

Franklin, S., and F. D. Ginsburg. 2019. "Reproductive Politics in the Age of Trump and Brexit." *Cultural Anthropology* 34 (1): 3–9.

Ginsburg, F. D., and R. Rapp. 1995. *Conceiving the New World Order: the Global Politics of Reproduction*. Berkeley: University of California Press.

Gutkowski, N. 2020. "Bodies that Count: Administering Multispecies in Palestine/Israel's Borderlands." *Environment and Planning E: Nature and Space*, doi:10.1177/2514848620901445.

Hamayel, L., D. Hammoudeh, and L. Welchman. 2017. "Reproductive Health and Rights in East Jerusalem: The Effects of Militarisation and Biopolitics on the Experiences of Pregnancy and Birth of Palestinians Living in the Kufr 'Aqab Neighbourhood." *Reproductive Health Matters* 25 (1): 87–95.

Hamdan, M. 2019. "'Every Sperm Is Sacred': Palestinian Prisoners, Smuggled Semen, and Derrida's Prophecy." *International Journal for Middle East Studies* 51: 525–545.

Hirsch, D. 2009. "'We Are Here to Bring the West, Not Only to Ourselves': Zionist Occidentalism and the Discourse of Hygiene in Mandate Palestine." *International Journal of Middle East Studies* 41 (4): 577–594.

Inhorn, M. C., and Z. B. Gürtin. 2011. "Cross-border Reproductive Care: A Future Research Agenda." *Reproductive Biomedicine Online* 23 (5): 665–676.

Ivry, T. 2010. *Embodying Culture: Pregnancy in Japan and Israel*. New Brunswick: Rutgers University Press.

Kanaaneh, R. 2002. *Birthing the Nation. Strategies of Palestinian Women in Israel*. Berkeley: University of California Press.

Keshet, Y., and A. Popper-Giveon. 2017. "Neutrality in Medicine and Health Professionals from Ethnic Minority Groups: The Case of Arab Health Professionals in Israel." *Social Science & Medicine* 174: 35–42.

Lentin, R. 2016. "Israel/Palestine. State of Exception and Acts of Resistance." In *Resisting Biopolitics: Philosophical, Political, and Performative Strategies*, edited by S. E. Wilmer, and A. Žukauskaitė, 271–287. New York: Routledge.

Lewis, S. 2019. *Full Surrogacy Now: Feminism Against Family*. London: Verso.

Lipkin, N., and E. Samama. 2010. "Surrogacy in Israel. Status Report 2010 and Proposals for Legislative Amendment." *The Women and Medical Technologies Program*, 1–32.

Majadle, G. 2020. "Healthcare in the Occupied Territory During COVID-19." In *COVID-19 Report. A Policy of Neglect. The First 100 Days of COVID-19 in Israels Healthcare System*, edited by Y. Rosner, H. Ziv, A. Litvin, Z. Gutzeit, and G. Majadle, 64–84. Physicians for Human Rights Israel.

Masalha, N. 2012. *The Palestine Nakba: Decolonising History, Narrating the Subaltern, Reclaiming Memory*. London and New York: Zed Books.

Mbembe, A. 2003. "Necropolitics." *Public Culture* 15 (1): 11–40. doi:10.1215/08992363-15-1-11.

Merleau-Ponty, N., S. Vertommen, and M. Pucéat. 2018. "I6 Passages: On the Reproduction of a Human Embryonic Stem Cell Line from Israel to France." *New Genetics and Society* 37 (4): 338–361. doi:10.1080/14636778.2018.1548269.

Mezzadra, S., and B. Neilson. 2013. *Border as Method, Or, the Multiplication of Labor*. Durham: Duke University Press.

Mitra, S., S. Schicktanz, and T. Patel. 2018. *Cross-Cultural Comparisons on Surrogacy and Egg Donation: Interdisciplinary Perspectives from India, Germany and Israel*. Basingstoke: Palgrave Macmillan.

Nahman, M. R. 2013. *Extractions: An Ethnography of Reproductive Tourism*. Basingstoke: Palgrave Macmillan.

Nahman, M. R. 2016. "Reproductive Tourism: Through the Anthropological 'Reproscope'." *Annual Review of Anthropology* 45 (1): 417–432.

Parsons, N., and M. B. Salter. 2008. "Israeli Biopolitics: Closure, Territorialisation and Governmentality in the Occupied Palestinian Territories." *Geopolitics* 13 (4): 701–723. doi:10.1080/14650040802275511.

Portugese, J. 1998. *Fertility Policy in Israel: The Politics of Religion, Gender, and Nation*. Westport: Praeger.

Puar, J. K. 2017. *The Right to Maim: Debility, Capacity, Disability*. Durham: Duke University Press.

Said, E. W. 1978. *Orientalism*. 1st ed. New York: Pantheon Books.

Salamanca, O. J., M. Qato, K. Rabie, and S. Samour. 2012. "Past is Present: Settler Colonialism in Palestine." *Settler Colonial Studies* 2 (1): 1–8. doi:10.1080/2201473X.2012.10648823.

Shalev, G. 2016. "A Doctor's Testimony: Medical Neutrality and the Visibility of Palestinian Grievances in Jewish-Israeli Publics." *Culture, Medicine and Psychiatry* 40 (2): 242–262. doi:10.1007/s11013-015-9470-7.

Shalhoub-Kevorkian, N. 2015a. "The Politics of Birth and the Intimacies of Violence Against Palestinian Women in Occupied East Jerusalem." *The British Journal of Criminology* 55 (6): 1187–1206.

Shalhoub-Kevorkian, N. 2015b. *Security Theology, Surveillance and the Politics of Fear*. Cambridge: Cambridge University Press.

Sowa, C. 2014. "Smoothing the Striated Space of Occupation – The Struggle over Space in the West Bank." *Rosa Luxemburg Stiftung Regional Office Palestine, PAL Papers*, 1–15.

Sperling, D., and Y. Simon. 2010. "Attitudes and Policies Regarding Access to Fertility Care and Assisted Reproductive Technologies in Israel." *Reproductive Biomedicine Online* 21 (7): 854. doi:10.1016/j.rbmo.2010.08.013.

Stoler, A. L. 2010. *Carnal Knowledge and Imperial Power: Race and the Intimate in Colonial Rule*. 2nd ed. Berkeley: University of California Press.

Stoler, A. L. 2016. *Duress: Imperial Durabilities in Our Times*. Durham: Duke University Press.

Tanous, O. 2020. "Covid-19 Fault Lines: Palestinian Physicians in Israel." *Journal of Palestine Studies* 49 (4): 36–46.

Tawil-Souri, H. 2011. "Qalandia Checkpoint as Space and Nonplace." *Space and Culture* 14 (1): 4–26.

Tawil-Souri, H. 2012. "Uneven Borders, Coloured (Im)mobilities: ID Cards in Palestine/Israel." *Geopolitics* 17 (1): 153–176.

Taylor, J. S. 2003. "Confronting 'Culture' in Medicine's 'Culture of No Culture'." *Academic Medicine* 78 (6): 555–559.

Teman, E. 2018. "A Case for Restrictive Regulation of Surrogacy? An Indo-Israeli Comparison of Ethnographic Studies." In *Cross-Cultural Comparisons on Surrogacy and Egg Donation. Interdisciplinary Perspectives from India, Germany and Israel*, edited by S. Mitra, S. Schicktanz, and T. Patel, 57–81. Basingstoke: Palgrave Macmillan.

Veracini, L. 2016. "Afterword: A History of the Settler Colonial Present." *Settler Colonial Studies* 6 (2): 174–179. doi:10.1080/00048623.2015.1024304.

Vertommen, S. 2017a. "Babies from Behind the Bars: Stratified Assisted Reproduction in Palestine/Israel." In *Assisted Reproduction Across Borders. Feminist Perspectives on Normalizations, Disruptions and Transmissions*, edited by N. L. Merete Lie, 207–218. New York: Routledge.

Vertommen, S. 2017b. "From the Pergonal Project to Kadimastem: A Genealogy of Israel's Reproductive-Industrial Complex." *BioSocieties* 12 (2): 282–306.

Weiss, M. 2002. *The Chosen Body: The Politics of the Body in Israeli Society*. Stanford: Stanford University Press.

Yurdakul, G., G. Rexer, S. Eilat, and N. Mutluer. 2019. "Contested Authorities over Life Politics: Religious-Secular Tensions in Abortion Debates in Germany, Turkey, and Israel." *Comparative Sociology* 18 (5-6): 706–734.

Zu'bi, H. 2018. "Palestinian Fertility in the Israeli Sphere: Palestinian Women in Israel Undergoing IVF Treatments." In *Bioethics and Biopolitics in Israel: Socio-Legal, Political, and Empirical Analysis*, edited by Y. H.-D. Hagai Boas, Nadav Davidovitch, Dani Finc, and Shai J. Lavi, 160–180. Cambridge: Cambridge University Press.

"We're dating after marriage": transformative effects of performing intimacy in Vietnamese "marriage fraud" arrangements

Grace Tran

ABSTRACT

Drawing on narratives of three Vietnamese women who agreed to participate in *đám cưới giả* ("fake wedding") arrangements with Canadian citizens to enter Canada, this paper examines the paradoxical consequences of marriage migration policies. I introduce the concept of *strategic intima*cies to highlight the ways that Vietnamese women in these arrangements deliberately draw on social and economic capital to perform intimacy under manufactured settings to navigate securitized and racialized border regimes. Ironically, through deploying strategic intimacies catering to classed and gendered ideals of love and intimacy to present evidence of their "genuine" marriages, participants developed romantic attachments and pursued long-term relationships with their sponsors. I argue that, in trying to regulate migration, the state sets the conditions for and necessity of "marriage fraud", blurring boundaries between what constitutes as "real" and "fake" for participants. This contribution prompts for a rethinking of the heteronormative and racialized practices of contemporary border regimes.

Introduction

My first meeting with Kimmy took place in a tea shop on the fourteenth of February. She motioned to her dress and asked me timidly: "Is too fancy for *ngày lễ tình nhân?*" After reassuring Kimmy that her dress was well-suited for a Valentine's Day celebration in Canada, we began our interview. An informant had arranged the meeting, but had told me little about Kimmy other than that she had participated in a *đám cưới giả* (DCG) arrangement. Loosely translated to "fake wedding",[1] Kimmy's case followed a similar trajectory to that of other "successful" DCG arrangements, whereby she had paid a Vietnamese-Canadian man a significant sum of money to sponsor her as his spouse to gain admission into Canada as a permanent resident.

As our interview drew to what I thought was a close, I returned to Kimmy's question and asked whether, after two years of residing in Canada, she had developed romantic feelings for someone. Kimmy nodded and giggled: "Yes – the man who pretend to marry me so I can come here … I guess you can say, we are dating after marriage!"

Kimmy's admission that she had a Valentine's date with the man who had sponsored her to Canada as his wife was intriguing for several reasons. Within the past decade, nation-states have clamped down on family reunification and spousal sponsorship as legitimate pathways to citizenship (Luibheid 2002; Wray 2006; Abrams 2007, 2012) Moral panics surrounding increasing rates of "marriage fraud" spotlight the undermining of not only border securitization, but the integrity of immigration systems, in turn enabling states to violently police borders, reproducing heteronormative gender roles at large (Constable 2009; Chen 2015; Friedman 2015; Kim and Kim 2020). In 2011, the Canadian government's Conservative party claimed an acute rise in marriage fraud cases, and launched a nation-wide anti-marriage fraud campaign despite lacking empirical evidence to support its claim (D'Aoust 2013; Gaucher 2018). Politically and discursively, this campaign constructed marriage fraud as a "serious crime" that justified amplified state attention and resources (Bhuyan, Korteweg, and Baqi 2018, 359).

The Canadian government defines "marriage fraud", alternatively referred to as "marriages of convenience", as any marriage entered into solely for immigration purposes (ICC 2017). According to this definition, Kimmy and her husband's case would be considered one of "marriage fraud": their primary intention for knowingly entering into a *DCG* arrangement was to secure permanent residency for Kimmy, with an exchange of money at the core of this arrangement. However, Kimmy's case is incongruous with the Canadian government's definition of "marriage fraud", as she and her sponsor developed feelings for each other and chose to remain married after her resettlement in Canada. The trajectory of their relationship not only challenges the parameters of their *DCG* arrangement, but also challenges dichotomous understandings of love as either genuine and "true", grounded in sentiment, or "fake" and cunning, driven by instrumentality (Simoni 2015, 33). Cases like Kimmy's remind us that "fake" marriages only come into being and are rendered necessary through exclusionary and racialized border policies of the state. Moreover, they remind us that the messiness of intimate relationships do not fit neatly into the migration policies and logics of nation-states, and that such intimate relationships are also, in turn, catalyzed and transformed by said logics and policies.

In this paper, I argue that participants in *DCG* arrangements deploy what I refer to as *strategic intimacies* both before, during, and after preparing their spousal sponsorship applications with their husbands to merit access to state membership. By strategic intimacies, I refer to the purposeful and planned performances of intimacy, reflecting idealized models of love and marriage, undertaken by individuals who must draw on social and economic capital to navigate securitized border regimes. This article situates the concept of strategic intimacies in the development of three relationships that were initiated to secure Canadian citizenship for a Vietnamese spouse. In doing so, it demonstrates how the deliberate presentation of a "legitimate" relationship to external sources can create the very conditions for what one might consider "authentic" intimacy, and highlights the patterned yet nuanced ways that migrants actively reconfigure understandings of intimacy in response and resistance to restrictive border regimes.

This paper begins with an interdisciplinary overview of literature on marriage and partner migration, self-presentation, intimacy, and authenticity, followed by a discussion of my methodological approach. I illustrate how, by preparing to present "real", legitimate transnational marriages to the Canadian government and evade governmental efforts to police for marriage fraud, participants by necessity engage in emotional entanglements that often blur the boundaries between what constitutes as "real" and "fake" love, marriage, and intimacy. The Canadian immigration system holds all transnational couples under close scrutiny as immigration officers police spousal sponsorship applications for fraudulent marriages; these screening practices have the paradoxical effect of bringing participants in arrangements like *DCG* closer together. Consequently, despite initially deploying strategic intimacies to gain legal entry into Canada, interviewees' undertakings of strategic intimacies instead become transformative moments that mediate their understandings of themselves and their relationships.

Literature review: marriage fraud, self-presentation, and authenticity

Migration scholarship highlights how nation-states have increasingly restricted family reunification policies in an effort to regulate cross-border relationships that seek to assert claims to state membership, instead shifting to exclusionary and racialized border politics which construct the ideal immigrant as high-skilled and economically useful (Wray 2006; Bonjour and de Hart 2013; D'Aoust 2013; Eggebø 2013). As few possess the credentials to demonstrate their economic utility to the state, the importance of marriage as a citizenship-delineating institution (Kim and Kim 2020) comes to the forefront, as it enables states to confer citizenship to individuals whom the state would not otherwise choose. Consequently, fake marriages are rendered necessary and manifest through and because of exclusionary border politics as a tool of resistance against restrictive border regimes which render it increasingly difficult for individuals to migrate legally.

Echoing international trends to regulate marriage and partner migration through screening for marriages of convenience in growingly securitized border regimes (Luibheid 2002; Abrams 2012; D'Aoust 2013; Carver 2016), the Canadian government subjected all transnational relationships to intensified surveillance beginning in the early 2000s. This shift in policy and practice highlights how nation-states process sponsorship applications in ways that are far from neutral, inadvertently discriminating against couples who lack the resources to provide adequate "proof" of their relationship (Gaucher 2014; 2018). For instance, the Canada Border Services Agency identifies China, India, and Vietnam as "high risk" source countries for marriage fraud (O'Neil 2015), inevitably placing transnational couples from Asia under heightened moral suspicion (Hwang and Parreñas 2018).

One need not look for further proof that marriage and partner migration is a site of legal, socio-economic, racial, and moral scrutiny than in recent legislation passed by the Canadian government, which launched its anti-marriage fraud campaign to "crack down" (D'Aoust 2013, 259) on marriages of convenience in 2012. As part of its campaign, the government introduced a two-year conditional permanent residency rule requiring partners of Canadian citizens without children to cohabit with their sponsor for at least two years to demonstrate the authenticity of their relationship. This reflects Illouz (2007)'s observation that despite modern, romantic love being characterized as liberating and spontaneous, understandings of "love" remain deeply entrenched in classed, gendered, and racialized ideals that must take on a procedural form in order to be witnessed, understood, and consumed.

This paper answers to scholars' calls for more in-depth, empirical studies that examine how borders, race, and intimacy are in dialogue with economic flows of capital (Constable 2009; Hoang 2015; Simoni 2015; Groes 2018; Parreñas, Thai, and Silvey 2016). While the field of migration studies stemmed from economic interrogations into why people move, attributing the motivations for migration to economic stimuli and the mitigation of economic risk (Harris and Todaro 1970; Piore 1979; Massey 1999), recent scholarship on marriage and partner migration challenges the degree to which money motivates and sustains migration flows. As exemplified by terms such as "intimate mobilities" (Groes and Fernandez 2018, 1), scholars are beginning to recognize the complex ways that affect, emotion, and intimacy can be mapped on to, facilitated by, reproduced, or challenged in relationships that reckon with and traverse borders (D'Aoust 2013; Gaucher 2014, 2018; Illouz 2007; Groes and Fernandez 2018). What we know about restrictive immigration policies is that they are responded to by immigrants in ways that cannot be captured nor predicted by rational choice and economic migration models (Ryo 2015). In light of this, how might we make sense of situations like Kimmy and her husband's, in which both parties enter into a "marriage of convenience" with the intention of divorcing shortly after securing permanent residency, but who become emotionally entangled in something more?

What we know about irregular migrant behaviour and what Goffman refers to as "presentation of self" also remains limited to studies of unauthorized Mexican immigration to the U.S. (Goffman 1959; García 2014; Chávez 2016; Enriquez 2020) and cross-Straight marriages from Southeast Asia and mainland China to Taiwan, South Korea, and Japan (Friedman 2015; Kim and Kim 2020). However, the rising significance of access to citizenship, paralleled by the high threshold of requirements for obtaining citizenship, necessitates research on how the process of gaining legal recognition and status affects people's everyday lives (Menjívar and Lakhani 2016). This is especially important in the context of marriage and partner migration, as conjugality serves as grounds for access to Canadian citizenship (Gaucher 2018) and surveillance apparatuses of the state have the power to shape intimacy by conferring legal status and legitimizing transnational relationships (Abrams 2012; D'Aoust 2013). Beyond legal legitimation, marriage and partner migration policies serve as a form of normative social control by legitimizing transnational relationships when they reflect Westernized ideals of marriage, love, and intimacy (Wray 2015). In applying for spousal sponsorship, couples must answer specific questions about their relationship and provide documented "evidence" of it in order for their relationship to gain legal recognition as authentic, deserving, and thus "safe" enough to admit past state borders.

Far from being delimited to the domestic sphere, scholars have also demonstrated that marriage and intimacy are just as much public colonial enterprises as they private (Stoler 1989, 2006; Dua 2007). For instance, the Canadian government's flagging of Asian countries as "high risk" marriage fraud sources plays into longer histories of the Canadian government controlling, gendering, and racializing migration from this region by admitting migrants solely for their labour power and not for their ability to participate in nation-building (Dua 2007). Thus, historically and contemporarily, race and colonialism shaped and continue to shape the interrelationships between border controls and intimacy.

Recent scholarship sheds light on the ways that intimacy is inextricably tied to money through processes of commodification, presentation, and performances of "authentic" love (Brennan 2004; Bernstein 2007; Constable 2009). Friedman (2015) argues that authenticity has "become the dominant register for evaluating intimacy in cross-border relationships" (206), coining the regulations, norms, and knowledge forms that mediate state recognitions of intimate relationships as "authenticity paradigms." As authenticity paradigms widen the gap between lived intimacies and the narrow construction of intimacy that state authorities screen for in assessing relationships, individuals may resort to presenting their cross-border relationships to authorities in ways that are regarded by the state as inauthentic.

The establishment of "authentic" intimacy also relies heavily on the presentation of a specific self – that is, an "authentic" self, which is essential in mediating all forms of relationships, from securing membership in social groups to ensuring the effective selling of consumer goods (Ivory 2017). Synthesizing self-presentation scholarship (Goffman 1959; García 2014) with literature on migration, intimacy, and authenticity (Stoler 1989, 2006; Friedman 2015; Simoni 2015; Ivory 2017), I develop the concept of *strategic intimacies* in this analysis to contribute to the aforementioned literatures and to highlight various contours of intimacy in the context of marriage and partner migration that challenge and reflect what it looks like to be in an "authentic" marital relationship that enables individuals to gain admission past state borders.

Methods

The larger project from which this article is drawn involves in-depth interviews conducted with eighteen Vietnamese-Canadian participants in *DCG* arrangements, or what the Canadian government would consider "marriage fraud". I met interviewees through social networks, snowball sampling, and volunteer work with migrant community organizations. While my participants consisted of men and women, this paper focuses on the narratives of three women in particular, all of whom were born in Vietnam and paid between $55,00 and $65,000 USD to Vietnamese-Canadian men to "marry" them. I conducted these interviews in English and Vietnamese at various spaces including participants' homes, nail salons, and coffee shops, switching between both languages as interviewees felt comfortable. To mitigate risk and protect participants' identities, I did not record interviews, but jotted down notes that were later retyped on a laptop, with the original notes destroyed. Typed notes were anonymized and coded on NViVo, with identifying details redacted.

Interviewees ranged from their early twenties to late fifties, and were employed in low-skilled occupations. These interviews are also informed and supplemented by fifteen months of ethnographic research that I conducted between 2018 and 2019 while working part-time at an immigration law and consulting firm as a legal assistant. In this capacity, I met with clients from diverse socio-economic backgrounds who were in relationships with Canadian citizens, and who were interested in submitting spousal sponsorship applications. With extensive training, I oversaw the process of compiling a variety of supporting documents and government forms necessary for spousal sponsorship applications. This experience familiarized me with the application process and enabled me to draft interview questions that captured transnational couples' experiences with the Canadian immigration system before, during, and after applying for spousal sponsorship.

My positionality as a Vietnamese-Canadian woman in a relationship with a non-Canadian enabled me to develop a strong rapport with participants, as they saw me as both "like" them (self-identified female, Vietnamese-speaking, experienced with the Canadian immigration system) and not like them (Canadian-born, native English speaker). In learning more about their experiences with a complex immigration system, I was forced to reckon with my own privileges as someone who had been fortunate enough to be born in Canada and who never had to resort to *DCG* to merit access to another country.

My positionality also reminded me to consider the unintended consequences of producing knowledge on this topic, including romanticizing the nature of these seemingly "successful" relationships or exposing the Vietnamese-Canadian community – already under intensified state scrutiny – that had given me access to their experiences. While the potential consequences of drawing on strategic intimacies in cross-border marriages, whether for citizenship purposes or otherwise, has received wide scholarly attention, ranging from intimate partner violence and sexual coercion (Chiu 2017; Cheung and Chiu 2019) to international trafficking (Constable 2012; Lee 2014), the women in my study proactively rejected the notion that they had been coerced or trafficked in their *DCG* arrangements. I reiterate here that interviewees' narratives and experiences are not generalizable and may well be the minority in the trajectory of *DCG* arrangements. However, while it remains possible that the romantic feelings that interviewees candidly expressed to me about their now-husbands can themselves be a part of the performance of strategic intimacies, and performativity colours every form of communication (Goffman 1959), interviewees had little to gain by presenting a convincing romantic narrative to me, considering the confidentiality of these interviews and the fact that the majority of them had surpassed the two-year conditional residency requirement.

I was also concerned with whether, by writing about these cases of *DCG*, I would risk playing into a moral panic about marriages of convenience that discredits all spousal sponsorship applications, and whether I would be providing political ammunition to immigration officers and policymakers. However, through conducting supplementary interviews with immigration officials, I was reassured that I am not providing a level of detail about strategies deployed by transnational couples in this analysis that officials are not already aware of. While it is true that officials operate within a culture of suspicion, it would be naïve for those reading this analysis to assume that cases of *DCG* do not exist, or that I should not discuss them because to do so would occupy too great of a place in the public imagination. Rather, in my analysis, I stress the importance of unpacking the narratives and trajectories in these cases to acknowledge that they happen rather than to deny that they do not, and to discuss them in ways that destabilize the rush to judgement for those who participate in "marriage fraud" arrangements. Rather than being representative, this analysis focuses on three narratives to add complexity to normative understandings of "marriage fraud" by recasting *DCG* participants and practices in different hues to highlight the nuanced ways that border controls and intimate relationships intersect.

DCG arrangements and trajectories

Kimmy

Upon graduating high school, Kimmy's neighbours recommended that she meet Trinh, a Canada-based DCG broker who specialized in recruiting Canadian men for *DCG* arrangements. Kimmy recalls of her first phone call with Trinh:

> She ask me why I want to come to Canada. I said, to live there because I am from a small village, my family is not rich, and I am not good in school. There is not much for me in Vietnam, but in Canada I can *lám móng tay và chân* [do manicures and pedicures] and work for nail store, then I send money back home. Trinh ask me what I like to do for fun, how tall and old I am, if I have boyfriend. Then she say, okay, I will find someone for you that looks like good match on paper.

In less than two weeks, Trinh called Kimmy's parents to inform them that she had met a man named Quoc who agreed to sponsor Kimmy to Canada as his "spouse" for $55,000 USD. Quoc and Kimmy were close in age, and Quoc had a stable job, which meant that he possessed enough funds to demonstrate to the Canadian government that he could support Kimmy as his wife in Canada, thus increasing their chances for a sponsorship approval.

Kimmy admitted that she did not initially think Quoc was attractive, "just *cường được*" [okay, so-so]. During the two trips that Quoc made to Vietnam to mimic the stages of a cross-border courtship with Kimmy, she was struck by what they did share in common, including a love for movies and an aversion to nightlife. At Trinh's suggestion, Kimmy and Quoc brought outfit changes and posed for photos both together as a couple in group outings at various tourist hotspots. As is common across most *DCG* arrangements, Kimmy and Quoc's *DCG* involved a traditional Vietnamese tea ceremony, followed by a large wedding reception attended by over fifty guests, and a "honeymoon" trip to another city in Vietnam with a hired photographer.

Upon their sponsorship application approval in 2018, Kimmy and Quoc acknowledged that they had developed feelings for each other, and decided not to file for divorce. They are now in a long-term, committed relationship, currently reside together, and are planning to have their first child.

My-Linh

My-Linh, a fifty-year-old woman from a densely populated city in Vietnam, asserted that she did not choose to participate in a *DCG* arrangement for herself, but rather, for her sons. Unlike Kimmy, My-Linh relied on her cousin, who resided in Canada, to take on the role of a DCG broker by helping her find someone in Canada to "marry" her:

> I could not afford a broker because my kids are in school in Canada, which is expensive for international. School is cheaper if they are Canadian. My [Canadian] cousin knows many people … she is a *bà tám* [meddling woman], she knows everyone's business! She called me and said, "I found someone who will "marry" you for $65,000. Ben Vietnamese, older, and divorced, like you. The government will think it is a believable match."

On My-Linh's second trip to Canada to visit her sons, she and Ben held a relatively small "fake" wedding reception at a restaurant. They maintained regular contact after their spousal sponsorship application was approved, and decided to move in together after a year of My-Linh residing in Canada. The couple recently celebrated their sixth wedding anniversary and renewed their vows with friends and family at a larger reception than their "fake" one.

Jasmine

Equipped with a degree in the sciences, Jasmine was more educated than the average man in her coastal hometown, which made it difficult for her to date – a common issue for educated women in Vietnam that Thai (2008, 51) refers to as the "marriage gender bind." As social media began attracting tourists from overseas to her hometown, Jasmine met foreigners whose open-minded attitudes she enjoyed, and which rendered Canada appealing to her.

Like Kimmy, Jasmine's parents also hired a reputable DCG broker who introduced Jasmine to Nam, a Vietnamese-Canadian man a few years her senior. Jasmine admits that she originally had no interest in Nam until a turn of events at their staged wedding. The couple have been legally married for four years, do not have plans to file for divorce, and maintain an open and intimate relationship.

From strategic intimacies to transformative moments

All interviewees rejected the idea of "love at first sight" and pointed to moments during which they enacted strategic intimacies with their sponsors, prompted by bureaucratic immigration requirements and tertiary actors, as pivotal turning points in their respective relationships. The social process of responding to and completing bureaucratic immigration requirements, as well as engaging with brokers and tertiary actors, significantly buttressed the transformation of their *DCG* arrangements into long-term relationships.

As the case studies above highlight, strategic intimacies heavily depend on "networks of complicity" (Sadiq 2009, 58) or individuals outside of the couple who aid in the formation, construction, and moderation of strategic intimacies. Members of these networks include DCG brokers, who systematically facilitate the presentation of a "real" relationship to state authorities by helping couples rehearse the "love" story of how they met in preparation for interviews with immigration officers, and by securing guests and attire for wedding receptions and ceremonies. As I have detailed elsewhere (Tran forthcoming), in addition to recruiting sponsors, DCG brokers connect Vietnamese families interested in *DCG* to Canadian nationals who may be interested in sponsoring for a wide range of reasons, including but not limited to monetary gain; brokers also cross-check information about both parties in a *DCG* arrangement to ensure a believably sustainable performance of intimacy.

Moreover, *DCG* brokers introduce couples to other tertiary actors who are often aware of the nature of these arrangements, and who play critical roles in the successful deployment of strategic intimacies, including: "fake" wedding guests, who bear witness to the couple's union and provide supporting letters; photographers, who encourage couples to enact physical displays of affection with a focus not only on capturing the couple's intimacy, but the attendance of third parties including relatives and wedding guests; merchants and dressmakers, who rent out wedding rings and attire; and immigration lawyers and consultants, who guide couples through the process of submitting spousal sponsorship applications by advising them on how to best navigate required government forms and document their "authentic" relationship for government evaluation (Tran forthcoming).

The process of providing tangible evidence of an "authentic" relationship to the Canadian government to meet spousal sponsorship requirements significantly shapes how individuals in *DCG* arrangements interact with each other. Jasmine noted that she first felt genuinely attracted to Nam when they sang together at their wedding reception. Their photographer repeatedly urged them to interact physically to achieve a more believable wedding album:

> Our photographer said, "Look like you are having fun! You are "married" now. Sing together, kiss her." After singing karaoke together, [Nam] kissed me for the photographer. Then he picked me up ... he made a speech: "To my beautiful wife, a good singer!" We knew it was fake, but it was funny, I had a good time. It felt like we were on a date and he was proud I'm his girlfriend, even though it was pretend. Even though I did not like him a lot at first, that was the first time I felt real feelings for him.

The couple's awareness that they needed to deploy strategic intimacies to provide "proof" of their relationship to Canadian immigration officials motivated them to mimic physical displays of affection. The moment of "pretend" kissing that their photographer knowingly encouraged became a transformative moment that prompted Jasmine to consider Nam as more than a man in a transactional arrangement who could help her merit Canadian residency.

Similarly, although previous photos taken by Kimmy's photographer showcased Kimmy air-kissing Quoc on the cheek, Kimmy's DCG broker rebuked her for not being aggressive enough in her photos by insisting: "Real Canadians, they are not afraid to kiss on the lips." Kimmy was visibly nervous, as she had never kissed a boy before, but recalls how Quoc reassured her:

> He took my hand and goes [patting gently] and say, "*Em*, what is your favourite romance movie? For this picture, we just pretend to be people in that movie ... don't worry." I saw how [Quoc] is sweet, he take good care of me. When I kiss him, it is not a bad first kiss. From that, I start to think, he would make a good real husband.

The crucial role that external actors have in transforming DCG relationships is notable in these two recollections. As Kimmy and Quoc's DCG broker and photographer were aware that enacting stronger physical displays of affection would help the couple's spousal sponsorship application appear more "Canadian" and thus convincing to immigration officers, they manufactured the setting and conditions under which the couple could deploy strategic intimacies to increase their chances for a sponsorship approval. However, these conditions rendered the couple's intimacy more "real" than either expected: Quoc was Kimmy's first real "kiss", and his patience and understanding for their situation concretized her feelings towards him not only as a short-term *DCG* partner, but as a lifelong partner whom she could rely on for emotional support.

The social process of preparing to meet bureaucratic immigration requirements also served as an influential mechanism in transforming couples' interactions with and feelings for each other. For instance, My-Linh recalled developing feelings for her sponsor, Ben, in the process of preparing for an interview with an immigration officer:

> Ben told me, don't worry. He said, "The officer will ask us questions to test that we know each other. So let's practice." We learned and memorized each other's favourite food and colour. I asked him how old his daughter was, and Ben said, "She is older now ... but to me she will always be my *công chúa* [princess]." I like that [Ben] loves his daughter like I love my kids. Ben told me that is what made him love me too, when he learned I did *DCG* to support my kids' study in Canada.

In the process of learning and memorizing facts about one another in preparation for their interview with immigration officers, Ben and My-Linh discovered shared interests and values that strengthened and transformed their relationship, tipping it from transactional into something more.

Similarly, Kimmy's feelings for Quoc were reaffirmed when, after being sponsored to Canada, she struggled to complete basic paperwork to secure a social insurance number. As instructed by their DCG broker and lawyer, Quoc called Kimmy daily to maintain a log of contact that they could include as part of their sponsorship application to provide "proof" of their consistent communication. During a scheduled phone call, Kimmy broke down crying: "I told him, I am all alone ... and my English is not good, I do not know how to do this [paperwork]." Ironically, the process of filling out mandatory administrative paperwork for immigration purposes helped solidify Kimmy's interest in pursuing a long-term relationship with Quoc:

> Quoc say no problem, he come over to explain the forms to me. He is a nice person, always happy ... he help me even though he did not have to. He is very good, not lazy. Whatever I ask him for help, he help me. I never feel alone in Canada anymore because he is there for me, a good husband ... showing me good places to eat, teaching me how to enjoy life here with him.

Like Kimmy, Jasmine also encountered unexpected difficulties adjusting to life in Canada. She regarded her age, English-speaking abilities, deployment of strategic intimacies, and participation in *DCG* as possibly detrimental to her ability to date other men:

> My English is good ... but will never sound like yours, right? I am thirty. I could not find a job right away and I did not want to go places alone, so I could not meet people. I felt lonely ... and who would want to date a married woman? Whoever I am interested in ... they will have to know that I married someone to come to Canada ... that does not look good for me. One day, it was so cold, *muốn chết* [want to die]! I was miserable. I called Nam. He told me, "You are Canadian now, let's go skating!" He took me to skate ... and showed me the city. It was the first time I felt happy here. I asked [Nam] if I could sleep with him ... that was when I knew I want something more with him.

Unlike DCG brokers, who facilitate multiple *DCG* arrangements, the majority of men who participate in DCG as sponsors do so only once, as to sponsor in more than one cross-border relationship would draw additional government attention and prove too risky. Perhaps because it was their first and only time participating in a DCG arrangement, all three sponsors transcended their agreed-upon roles and responsibilities by offering transportation, paperwork assistance, dining and recreational accompaniment, and friendship to interviewees. Although these interactions may have initially been motivated by the need to document their relationships to meet bureaucratic immigration requirements, in all three cases, undertakings of strategic intimacies challenged the parameters of *DCG* arrangements by intersecting with ideals of love and companionship, ultimately transforming into emotional entanglements that were less strategic and performed for the sake of helping interviewees secure citizenship. Participants' narratives demonstrate how the government's efforts to screen and police for marriage fraud by holding all transnational couples up to specific expectations around "intimacy" can have the paradoxical effect of bringing couples, especially ones in *DCG* arrangements, closer together through the social process of fulfilling bureaucratic immigration requirements and engaging with networks of complicity in order to do so.

Discussion and conclusion

Interviewees' experiences with Canadian immigration processes shed light on how structural factors in increasingly globalized and securitized border regimes can both dictate and be dictated by micro-level relationships and articulations of marriage and intimacy. As Kimmy summarized her frustration with the dichotomy of "real" and "fake" marriages:

> My first "fake" kiss with Quoc is my *first real kiss*! I never kiss a boy before, never. So why the government think what I do is wrong? If Quoc and I are in real love now, and that kiss and our relationship is real, then even if our *DCG* is not, why it is a crime?

Kimmy's experience speaks to the paradoxical conditions that *DCG* participants can find themselves in, and affirms scholars' calls for more theoretical attention to be paid to conjugal relationships in transnational contexts that trouble globalized ideals, temporal understandings, and dichotomies of love, marriage, and intimacy as they intersect with money (Constable 2009; Friedman 2015; Simoni 2015). In all three cases, "backstage" and "frontstage" are blurred and deconstruct themselves through the "staging talk" (Goffman, 1959) and strategic intimacies that participants must employ to provide believable documentation of their "authentic" relationships to state authorities.

This blurring of backstage and frontstage, and the transformative effects that *DCG* participation may have on couples who decide to stay together, is particularly evident when interviewees discuss how they divided the sponsor's *DCG* money after they decided to stay together. While interviewees were ultimately able secure jobs in Canada and remit back to their families in Vietnam, their recollections of moments when they realized that their enactment of strategic intimacies transcended or troubled what qualified as "real" or "fake" emotions effectively demonstrate a breakdown in ways that the self is presented. For instance, although Jasmine's DCG broker had arranged for

Jasmine's parents to pay Nam half of the sponsorship money upfront and the remaining half after Jasmine secured permanent residency, the couple's decision to remain married "for real" prior to her securing permanent residency complicated the couple's approach to discussing financial matters:

> I did not want to even talk about the money my parents owed Nam for sponsoring me to Canada. Not because I do not want to pay him, but because I am worried Nam will think, "Oh, she is always thinking about money, maybe she is staying with me to save money." Finally, I asked him, "Do you want my parents to still pay you?" Nam said, "No, we are together now and that's worth more than money." Still, I try to pay when we go out, I never want him or other people thinking I am with him just for money, that is not true.

For Jasmine, avoiding the topic of money completely enabled her to present herself to others as one-half of a relationship based on genuine love and prove the authenticity of her relationship to Nam. All interviewees agreed that, once they decided to stay with the man who sponsored them, broaching the topic of money was difficult, as they had to transition to discussing finances in a way that was distinct from the transactional manners with which they negotiated money at the beginning of their *DCG* arrangements. Residues of the transactional roots of their *DCG* arrangements continue to shape and constrain how couples perform "genuine" intimacy, as exemplified in Kimmy and My-Linh's husbands decisions to accept but reinvest the money that they received from their roles as sponsors to purchase bigger diamond rings for their wives and host larger, more extravagant weddings to distinguish their "fake-turned-real" relationships.

Here, participants demonstrate once again how modern, Westernized ideals of love are sustained along a real/instrumental dichotomy, one that relies on the idea of money as being inherently incompatible with ideas of "true" love (Constable 2009; Simoni 2015). In re-investing those payments into rings and ceremonies, or foregoing those payments altogether, DCG participants reaffirm and reinforce "authenticity paradigms" (Friedman 2015, 206) by using the money that sponsors received through instrumental means for seemingly non-instrumental purposes.

As the Canadian government's spousal sponsorship requirements increasingly necessitate that transnational couples provide tangible "proof" of their relationships to gain admissibility past state borders (D'Aoust 2013; Gaucher 2014, 2018), *DCG* participants must deploy strategic intimacies and interact with one another in manufactured settings which require a suspension of disbelief to demonstrate that they are coherent halves of an intimate marital relationship. In the process of circumventing, contesting, and destabilizing state borders through their participation in "marriage fraud", participants in *DCG* arrangements both challenge the immigration requirements and authenticity paradigms (Friedman 2015) that sustain restrictive immigration regimes, at the same time as they reaffirm them by experiencing and internalizing elements of these requirements and paradigms. In pursuing long-term, committed relationships with their sponsors rather divorcing them, and by cautiously approaching the ways that they discuss money with their sponsors-turned-husbands, interviewees "apply state power to themselves" (Menjívar and Lakhani 2016, 1820). Their decisions highlight how undergoing formal immigration processes can trigger and sustain enduring effects on migrant behaviours and identities, as the process of undertaking strategic intimacies becomes transformative in shaping participants' lives, thus "self-perpetuating" (Menjívar and Lakhani 2016, 1819) global ideals of what marriage, love, family, and intimacy are and ought to look like.

At the same time as their engagement with intimate aspects of their lives are shaped by borders, I argue that *DCG* participants also actively *shape* border controls by challenging the permeability of access to Canadian citizenship. Strategic intimacies deployed by *DCG* participants point to the irony and fallibility that characterize the securitized border regime as a whole: one that, in attempting to police and screen for transnational marriages by separating fake marriages from "real" ones, can also facilitate, enable, and transform the very "fraudulent" and "unworthy" relationships that it seeks to curb. Interviewees' experiences highlight variation in ways that they navigated their respective *DCG* arrangements and formal Canadian immigration processes, providing examples of how borders can both shape and be shaped by strategic intimacies.

Ironically, despite institutional immigration policies and documents advocating for marriages that are consensual, unarranged, and characterized by the freedom, liberty, and "spontaneity" (Illouz 2007, 114) of modern love, *DCG* participants' enactments of strategic intimacies, systematically facilitated by tertiary actors under manufactured conditions, highlight just how important class, gender, race, and ethnicity are to legitimizing discourses surrounding love and marriage. While strategic intimacies can be understood as a tool of resistance deployed against increasingly restrictive border regimes, they remain practices confined to more elite groups who possess a certain threshold of social and economic capital. *DCG* arrangements would not have been possible if, for instance, interviewees' families did not have access to someone living overseas who could mediate and secure a willing sponsor in the first place, and the staging of "fake" weddings, tea ceremonies, and honeymoon nights came at the expense of *real* money needed to secure venues, wedding guests, attire, and legal consultations. The capacity to provide "evidence" of a legitimate relationship requires participants to have access to social networks that they can rely on, the ability to navigate transnational spaces unfamiliar to them, and social capital to manufacture the settings and conditions for strategic intimacies to be believable.

The processes by which participants prepared to present evidence of authentic relationships that enabled their spousal sponsorship applications to be approved by state officials also highlights the gendered and heteronormative assumptions underlying idealized notions of marriage, love, and intimacy deemed acceptable by the state. For instance, couples intentionally changed from traditional *áo dài* in their tea ceremonies to white wedding dresses and suits for their staged wedding receptions, an expense that caters to Westernized wedding norms. Participants were also encouraged by DCG brokers and legal consultants to highlight their wedding bands in spousal sponsorship applications, which symbolically demonstrate their emotional and financial investments in each other. Moreover, to justify why the sponsor would marry a foreigner, couples relied on discourses of what constitutes an ideal partner that can be admitted past state borders, reinforcing gendered roles within the patriarchal family (Kim and Kim 2020). For instance, in the process of preparing for their interview with an immigration officer, My-Linh and Ben practiced emphasizing how My-Linh could cook Vietnamese food for Ben that a Canadian-born Vietnamese woman could not.

Although the primary function of DCG brokers is to match individuals in short-term, transactional relationships that are plausible enough to warrant state recognition for citizenship purposes, the work of DCG brokers often overlaps with the role of traditional overseas matchmakers, as both are preoccupied with questions of plausibility and compatibility. Because brokers match prospective DCG participants according to how similar participants' values and characteristics are in order to maximize the couple's ability to deploy strategic intimacies that highlight their compatibility and authenticity in spousal sponsorship applications, it is unsurprising that interviewees developed feelings for their partners. Future research should pay attention to contours of intimacy, love, and citizenship as they are mediated by transnational marriage brokers and matchmakers, whose identities are "not fixed" but rather, can be re-evaluated "in relation to location, time and power" (Lindquist, Xiang, and Yeoh 2012, 10). Regardless of whether they intend to facilitate "real" or "fake" marriages, transnational marriage brokers play important roles and occupy highly demanded, niche spaces in globalized markets that cannot be underestimated (Yeoh et al. 2017).

I argue and have demonstrated here how, ironically, the "procedural quality" (Illouz 2007, 39) that documenting and presenting "proof" of love-based relationships takes on through formal Canadian immigration processes sets the very conditions for *DCG* arrangements to flourish and transform into something more than just "faked" for immigration purposes. The narratives above highlight how fake marriages are rendered necessary and only manifest through and because of exclusionary and racialized border policies.

While my concept of strategic intimacies does not account for the unexpected turn of events and spontaneity with which the *DCG* arrangements developed, this analysis focuses on the three cases above to shed light on the complex and nuanced ways that *DCG* arrangements, relying on the deployment of strategic intimacies, can unfold, as well as the transformative effects that they can yield in response to, but also as a result of, border regimes and state powers which attempt to control for intimacy and mobility. While these trajectories may only apply to a marginal number of cases, they are not unusual, and thus highlight how the concepts of "true" and "instrumental" love are not antithetical nor mutually exclusive to each other, and cannot be characterized as such.

Migration scholarship would benefit from remaining attuned to empirical and intersectional undertakings of research on the variety of other forms that transnational intimate relationships can take, including common-law relationships. While the present study examines a minority of "successful" cases in which *DCG* arrangements are transformed into relationships that both parties remain in and pursue based on "love", an examination and juxtaposition of genuine cross-border marriages and both successful and unsuccessful (rejected) spousal sponsorship applications would help to expand and develop theorizations of strategic intimacies.

Paying careful attention to the nuances of how relationships shape and inform individuals' articulations about themselves and others, especially in the context of marriage and partner migration, is especially important in rethinking configurations of what it means to be in a relationship worthy of state recognition. Acknowledging the inadequacies in dichotomous views of love and money paves the way for new understandings of transnational emotional entanglements in an increasingly globalized world.

Note

1. The term commonly used to denote marriage fraud in Vietnam, *đám cưới giả*, combines the words *đám cưới* ("wedding") with *giả* ("fake"), thus translating to "fake wedding" in English.

Acknowledgements

I am indebted to the courageous women in this article who trusted me enough to share their nuanced cross-border stories in detail with me. This paper would not have been possible without them, nor the expertise and unwavering support of Dr Neda Maghbouleh, Dr Juan Pedroza, Dr Naveen Minai, Dr Alex Lee, and Laila Omar, all of whom were incredibly generous with their time and rich insights. I would also like to thank the faculty members and my cohort at the University of Toronto's Centre for Criminology & Sociolegal Studies, who encouraged me throughout this research and writing process, as well as the anonymous peer reviewers at *Ethnic and Racial Studies* for their engaged and thoughtful feedback.

Disclosure statement

No potential conflict of interest was reported by the author(s).

ORCID

Grace Tran 🕩 http://orcid.org/0000-0002-2460-6520

References

Abrams, Kerry. 2007. "Immigration Law and the Regulation of Marriage." *Minnesota Law Review* 91 (1): 1625–1709.

Abrams, Kerry. 2012. "Marriage Fraud." *California Review* 100 (1): 1–68.

Bernstein, Elizabeth. 2007. *Temporarily Yours: Intimacy, Authenticity, and the Commerce of Sex.* Chicago: University of Chicago Press.

Bhuyan, Rupaleem, Anna Korteweg, and Karin Baqi. 2018. "Regulating Spousal Sponsorship Through Canada's Multiple Border Strategy: The Gendered and Racialized Effects of Structurally Embedded Borders." *Law and Policy* 40 (4): 346–370.

Bonjour, Saski,a and De Hart, Betty. 2013. "A Proper Wife, a Proper Marriage: Constructions of 'Us' and 'Them' in Dutch Family Migration Policy." *European Journal of Women's Studies* 20 (1): 61–76.

Brennan, D. 2004. *What's Love Got to Do with It? Transnational Desires and Sex Tourism in the Dominican Republic.* Durham: Duke University Press.

Carver, Natacha. 2016. "For Her Protection and Benefit: The Regulation of Marriage-Related Migration to the UK." *Ethnic and Racial Studies* 15 (39): 2758–2776.

Chávez, Sergio. 2016. *Border Lives: Fronterizos, Transnational Migrants, and Commuters in Tijuana.* Oxford: Oxford University Press.

Chen, Mei-Hua. 2015. "The 'Fake Marriage' Test in Taiwan: Gender, Sexuality, and Border Control." *Cross-Currents: East Asian History and Culture Review E-Journal.* http://cross-currents.berkeley.edu/e-journal/issue-15.

Cheung, Adam Ka-Lok, and Tuen Yi Chiu. 2019. "Husband-to-wife Sexual Coercion in Cross-Border Marriage: A Relationship Power Perspective." *Current Sociology* 1–22.

Chiu, Tuen Yi. 2017. "Marriage Migration as a Multifaceted System: The Intersectionality of Intimate Partner Violence in Cross-Border Marriages)." *Violence Against Women* 23 (11): 1293–1313.

Constable, N. 2009. "The Commodification of Intimacy: Marriage, Sex, and Reproductive Labor." *Annual Review of Anthropology* 38: 49–64.

Constable, Nicole. 2012. "International Marriage Brokers, Cross-Border Marriages and the U.S. Anti-Trafficking Campaign." *Journal of Ethnic and Migration Studies* 38 (7): 1137–1154.

D'Aoust, Anne-Marie. 2013. "In the Name of Love: Marriage Migration, Governmentality and Technologies of Love." *International Political Sociology* 7 (3): 258–274.

Dua, Enakshi. 2007. "Exclusion Through Inclusion: Female Asian Migration in the Making of Canada as a White Settler Nation." *Gender, Place & Culture* 14 (4): 446–466.

Eggebø, H. 2013. "A Real Marriage? Applying for Marriage Migration to Norway." *Journal of Ethnic and Migration Studies* 39 (5): 773–789.

Enriquez, Laura. 2020. *Of Love and Papers: How Immigration Policy Affects Romance and Family*. Oakland: University of California Press.

Friedman, Sara. 2015. "Regulating Cross-Border Intimacy: Authenticity Paradigms and the Specter of Illegality among Chinese Marital Immigrants to Taiwan." In *Immigrant Encounters: Intimate Labor, the State, and Mobility Across Asia*, edited by Sara Friedman and Pardis Mahdavi, 206–230. Philadelphia: University of Pennsylvania Press.

García, Angela S. 2014. "Hidden in Plain Sight: How Unauthorised Migrants Strategically Assimilate in Restrictive Localities in California." *Journal of Ethnic and Migration Studies* 40 (12): 1895–1914.

Gaucher, M. 2014. "Attack of the Marriage Fraudsters!: An Examination of the Harper Government's Antimarriage Fraud Campaign." *International Journal of Canadian Studies* 50 (1): 187–205.

Gaucher, M. 2018. *A Family Matter: Citizenship, Conjugal Relationships, and Canadian Immigration Policy*. Vancouver: UBC Press.

Goffman, Erving. 1959. *The Presentation of Self in Everyday Life*. New York: Anchor Books.

Groes, Christian. 2018. "Mobility Through Sexual Economy: Exchanging Sexual Capital for Respectability in Mozambican Women's Marriage Migration to Europe." In *Intimate Mobilities: Sexual Economies, Marriage and Migration in a Disparate World*, edited by Christian Groes and Nadine Fernandez, 118–139. New York: Berghahn Books.

Groes, Christian, and Nadine Fernandez. 2018. "Intimate Mobilities and Mobile Intimacies." In *Intimate Mobilities: Sexual Economies, Marriage and Migration in a Disparate World*, edited by Christian Groes and Nadine Fernandez, 1–27. New York: Berghahn Books.

Harris, J. R., and M. P. Todaro. 1970. "Migration, Unemployment and Development: A Two-Sector Analysis." *The American Economic Review* 60 (1): 126–142.

Hoang, K. K. 2015. *Dealing in Desire: Asian Ascendancy, Western Decline, and the Hidden Currencies of Global Sex Work*. Oakland: University of California Press.

Hwang, Maria Cecilia, and Rhacel Salazar Parreñas. 2018. "Intimate Migrations: The Case of Marriage Migrants and Sex Workers in Asia." In *Routledge Handbook of Asian Migrations*, edited by Gracia Liu-Farrer and Brenda S.A. Yeoh, 64–74. New York: Routledge.

Illouz, Eva. 2007. *Cold Intimacies: The Making of Emotional Capitalism*. Cambridge: Polity Press.

Immigration and Citizenship Canada. 2017. "Protect Yourself From Marriage Fraud. Retrieved from the Government of Canada website". https://www.canada.ca/en/immigration-refugees-citizenship/services/protect-fraud/marriage-fraud.html

Ivory, Tristan. 2017. "Strategic Ethnic Performance and the Construction of Authenticity in Urban Japan." *Ethnic and Racial Studies* 40 (1): 172–189. doi:10.1080/01419870.2016.1206587.

Kim, Nora Hui-Jung, and Hyemee Kim. 2020. "From a Spuse to a Citizen: The Gendered and Sexualized Path to Citizenship for Marriage Migrants in South Korea." *Law and Society Review* 54 (2): 423–452.

Lee, Hyunok. 2014. Trafficking in Women? Or Multicultural Family? The Contextual Difference of Commodification of Intimacy." *Gender, Place & Culture* 21 (10): 1249–1266.

Lindquist, J., B. Xiang, and B. S. A. Yeoh. 2012. "Opening the Black Box of Migration: Brokers, the Organization of Transnational Mobility and the Changing Political Economy in Asia." *Pacific Affairs* 85 (1): 7–19.

Luibheid, Eithne. 2002. *Entry Denied: Controlling Sexuality at the Border*. Minnesota: University of Minnesota Press.

Massey, Douglas. 1999. "Why Does Immigration Occur?: A Theoretical Synthesis." In *The Handbook of International Migration: The American Experience*, edited by C. Hirschman, P. Kasinitz, and J. Dewind, 34–52. New York: Russell Sage Foundation.

Menjívar, Cecilia, and Sarah M. Lakhani. 2016. "Transformative Effects of Immigration Law: Immigrants' Personal and Social Metamorphoses Through Regularization." *American Journal of Sociology* 121 (6): 1818–1855.

O'Neil, Peter. 2015. "Federal Report Warns 'Marriages of Convenience' a Threat to Immigration System." *Vancouver Sun*. April 8.

Parreñas, R. S., H. C. Thai, and R. Silvey. 2016. "Guest Editors' Introduction: Intimate Industries: Restructuring (Im) Material Labor in Asia." *Positions* 24 (1): 1–15.

Piore, M. J. 1979. *Birds of Passage: Migrant Labor and Industrial Societies*. Cambridge: Cambridge University Press.

Ryo, Emily. 2015. "Less Enforcement, More Compliance: Rethinking Unauthorized Migration." *UCLA Law Review* 62: 622.

Sadiq, Kamal. 2009. *Paper Citizens: How Illegal Immigrants Acquire Citizenship in Developing Countries*. New York: Oxford University Press.

Simoni, Valerio. 2015. "Intimacy and Belonging in Cuban Tourism and Migration." *The Cambridge Journal of Anthropology* 33 (2): 26–41.

Stoler, A. L. 1989. "Making Empire Respectable: The Politics of Race and Sexual Morality in 20th Century Colonial Cultures." *American Ethnologist* 16 (4): 634–660.

Stoler, A. L. 2006. *Haunted by Empire: Geographies of Intimacy in North American History*. Durham: Duke University Press.

Thai, Hung Cam. 2008. *For Better or For Worse: Vietnamese International Marriags in the New Global Economy*. Piscataway: Rutgers University Press.

Tran, Grace. Forthcoming. ""I'm Not a Bad Guy, I Swear:" Analyzing Emotion Work and Negotiations of Criminality and Masculinity in Vietnamese-Canadian Men's Participation in 'Fake Wedding' Arrangements." In *Transnational Marriage and Partner Migration: Constellations of Security, Citizenship, and Rights*, edited by Anne-Marie D'Aoust. New York: Rutgers Press.

Wray, Helena. 2006. "An Ideal Husband? Marriages of Convenience, Moral Gatekeeping and Immigration to the UK." *European Journal of Migration and Law* 8 (3-4): 303–320.

Wray, Helena. 2015. "The 'Pure' Relationship, Sham Marriages and Immigration Control." In *Marriage Rites and Rights*, edited by Joanna Miles, Pervees Mody, and Rebecca Probert, 141–165. Oxford and Portland: Hart.

Yeoh, B., H. L. Chee, and G. Baey. 2017. "Managing Risk, Making a Match: Brokers and the Management of Mobility in International Marriage." *Mobilities* 12 (2): 227–242.

Border panic over the pandemic: mediated anxieties about migrant sex workers and queers during the AIDS crises in Turkey

Yener Bayramoğlu [ID]

ABSTRACT
Looking back to remember the "arrival" of AIDS in Turkey, this article explores how the spread of the new disease fueled border panic in Turkey from the mid 1980s to the mid 1990s. Drawing on a rich array of material from the archives of national newspapers and magazines, this article analyzes the media discourse on migrant sex workers from the former USSR and the first HIV-positive men. It shows how both groups were seen as intruders bringing the virus from outside Turkey's borders to its territory. In both cases, I argue, fear of the spread of the virus across borders became entangled with anxieties about the movement of ideas, images, lifeworlds, and meanings relating to sexuality that were discursively constructed as fundamentally alien to Turkish ones. The movement of sexually and racially "other" bodies across borders was seen as a threat to the fragile construed border between "Turkishness" and "foreignness".

Introduction: the "Arrival" of AIDS

> "The danger of AIDS brought by *nataşa*s working in the Black Sea region represents the greatest challenge to be faced by the authorities of the Black Sea Region since the Chernobyl disaster"[1]

This short excerpt from an article published in *Milliyet,* one of Turkey's bestselling national newspapers in the 1990s, synthesizes several aspects of "border panic": a state of public anxiety and panic in response to perceived border insecurity. Here, the movement of a virus across borders is compared with another nonhuman intrusion: the effects of a nuclear disaster that transcended national borders. What is striking in this sentence is that two nonhuman movements — of a virus and of nuclear radiation – seen to threaten public health are brought into the same frame as migrant sex workers from former Soviet states (*"nataşa"*). This echoes the long tradition of media images, metaphors, and discourses that portray migration as a natural disaster (Musolff 2011). The constructed nature of political borders is underplayed when media discursively entangle the migration of people with the mobility of the nonhuman.

In this article, I trace mediated anxieties about AIDS as a contagious disease spreading across borders, and explore how journalists invoke fear of the disease to impose meanings upon bodies marked as sexually, ethnically and/or racially different. Drawing on an archive of media texts and images, I revisit the peak decade of panic over AIDS: the period from the mid-1980s to the mid-1990s. While there have been innumerable studies on HIV/AIDS in European and North American contexts, and on borders and migration researched from the perspectives of the Global North, here, I turn my attention to Turkey, a country that is predominantly Muslim and has borders with both Europe and the Middle East. Furthermore, while previous studies on racialized and migrantized constructions of HIV/AIDS have often focused on discriminatory discourse on Blackness (Cohen 1999; Phillips 2005) and Haitiness (Dubois 2009), my investigation concentrates on Turkish public anxieties about "Westernness", "Russianness", and "whiteness" at the time when AIDS reached Turkey.

And yet, the disease never actually did reach Turkey in the 1980s. The relevant literature (Erbaydar and Erbaydar 2012; Çetin and Bänziger 2019) reveals that AIDS never became a truly threatening epidemic in Turkey with huge numbers of deaths, as it did in many countries in the Global North in the 1980s and early 1990s. Yet the disease did arrive at a discursive level; defined and disseminated by the Turkish media. What came were new images, meanings, and anxieties that had been hitherto unheard of in Turkey. In reports, associations were made between the virus and bodies marked as sexually and ethnically / racially different. The conclusions drawn by the Turkish press were not grounded in actual experiences or events in Turkey, but were simply meanings, anxieties, and images of AIDS imported from Western media. Borrowing Sara Ahmed's (2004a) concept, I argue that public discourse circulating in the Global North had already established *stickiness* between the concepts of "AIDS" and "the queer body" as well as between "AIDS" and "the migrant body". Turkish journalists simply adopted that *stickiness* from the West and presented it to the Turkish public, thereby inciting a sense of border panic at the height of the international AIDS crisis, while making migrant sex workers and queers the objects of public fear and hate.

By bringing sexuality, race, ethnicity, and disease into the same frame, this article proposes rethinking the meaning of borders. I argue that, in the context of the AIDS crises, borders were not only conceptualized as physical barriers that were supposed to prevent the invisible virus entering Turkish territory, but also as a discursive border between knowable Turkish society and alien ideas and practices. This discursive border was underpinned by violent images and meanings imposed upon Others, and was even integrated into biopolitics and surveillance mechanisms. It was a border that was supposed to protect public health as well as public morality, to defend "Turkishness" from the dangers of a publicly imagined scandalously "foreign" lifeworld of uninhibited sexuality. In this framework, sexually, ethnically and racially "other" bodies that transgressed geographical as well as "moral" borders, such as migrant sex workers from the former Soviet Union, and queer men who visited and returned from Europe, were presented in the mediated public sphere as potential virus carriers who also threatened Turkish sexual moralities.

Before I discuss my central arguments in greater detail, I would like to first summarize my theoretical engagement with border studies. I will then briefly outline the methodological approach I took to study the texts and images I gathered from different archives. By exploring mediated anxieties about two prominent figures – of Turkey's first HIV-positive man and of migrant sex workers– I will map out how sexualized and racialized bordering regimes operated to protect "Turkishness" and "Turkish sexual mores" from "foreign intruders".

Mediated bordering, contagious diseases

Contemporary scholarly interest in borders emerged in disciplines such as geography, history, political science, and sociology, with a number of researchers expressing hope that borders might become less rigid in the wake of events such as the fall of Berlin Wall, the end of the Cold War, or the expansion of the EU (Wilson and Donnan 2012, 3). Despite this initial optimism, there are now more international borders than ever before (ibid. 5), and understanding borders as manifestations of national identity (Rabinowitz 2012), surveillance, control of mobility (Mountz 2011), violence (Andersen and Bergmann 2019), and intersectional sociocultural boundaries (Altay, Yurdakul, and Korteweg 2020) has become all the more expedient with the rise of anti-immigration policies and discourses (Van Houtum and Pijpers 2007; Saddiki 2014; Castro Varela and Mecheril 2016). This has sparked researchers not only to revisit already well-studied and theorized borders such as that between Mexico and the USA, the EU's borders, and the Mediterranean Sea (Saddiki 2017; Madörin 2019; Strasser and Tibet 2019; M'charek 2020), but also to shift their attention to other, under-researched borders, such as the borderland between Georgia and Turkey (Akyüz 2017) and the border between Thailand and Myanmar (Joliffe 2015).

Rather than focusing on borders as a geopolitical concept, my primary concern here is to understand how borders operate in the discursive sphere. Turning towards discourse illustrates how border regimes operate not only physically – manifested in walls, fences, and surveillance technologies – but also as symbolic entities. Dan Rabinowitz's (2012) analysis, for instance, sheds light on how language has become central to establishing, justifying, and maintaining borders in Israel since the state's establishment. On the other hand, scholars such as Bilgin Ayata (2012) and Jaffer Sheyholislami (2010) show how Kurdish media help to establish transnational belongings and identities that stretch across borders. But not only do media technologies, particularly digital media, facilitate the forging and sustaining of transnational belongings and identifications (Bayramoğlu and Lünenborg 2018); they also serve to intertwine borders with data and code, creating a condition of "postvisuality" that helps to secure racialized border regimes (Madörin 2019). Kira Kosnick (2014), for instance, discusses the new roles played by media technologies in reinforcing borders, not only in the form of surveillance technologies, but also in the circulation of images, texts, and meanings that serve to prevent refugees from migrating to the Global North. In *Mediating Migration* (2016), Radha Hegde observes that media reflect and reinforce the logic of the security state's bordering techniques by setting and disseminating definitions of who belongs to a certain territory. This often goes hand in hand with racialized anxieties about the changing demographics of nations (Hegde 2016, 112).

What must be noted here is that "borderscapes" operate as racialized spaces that are shaped by the state's efforts to control the transnational movement of humans (Dell'Agnese and Amilhat Szary 2015) as well as that of nonhumans, such as animals, plants, and viruses. Quarantine is one example of a bordering technique that has been implemented to prevent and control the movement of nonhumans for centuries (Smart and Smart 2012). In the case of viruses and diseases, the human and nonhuman become messily entangled with one another, making it convenient for media and political discourses to implicate certain bodies as the visible embodiment of an invisible epidemic. For instance, as Seçil Yılmaz (2017) argues, at the peak of the syphilis pandemic the Ottoman authorities were primarily concerned with regulating the cross-border movement of refugees, of immigrant men from the empire's peripheries, and of migrant workers, soldiers, and urban dwellers (Yılmaz 2017, 224). Migrant workers were obliged to carry their travel documents together with certificates proving they were syphilis free (ibid. 228). As Murat Arpacı (2014) writes, in mediated discussions in the early Turkish Republic, syphilis was often portrayed as an "enemy" – just as "Greeks" were – that threatened public health and the entire nation (Arpacı 2014, 67). Furthermore, the commonly used Turkish term for syphilis was "frengi", derived from the word "Frenk", which meant "the Western". Thus, the source of syphilis was not only discursively located outside Turkey's physical borders, but also linked to the "Western" "European"

THE SEXUAL POLITICS OF BORDER CONTROL

lifestyle with its imagined liberal sexual morals that threatened the so-called "Turkish race" (Ibid. 76).

Many scholars have written about how borders became an integral part of biopolitics during epidemics such as Ebola (Honigsbaum 2017; Pieri 2019), H1N1, or SARS (Keil and Ali 2006); highlighting the significance of the borderscape for sexualized and racialized regimes of policing and surveillance (Luibhéid 2002). I will not revisit this body of work here, but turn my attention to a particular moment and space in the history of pandemics: the peak period of AIDS in Turkey. In order to interrogate the public anxieties of that time, I decided to focus on two figures: migrant sex workers and Murtaza Elgin, the first publicly known HIV-positive man. As I will elaborate in more detail in the following pages, both of these figures represented "foreignness" in Turkish public consciousness. As well as literally crossing national borders, like other "borderlanders" (Anzaldúa 2007) they conflated, mixed, and disrupted the sexualized and racialized categories that borders were supposed to uphold. Furthermore, these two cases are important in showing how Turkey's borders are publicly imagined as fragile and vulnerable to seduction and abuse by bodies that are sexually and ethnically / racially marked as "other". Following Sara Ahmed (2004b), I trace how the movement of sexually and ethnically / racially "other" bodies across borders evoked emotions such as panic, fear, and anxiety among the general public during Turkey's AIDS crises.

My study is based on an examination of texts and images that I gathered during my archival research in Istanbul Atatürk Kitaplığı, the state press archive in Istanbul, Turkey, and the archive of Berlin's Schwules Museum in Germany. Key to my exploration of the 1980s discourse is material from *Hürriyet*. *Hürriyet* was the best-selling newspaper of that period (Sezgin and Wall 2005), and also played a leading role in stoking public anxiety about AIDS in Turkey. The newspaper was the first to publish a scandalizing report on the first known HIV-positive man – without his consent. I expanded my archive by including images and texts from *Nokta*, a tabloid magazine that played an important role in addressing formerly taboo topics such as sex work and homosexuality in Turkish media in the 1980s (Çeler 2011) as well as material from the digital archive of *Milliyet* relating to migrant sex workers during the AIDS crises. In developing my methodology, Fairclough's (2013) concept of critical discourse analysis helped me not only to understand how discursive elements of texts such as metaphor, voice, and argumentation work together to build the architecture of narratives, but also to locate such discourses in their historical and socio-political contexts. I used the figures "Nataşa" and "first HIV positive men", and the topic "AIDS in Turkey" to open specific windows of time within the temporal flow of discourse, which enabled me to sample fragments of discourse from particular moments in the history of the AIDS crises. By using border theory as an analytical framework for deductive coding, I singled out specific patterns of journalistic narrative. In the second phase, I elaborated the analysis by using inductive coding to identify commonalities and contrasts within the material (Mayring 2004).

The Virus Embodied

Stories of the first men to be diagnosed HIV-positive in Turkey tended to be told with reference to mobility or to the crossing of national borders.[2] Often, it was implied that a trip to Europe (usually to Germany) had led to their HIV status. By focusing on the stories told about Turkey's first HIV-positive man, Murtaza Elgin, I would like to discuss how panic over AIDS unfolded in relation to queer sexualities, and how the queer body was connoted as an intruder bringing the virus from Europe to Turkey. Although Elgin was Turkish, there is a long history of queer sexualities been presented as a danger to "Turkishness", Turkish "public sensitivities", and "sexual moral" by the Turkish authorities (Sarı et al. 2018).

In 1985, Murtaza Elgin became the first publicly known HIV-positive person, and his story provides a typical example of how AIDS-related anxieties led to violent bordering processes. Until then, all articles about HIV/AIDS had been about cases in Europe or North America. Based upon the absence of any known case in the country, the then Prime Minister Turgut Özal had told journalists at a press conference that there was no AIDS epidemic in Turkey. Offering an explanation for this, he claimed that unlike in Western countries "the traditional Turkish family structure" did not allow for deviant sexualities.[3] In such statements, not only AIDS, but also the existence of sexual and gender identities that did not fit within "traditional" heteronormative "Turkish society" were discursively located in the West. Despite the homo- and transphobic nature of such press releases, the Turkish authorities were accurate in one point: at that time, AIDS did not constitute a threatening epidemic for Turkish society as a whole or for its gay men (Erbaydar and Erbaydar 2012; Çetin and Bänziger 2019).

Seizing the chance for a scandal, Murtaza Elgin's doctor Dr. Hüseyin Sipahioğlu contacted *Hürriyet* without his patient's consent and told the newspaper that the Minister of Health was wrong – Turkey had its first case.[4] Since Murtaza Elgin was a public figure, *Hürriyet* capitalized on the scoop. Elgin was particularly well known in the Turkish music scene; he was a friend of popular singers such as Ibrahim Tatlises and Ferdi Tayfur, and often accompanied singers on concert tours as a backing vocalist. *Hürriyet*'s reporter's conclusion as to how Murtaza Elgin had become infected by the virus is key to my argumentation:

> After attending concert tours with many singers in Germany, Murtaza Elgin panicked that he might have AIDS and initially got tested under the fake name of Namık Oktay[5]

Without overtly stating so, this sentence implies that Elgin may have become infected with HIV while on concert tours in Germany. This is indeed a typical discursive strategy of journalistic rhetoric: meanings are suggested by combining disparate pieces of information to imply a connection between them. The history of queer representations in Turkish tabloids sees repeated use of such discursive strategies, which create pathologizing, criminalizing, or scandalizing meanings (Bayramoğlu 2018, 160–161). Here, the discursive strategy serves to imply that the source of the disease lay beyond Turkey's borders.

When the Ministry of Health was seen to be slow to take measures to prevent a potential new epidemic from spreading, the sense of border panic became even more intense. *Hürriyet* cited Dr. Sipahioğlu, who warned the public:

> "Today, many patients with AIDS walk and work freely in America and Europe. If preventive measures are not taken immediately, here too, everyone will witness the spread of AIDS."[6]

Ministry of Health reacted immediately. It announced it would put Elgin in quarantine just a couple of days after the first media reports were published.[7] Elgin, however, was unwilling to be quarantined, and hid at different addresses while secretly applying for a visa to flee to Germany.[8] As Elgin was sought, Turkish newspapers warned the public that anyone who helped him hide would be in danger of getting infected by the virus.[9] They even published the addresses where he was believed to be staying.[10]

Eventually, Turkish police apprehended Elgin at a physical border. On November 6, 1985, Elgin was trying to take a Lufthansa flight to Munich when police recognized him at the customs of Istanbul Atatürk Airport. He was then forcibly put into quarantine.[11] The fact that Elgin was arrested at a physical border, at the airport customs checkpoint, reflects and reinforces the border panic that was at least partially created by the media. Furthermore, even if he had not been recognized by the customs authorities, Lufthansa might not have allowed him to take the flight. According to one report, it was Lufthansa's policy in 1985 not to accept HIV-positive passengers.[12] This can be read as one of the early signs of biosecurity measures taken to secure borders in response to the AIDS pandemic, while some countries such as the USA adopted policies to deny entry to HIV-positive immigrants (Luibhéid 2002, 26). So, the border panic created by the media over Elgin's case was multi-layered: at the beginning, the danger was discursively projected beyond Turkey's borders with the implication that Elgin had brought the virus from Germany, and ultimately, media played an important role in forcing Turkish authorities to capture Elgin, and to hinder his mobility.

Let me return to the question of the *stickiness* between AIDS and queer sexualities. What must be noted here is that from the very beginning, Murtaza Elgin's sexuality was represented as outside the realm of heteronormativity. Although he was married to a woman, newspapers circulated rumors about his sexuality and implied that he might have caught the virus from his queer friends.[13] He was recurrently represented as effeminate. Furthermore, as I will show in the following, not only the insinuation that he might be homosexual, but also violent representations, exposure to public scrutiny, and the shaming of his sexuality made his story a queer story.

When Elgin died, his corpse became a stage upon which necropolitical violence (Mbembe 2003) was enacted in order to ease public anxiety by showing that the state was taking action to protect its citizens. While Achille Mbembe (2003) uses the concept of necropolitics to address power in relation to destruction and killing, Banu Bargu (2016) uses the term "necropolitical violence" to refer to acts performed upon dead bodies. Bargu writes how necropolitical violence transforms the dead body into a public display, similar to what Suvendrini Perera (2014) terms the "trophy body": the murdered absolute Other exhibited to the public. The mediated necropolitical violence that was posthumously inflicted upon Elgin's body still haunts people who are old enough to remember the 1980s. In a recent oral history project with Turkish HIV activists (Çetin and Bänziger 2019), the story of Murtaza Elgin's death is remembered in poignant detail:

> "Murtaza died of course, due to lack of treatment, and when he died, they first called an imam who was covered by a garbage bag. On his hands he wore dishwashing gloves, everything looked a bit like an astronaut. Then they gave him a bottle of bleach. Murtaza was ritually washed with it and then wrapped in plastic foil. Then he was placed in a zinc coffin that was nailed closed and sunk into a lime pit. And every single step was documented and published by the media." (Çetin and Bänziger 2019, 116)

This posthumous media performance was paradoxically a documentation of state violence enacted upon bodies with AIDS and the simultaneous effacement of that same violence; the body was completely obliterated in the process. All the materials used during the funeral – the plastic bags, bleach, gloves, zinc, and lime – were measures ostensibly taken to prevent the soil from becoming contaminated by Murtaza Elgin's body and disease. At the same time, they exerted symbolic violence upon Murtaza Elgin. In Islam, corpses are buried covered by nothing more than a cotton shroud. The natural material enables the body to merge with the soil during decomposition, returning it to nature. Symbolically, the plastic foil and zinc coffin functioned as further layers of a punitive border that prevented his body from merging into the earth. The violence inflicted upon Murtaza Elgin was perpetuated by his exclusion and isolation, even after his death (Bayramoğlu 2019,

300). As Asli Zengin (2019) shows in her ethnographic work on transgender funerals, similar necropolitical strategies operate to isolate dead transgender bodies from their communities.

The violent treatment of Murtaza's dead body served a further necropolitical function. The funeral took place under the glare of the media, which reported on it step by step, in order to secure the confidence of the general public. The violence staged for the public showed that all necessary measures had been taken to prevent contamination of the soil. To paraphrase Bargu (2016), necropolitical violence operates as a practice that not only targets the dead, but also the living: it disciplines and even dishonors the living by publicly displaying posthumous violence. I argue that the mediated necropolitical violence inflicted upon Elgin's corpse had a disciplinary function. While securing the stability of public health, sexual, and gender norms, it demonstrated what kind of an end a life outside heteronormativity was doomed to.

Migrant Sex Workers Disrupting Borders

I now want to move on in time to when the focus of mediated anxieties about the arrival of AIDS shifted to the migrant sex workers who had started coming from the Balkans and former USSR countries from the late 1980s. Most studies (e.g. Hughes 2001) on sex workers from former USSR countries address the organized crime of human trafficking in which women are tricked into the sex industry without their consent. Media portrayals and academic research concerned with the migration of women from post-Soviet states to Turkey for work often reductively equates the women's migration with "human trafficking" (Bloch 2017, 21–22). Many such studies lack empirical evidence, and reproduce anti-sex work discourse, rarely acknowledging sex workers' own agency (Zhang 2009). However, some scholars (Gülçür and İlkkaracan 2008; Bloch 2017) who have conducted fieldwork in Turkey emphasize migrant women's agency, noting that some value the economic opportunities, freedom to travel, or the opportunity to encounter other cultures that transnational sex work offers.

Turkey has become an attractive destination for migrant sex workers from former USSR countries because of its weak border surveillance and undemanding visa requirements (Gülçür and İlkkaracan 2008, 206). The border between Georgia and Turkey is particularly significant in discussions on migrant sex workers. The border was opened in 1988 to citizens of Turkey and the former Soviet Union to encourage small-scale trade across the border (Bellér-Hann 1995, 221). This allowed some migrant sex workers to commute between Turkey and their countries of origin and to conduct sex work, largely in borderland areas such as Georgia/Turkey and the East Black Sea Region (Günçıkan 1995). Sex work is legal in Turkey when carried out by cisgender women in registered brothels. Nonetheless, it is strongly monitored by the state and police (Zengin 2011) and the law does not allow migrants to conduct sex work. When migrant women are apprehended for conducting sex work they have no legal rights and are deported immediately. This situation often makes migrant sex workers vulnerable to state-sanctioned violence and discrimination (Gülçür and İlkkaracan 2008, 204). In addition, they also face discrimination, violence, and racism from local communities (Bellér-Hann 1995; Coşkun 2018).

Existing literature on HIV/STDs among migrant sex workers mainly focuses on prevention (Aral and Fransen 1995) or highlights the high STD rates among migrant sex workers (Agacifidan, Badur, and Gerikalmaz 1993) without critical contextualization or recognition of the hurdles that often prevent undocumented migrant sex workers from accessing social security, health services, or prevention measures. Rather than calculating HIV rates among migrant sex workers or asking why migrant women get involved in sex work, here I am more interested in exploring how the migrant sex worker became understood in relation to public anxieties in the 1980s and 1990s, like the queer body, as an intruder: a border-crosser that threatened to bring virus and disease from outside Turkey. The first reports to suggest such ideas were predominantly about migrant sex workers in the East Black Sea Region. Such women were often derogatively referred to as "Nataşa" – both in everyday speech and in media representations. Subsuming all migrant sex workers under the supposedly typical Russian female name Nataşa served to construct a racialized and sexualized category with no space for individual narratives.

The media coverage of the time implied strong links between the presence of migrant sex workers and the spread of AIDS across national borders. As I briefly mentioned at the beginning of this article, Turkish media went so far as to proclaim that the arrival of "Nataşas" and AIDS constituted the second greatest threat ever experienced by the Black Sea Region – surpassed only by the Chernobyl disaster.[14] In the late 1980s and early 1990s, the impact of the Chernobyl disaster on the Turkish Black Sea Region was one of the most widely discussed topics in the media. It is interesting to see how a nuclear disaster that had impacts across borders became discursively linked with a pandemic that also transcended national borders. While the effects of Chernobyl were transmitted climatically, AIDS was seen to cross borders with the mobility of people. The presence of "Nataşas" in Turkey was seen to be strongly associated with the arrival and spread of AIDS, as well as with other sexually transmitted diseases. Hence, when police raided houses where migrant sex workers met their clients, the sex workers were often forced to take HIV tests.[15] One article reported that 80% of migrant sex workers had diseases, and that AIDS was spreading in the wake of migrant sex work.[16] Many such media portrayals read as exemplary models of scandalizing journalistic rhetoric; lacking any scientific evidence they simply served to incite panic: border panic. The inadequacy of border surveillance and/or the failure of authorities to curb transnational sex work were presented as reasons why Turkey had become an attractive destination for women from former USSR countries.

One such text that invoked a sense of border panic was an article entitled "Kimdir bu Nataşa?" ("Who is this Nataşa?") in *Milliyet* in 1993.[17] A photograph of a young white woman is presented in the middle of the article. With its title asking who "Nataşa" is, the implication is that the woman pictured is the "Nataşa" written about. Another question is posed by the caption under the picture: "Who knows what storms break inside these small lives?" The representative "Nataşa" is thus portrayed as young, pure, and naïve; the victim of misfortunate events. This resonates with the humanitarian narrative of sex work as a consequence of human trafficking in which innocent migrant women become trapped without their knowledge or consent (Ticktin 2017). Furthermore, such representations of migrant sex workers from the former Soviet Union connoted their "whiteness" with purity, innocence, and naivety. Yet the racialized representations of migrant sex workers were multi-layered: Russians, for instance, are perceived as "whiter" and hence more "beautiful"; intrinsically "superior" to "darker skinned" Georgians (Bellér-Hann 1995, 222). Furthermore, "whiteness" was intensely sexualized in the context of AIDS, either connoted with migrant sex workers or with supposedly uninhibited European tourists visiting Turkey.[18] The article "Kimdir bu Nataşa?" reported that "Nataşas" entered Turkey via its border to the Black Sea or by crossing the northeastern borders to Georgia. They started by conducting sex work in the East Black Sea Region before moving to bigger cities such as Istanbul, where they met richer clients. Crucial to my analysis here is that the text criticizes the ineffectiveness of border surveillance: although migrant sex workers got deported by the police, they still managed to reenter the country.

In addition to the discursively constructed threat they apparently posed to public health, migrant sex workers were often featured in relation to Turkey's supposedly troubled sexual culture.[19] In seeking to explain why migrant sex workers were able to find so many clients in Turkey, the repressive national sexual culture or unhappy marriages were often invoked. According to such narratives, Turkish men who were unable to satisfy their sexual needs due to the conservative local culture were driven to visit "Nataşas". And by engaging in sexual contact with migrant sex workers they brought the danger, i.e. AIDS, home to the Turkish family. This logic reveals continuity with historical narratives on STDs, such as the fear during the syphilis crises that men visiting brothels would contaminate the "traditional Turkish family" (Arpacı 2014).

In some cases, experts also expressed concerns about possible effects upon the morals of Turkish women: "The other side of the coin is the possible impacts of Nataşas on [Turkish] women in the Black Sea [Region]"[20] Such media portrayals identified the presence of migrant sex workers in rural areas as a danger in that they set a bad example to local Turkish women, who might be influenced to become more sexually open or even slide into the sex industry. In this way, the representation of the "Nataşa" as a border-crosser portrayed her as a threat to Turkey's sexual and gender mores. Migrant sex workers revealed the permeability of borders intended to protect the nation. Migrant women were not only allegedly bringing AIDS, but also different sexual experiences and practices, different perceptions of sexuality, and different morals from across the border. As in the representations of the first HIV-positive men, the perceived threat of AIDS contagion became entwined with the idea that different sexual mores could be contagious. Following their exhaustive visual representations of dying bodies, death, and the funerals of the first HIV-positive men in the mid 1980s[21], from the late 1980s, the media began showing police raids on brothels and the deportations of migrant sex worker. In both cases, the media offered documentation of the sexualized and racialized "public measures" imposed to prevent contamination.

As in their portrayals of the first HIV-positive people, the Turkish media were keen to publish pictures and the full names of migrant women who had been caught conducting sex work. For instance, in 1993, *Milliyet* reported that the Istanbul police department had arrested 23 Romanian and Russian sex workers. According to the report, 14 of them did not have passports and had managed to enter Turkey without documents. It was also reported that two of them "had AIDS". The newspaper published their full names and photographs. This violated their right to privacy and endangered them but nonetheless did not present them as individualized subjects.[22]

In such cases, public visibility was an integral part of the violence inflicted. As in the example of Murtaza Elgin, media coverage of migrant sex workers became a necropolitical strategy whereby "having AIDS" was punished with social death even before the physical death that was on the horizon. Furthermore, in the case of the "Nataşas", visibility was made an instrument of violent border regimes. Visibility put pressure on authorities to reinforce Turkey's borders, while punishing border-crossers by revealing their identities or their migration strategies.

The incapacity of borders and border surveillance to prevent the movement of the virus or to protect Turkey from foreign conceptions of sexuality or different lifeworlds was sometimes explained in relation to Turkey's geopolitical context, which was seen to be characterized by mobility and migration. For example, journalist Şahin Alpay described Turkey as a perfect ground for the virus to spread:

> Turkey is an ideal place for the disease to spread for multiple reasons. Turkey is open to the outer world due to our citizens living abroad, due to tourism, due to busy international highways, due to the "Nataşa syndrome", and due to foreign workers. Mobility within the country is also rife. We have a very young

population that is sexually active, and we therefore have high rates of sexually transmitted diseases.[23]

Turkey's openness to the outer world is represented here as a weakness, making its borders vulnerable and likely to fail as physical barriers to protect the nation from unwanted intrusions. Not only the messy entanglement of the human and the virus, but also high rates of mobility are seen to bordering regimes difficult to sustain. The extract is also noteworthy for its claim that migrant sex workers from the former Soviet Union ("Nataşa syndrome") are not the only potential carriers of the disease; others include the Turkish diaspora ("our citizens living abroad"), as well as tourists, migrant workers, and even Turkish citizens travelling within the country. With this diversification of potential threats, the journalist suggests that the situation is more complex than the public has assumed so far. Not only are migrant sex workers and homosexuals held responsible, but also the entire web of connections and mobilities of which Turkey is a part.

Conclusion

In this article, I have examined two specific cases in order to identify the multiplicity of meditated constructions of sexually, ethnically and/or racially "other" bodies that circulated during the peak decade of the AIDS crisis in Turkey. As my analysis has shown, media reports that associating the spread of the virus with the movement of sexually and ethnically / racially "other" bodies across borders forged a connection that generated panic about a perceived lack of border security. These reports portrayed borders as fragile, vulnerable, and susceptible to seduction and abuse. I focused on the case of one individual figure, Murtaza Elgin, to explore how border panic became discursively linked to queer sexualities. I did not concentrate on any single biography in my analysis of the central narratives formulated on migrant sex workers. This differentiated approach was called for by the material at hand: Elgin, as Turkey's first case, came to personify the virus, as the media projected all the circulating anxieties about AIDS onto him and the queerness he was made to stand for. No single migrant sex worker received such sustained individual attention; portrayal of the "Nataşas" was so undifferentiated that they were all subsumed under the same derogatory name. Despite the marked differences between the cases of Elgin and the "Nataşas", they share some essential commonalities. They were both seen as intruders bringing the virus from outside Turkey's borders into its territory. Furthermore, the anxiety and panic expressed about their stories were simultaneously about the danger they posed to public health and to "Turkish" sexual and gender norms. They were both seen as "foreign"; they represented non-Turkish values and lifeworlds. One might argue that "Western", "European", or "Russian" sexualities were portrayed as no less contagious than

118   THE SEXUAL POLITICS OF BORDER CONTROL

the virus itself. Significantly, in both cases, the media paid meticulous attention to how the stories ended: images of Elgin's dying body and funeral terminated his narrative absolutely, just as police raids and deportations of migrant sex workers removed them from Turkish society. I argue that violent representations of Elgin's death and of police raids and deportations of sex workers were similar techniques, deployed by authorities and media in an attempt to regain control over borders that were apparently becoming increasingly vulnerable in the wake of AIDS.

When humans and diseases become messily entangled, borders fail to function as protective barriers. As recent pandemics such as COVID-19, avian flu, and SARS have also shown, media play an important role in stoking public panic about border insecurity, the mobility of people and of the nonhuman, and the public presence of certain people who are discursively constructed to embody the respective diseases. Remembering and reflecting upon the border panic created at the height of the AIDS pandemic highlights how border panic in response to diseases becomes intertwined with other bordering processes such as discrimination based upon sexuality, gender, ethnicity, and race.

Notes

1. *Milliyet*, 1993. "Nataşalara çözüm" January 1, p.15 *My translation.*
2. *Hürriyet*, 1985. "AIDS'ten acı ibret." November 7, 1. *Hürriyet*, 1985. "AIDS'ten ölen Türk Almanya'da hastalanmıştı." November 6, 1. *Hürriyet*, 1985. "Ve işte AIDS-2" November 16, 6.
3. *Hürriyet*, 1985. "Bir musibet bin nasihatten iyidir", November 5, 11.
4. *Hürriyet*, 1985, "M için tecrit emri", November 6, 1.
5. *Hürriyet*, 1985, "M için tecrit emri", November 6, 11. *My translation*
6. *Hürriyet*, 1985, "Beyoğlu'na AIDS darbesi", November 5, 11. *My translation*
7. *Hürriyet*, 1985, "M için tecrit emri", November 6, 1.
8. *Hürriyet*, 1985, " ... Ve Murtaza'nın ümitsiz kaçışı", November 6, 6.
9. *Hürriyet*, 1985, "M'yi saklayanlar AIDS tehlikesinde", November 7, 8.
10. *Hürriyet*, 1985, "Beyoğlu'na AIDS darbesi", November 5, 11
11. *Hürriyet*, 1985, "Tecrit odası M'yi bekliyor" November 7, 8.
12. Ibid.
13. *Hürriyet*, 1985, "M Paniği". November 4, 11.
14. *Milliyet*, 1993, "Nataşalara çözüm," January 1, 15.
15. *Milliyet*, 1993, Nataşalara AIDS testi, January 1, 24.
16. *Milliyet*, 1993. Kimdir bu Nataşa?, January 19, 24.
17. Ibid.
18. *Nokta*, 1987, "AIDS'te kırmızı alarm: Turist akını başladı." May, 31.
19. *Milliyet* 1993 "Kimdir bu Nataşa?", January 19, 24. *Milliyet*, "AIDS ve namus", April 13, 20.
20. *Milliyet*, 1993 "Kimdir bu Nataşa?", January 19, 24. *My translation*
21. *Hürriyet*, 1985. "AIDS'ten acı haber" November, 7; *Hürriyet*, 1985, "AIDSten ölen Türk ... " November, 8.
22. *Milliyet*, 1994, "Laleli'de AIDS'li iki nataşa," November 16, 6.
23. Alpay, Şahin. 1996. "AIDS ve namus." *Milliyet*. April 13, 20.

Acknowledgement

The ideas expressed in this article were first presented at the *Sexuality and Borders Symposium* at New York University in April 2019. I would like to thank the organizers Michelle Pfeifer, Billy Holzberg, and Anouk Madörin for inviting me to that stimulating symposium and giving me the chance to discuss my thoughts with inspiring scholars such as Sabiha Allouche, Radha Hegde, Fadi Saleh, Elif Sarı, Miriam Ticktin, Alyosxa Tudor, and Paula-Irene Villa. I am also thankful to the German Academic Exchange Service (DAAD), which funded my trip to New York. In addition, I would like to thank Tunay Altay and Gökçe Yurdakul for inviting me to the Humboldt University in Berlin to present an earlier version of this paper. I am very grateful to Pip Hare, Anouk Madörin, and this journal's anonymous reviewers for their careful reading and thought-provoking comments. Their valuable suggestions have been crucial at various stages of editing. I very much appreciate my intellectual exchange on borders and media with Tanja Maier. I am also grateful to María do Mar Castro Varela for her mentorship and friendship.

Disclosure statement

No potential conflict of interest was reported by the author(s).

ORCID

Yener Bayramoğlu 🆔 http://orcid.org/0000-0003-2572-0939

References

Agacifidan, A., Selim Badur, and Özdem Gerikalmaz. 1993. "Syphilis Prevalence among Unregistered Prostitutes in Istanbul." *Sexually Transmitted Diseases* 20 (4): 236–236.
Ahmed, S. 2004a. "Affective Economies." *Social Text* 22 (2): 117–139.
Ahmed, S. 2004b. *The Cultural Politics of Emotion*. Edinburgh: The Edinburgh University Press.
Akyüz, L. 2017. *Ethnicity, Gender and the Border Economy: Living in the Turkey-Georgia Borderlands*. New York: Routledge.
Altay, T., G. Yurdakul, and A. C. Korteweg. 2020. "Crossing Borders: The Intersectional Marginalisation of Bulgarian Muslim Trans* sex Workers in Berlin." *Journal of Ethnic and Migration Studies* December: 1–18.
Andersen, R., and A. Bergmann. 2019. *Media, Central American Refugees, and the U.S. Border Crises: Security Discourses, Immigrant Demonization, and the Perpetuation of Violence*. New York: Routledge.
Anzaldúa, G. 2007. *Borderlands / La Frontera: The New Mestiza*. San Francisco: Aunt Lutte.
Aral, S., and L. Fransen. 1995. "STD/HIV Prevention in Turkey: Planning a Sequence of Interventions." *AIDS Education and Prevention* 7 (6): 544–553.
Arpacı, M. 2014. "Hastalık, Ulus ve Felaket: Türkiye'de Frengi ile Mücadele." *Toplum ve Bilim* 130: 59–86.
Ayata, B. 2012. "Kurdish Transnational Politics and Turkey's Changing Kurdish Policy: The Journey of Kurdish Broadcasting from Europe to Turkey." *Journal of Contemporary European Studies* 19 (4): 523–533.

Bargu, B. 2016. "Another Necropolitics." *Theory & Event* 19 (1). https://muse.jhu.edu/article/610222.

Bayramoğlu, Y. 2018. *Queere (Un-)Sichtbarkeiten: Die Geschichte der queeren Repräsentationen in der türkischen und deutschen Boulevardpresse*. Bielefeld: transcript.

Bayramoğlu, Y. 2019. "M. – Das Gespenst Einer Dystopie. Ein Essay." In *Aids und HIV in der Türkei*, edited by Zülfukar Çetin, and Peter-Paul Bänziger, 287–304. Gießen: Psychosozial Verlag.

Bayramoğlu, Y., and M. Lünenborg. 2018. "Queer Migration and Digital Affects: Refugees Navigating from the Middle East via Turkey to Germany." *Sexuality & Culture* 22 (4): 1019–1036.

Bellér-Hann, I. 1995. "Prostitution and its Effects in Northeast Turkey." *The European Journal of Women's Studies* 2: 219–235.

Bloch, A. 2017. *Sex, Love, and Migration: Postsocialism, Modernity, and Intimacy from Istanbul to the Arctic*. Ithaca: Cornell University Press.

Castro Varela, M.d.M., and P. Mecheril. 2016. *Die Dämonisierung der Anderen: Rassismuskritik der Gegenwart*. Bielefeld: Transcript.

Cohen, C. J. 1999. *The Boundaries of Blackness: AIDS and the Breakdown of Black Politics*. Chicago: The University of Chicago Press.

Coşkun, E. 2018. "Criminalisation and Prostitution of Migrant Women in Turkey: A Case Study in Ugandan Women." *Women's Studies International Forum* 68: 85–93.

Çeler, Z. 2011. "1980'lerde Türkiye'de Cinsellik ve Nokta Dergisi." *Çankaya University Journal of Humanities and Social Sciences* 8 (2): 283–291.

Çetin, Z., and P.-P. Bänziger. 2019. *Aids und HIV in der Türkei: Geschichten und Perspektiven Einer Emanzipatorischen Gesundheitspolitik*. Gießen: Psychosozial Verlag.

Dell'Agnese, E., and A. L. Amilhat Szary. 2015. "Borderscapes: From Border Landscapes to Border Aesthetics." *Geopolitics* 20 (1): 4–13.

Dubois, L. 2009. "A Spoonful of Blood: Haitians, Racism and AIDS." *Science as Culture* 6 (1): 7–43.

Erbaydar, T., and N. P. Erbaydar. 2012. "Status of HIV / AIDS Epidemic in Turkey." *Acta Medica* 1: 19–24.

Fairclough, N. 2013. *Critical Discourse Analysis: The Critical Study of Language*. New York: Routledge.

Gülçür, L., and P. İlkkaracan. 2008. "The 'Nataşa' Experience: Migrant Sex Workers from the Former Soviet Union and Eastern Europe in Turkey." In *Deconstructing Sexuality in the Middle East: Challenges and Discourses*, edited by P. İlkkaracan, 199–214. New York: Routledge.

Günçıkan, B. 1995. *Haraşo'dan Nataşa'ya*. Istanbul: Arion.

Hegde, R. 2016. *Mediating Migration*. Cambridge: Polity Press.

Honigsbaum, M. 2017. "Between Securitization and Neglect: Managing Ebola at the Borders of Global Health." *Medical History* 61 (2): 270–294.

Hughes, D. M. 2001. "The Nataşa Trade: Transnational Sex Trade." *National Institute of Justice Journal* 246: 9–15.

Joliffe, P. 2015. "Night-Time and Refugees: Evidence from the Thai-Myanmar Border." *Journal of Refugee Studies* 29 (1): 1–18.

Keil, R., and H. Ali. 2006. "Multiculturalism, Racism and Infectious Disease in the Global City: The Experience of the 2003 SARS Outbreak in Toronto." *Topia: Canadian Journal of Cultural Studies* 16: 23–49.

Kosnick, K. 2014. "Mediating Migration: New Roles for (Mass) Media." *The French Journal of Media Studies* 17 (5). https://doi.org/10.4000/inmedia.761.

Luibhéid, E. 2002. *Entry Denied: Controlling Sexuality at the Border*. Minneapolis: University of Minnesota Press.

Madörin, A. 2019. 'The View from Above' at Europe's Maritime Borders: Racial Securitization from Visual to Postvisuality." *European Journal of Cultural Studies* 23 (5): 698–711.

Mayring, P. 2004. "Qualitative Content Analysis." In *A Companion to Qualitative Research*, edited by U. Flick, E. Kardoff, and I. Steinke, 159–176. London: Sage.

Mbembe, A. 2003. "Necropolitics." *Popular Culture* 15 (1): 11–40.

M'charek, A. 2020. "Harraga: Burning Borders, Navigatin Colonialism." *The Sociological Review* 68 (2): 418–434.

Mountz, A. 2011. "Where Asylum Seekers Wait: Feminist Counter Topographies of Sites Between States." *Gender, Place, Culture* 18 (3): 381–399.

Musolff, A. 2011. "Migration, Media and "Deliberate" Metaphors." *Metaphorik* 21: 7–19.

Perera, S. 2014. "Dead Exposures: Trophy Bodies and Violent Visibilities of the Nonhuman." *Borderlands E-Journal* 13 (1): 1–26.

Phillips, L. 2005. "Deconstructing "Down Low" Discourse: The Politics of Sexuality, Gender, Race, AIDS, and Anxiety." *Journal of African American Studies* 9 (2): 3–15.

Pieri, E. 2019. "Media Framing and the Threat of Global Pandemics: The Ebola Crises in UK Media and Policy Response." *Sociological Research Online* 24 (1): 73–92.

Rabinowitz, D. 2012. "Identity, State and Borderline Disorder." In *A Companion to Border Studies*, edited by T. Wilson, and H. Donnan, 301–317. Malden: Wiley Blackwell.

Saddiki, S. 2014. "Border Fences as an Anti-Immigration Device: A Comparative View of American and Spanish Policies." In *Borders, Fences and Walls: State of Insecurity?*, edited by Elisabeth Vallet, 117–130. London: Ashgate.

Saddiki, S. 2017. *World of Walls: The Structure, Roles and Effectiveness of Separation Barriers*. Cambridge: Open Book Publisher.

Sarı, E., E. Savcı, S. Göknur, M. S. Birdal, and D. Aksoy. 2018, January 3. "A Critical Forum About LGBTI+ Prohibitions in Turkey." *Jadaliyya*. Accessed 1 February 2021. https://www.jadaliyya.com/Details/34951.

Sezgin, D., and M. A. Wall. 2005. "Constructing the Kurds in the Turkish Press: A Case Study of Hürriyet Newspaper." *Media, Culture & Society* 25 (7): 787–798.

Sheyholislami, J. 2010. "Identity, Language, and New Media: The Kurdish Case." *Language Policy* 9: 289–312.

Smart, A., and J. Smart. 2012. "Biosecurity, Quarantine and Life Across the Borders." In *A Companion to Border Studies*, edited by T. Wilson, and H. Donnan, 354–370. Malden: Wiley Blackwell.

Strasser, S., and E. E. Tibet. 2019. "The Border Event in the Everyday: Hope and Constraints in the Lives of Young Unaccompanied Asylum Seekers in Turkey." *Journal of Ethnic and Migration Studies* 46 (2): 1–18.

Ticktin, M. 2017. "A World Without Innocence." *American Ethnologist* 44 (3): 577–590. doi:10.1111/amet.12558.

Van Houtum, H., and R. Pijpers. 2007. "The European Union as a Gated Community: The two-Faced Border and Immigration Regime of the EU." *Antipode: A Radical Journal of Geography* 39 (2): 291–309.

Wilson, T. M., and H. Donnan. 2012. "Borders and Border Studies." In *A Companion to Border Studies*, edited by T. Wilson, and H. Donnan, 1–25. Malden: Wiley Blackwell.

Yılmaz, S. 2017. "Threats to Public Order and Health: Mobile Men as Syphilis Vectors in Late Ottoman Medical Discourse and Practice." *Journal of Middle East Women's Studies* 13 (2): 222–243.

Zengin, Aslı. 2011. *İktidarın Mahremiyeti: İstanbul'un hayat kadınları, seks işçiliği ve şiddet*. Istanbul: Metis.

Zengin, Aslı. 2019. "The Afterlife of Gender: Sovereignty, Intimacy, and Muslim Funerals of Transgender People in Turkey." *Cultural Anthropology* 34 (1): 78–102.

Zhang, S. 2009. "Beyond the 'Nataşa' Story – A Review and Critique of Current Research on sex Trafficking." *Global Crime* 10 (3): 178–195.

Migration, sex work and trafficking: the racialized bordering politics of sexual humanitarianism

Nicola Mai [ID], P.G. Macioti [ID], Calum Bennachie [ID], Anne E. Fehrenbacher [ID], Calogero Giametta [ID], Heidi Hoefinger [ID] and Jennifer Musto [ID]

ABSTRACT
The article presents the findings of the SEXHUM project studying the impact of the different policies targeting migrant sex workers in Australia, France, New Zealand, and the United States. It draws on the concept of sexual humanitarianism, referring to how neoliberal constructions of vulnerability associated with sexual behaviour are implicated in humanitarian forms of support and control of migrant populations. Based on over three years of fieldwork we examine the differential ways in which Asian cis women and Latina trans women are constructed and targeted as vulnerable to exploitation, violence and abuse, or not, in relation to racialized and cis-centric sexual humanitarian canons of victimhood. Through our comparative analysis we expose how the implication of sexual humanitarian rhetoric in increasingly extreme bordering policies and interventions on migrant sex workers impacts on their lives and rights, arguing for the urgent need for social reform informed by the experiences of these groups.

Introduction

This article addresses a key aspect of the link between borders and sexuality in contemporary times: the way humanitarian and racialized forms of governance focussed on gender and sexuality identify and target groups of migrants as specifically 'vulnerable' to exploitation and abuse (Ticktin 2008; Bernstein 2018). The concept of 'sexual humanitarianism' informs our understanding of the ways in which groups of migrants are strategically problematized, supported, and intervened upon by humanitarian institutions, representations and NGOs according to vulnerabilities that are supposedly associated with their sexual orientation and behaviour (Mai 2018). This concurs with a global rise of neo-abolitionist policies attempting to eradicate all sex work – framed as sexual exploitation – by ending the demand for sexual services, which translates into harmful policies exacerbating the exploitability and deportability of marginalized migrant groups.

Within this wider framework, and following our research evidence and findings, in this article, we will analyse the pivotal role played by racialized and sex-gendered criteria of victimhood in the sexual humanitarian justification and deployment of anti-migration rhetoric and bordering interventions. At the centre of our analysis is the concept of racialization, referring to deployment of racial categories to define and understand social issues (Murji and Solomos 2005). The strategic choice of the term sex-gendered acknowledges the ways in which the separation or conflation of these two specific and interlinked categories is implicated in the reproduction of cis- and hetero-centric hierarchies of victimhood within sexual humanitarian concerns and interventions (Mai 2018, 4). Both concepts are key to understand the workings of sexual humanitarianism and the way it operates by intersectionally racializing and sex-gendering target populations according to emerging and historical stereotypes of victimhood at a local, national and global level.

Drawing on original research evidence, we will analyse how sexual humanitarian rhetoric and interventions framed and were framed by increasingly "extreme bordering" dynamics. The latter result from the convergence between the ongoing reorganization of state sovereignty, borders and labour mobility by an increasingly globalized, polarizing and extreme form of neoliberal capitalism (Mezzadra and Neilson 2013; Mai 2018), and the global mainstreaming of extremist right-wing and xenophobic politics and policies. In this respect, whereas 'bordering' is inherent to the social reproduction and enforcement of governance, governmentality and belonging at a local, national and global level (Yuval-Davis, Wemyss, and Cassidy 2019), the shift towards 'extreme bordering' reflects the passage from 'progressive' forms of neoliberalism manipulating human rights discourses to legitimize securitizing and polarizing politics to the more directly exclusionary, xenophobic and nationalist discourse and practices characterizing the contemporary rise of authoritarian populism (Fraser 2016). Within this complex interplay, we will focus on the strategic role played by racialized and sex-gendered criteria of victimhood in the construction of sexual humanitarian target populations becoming specifically vulnerable to rhetoric and policies of 'extreme bordering' at a national and global level.

Although migrant sex workers in our sample comprise a much greater variety of nationalities, in this article we will concentrate on the experiences of Asian cis women and trans Latina women because these two migrant groups have been over-represented targets of racialized sexual humanitarian bordering rhetoric and interventions across the four national settings of the research project that generated its data in both specific and shared ways. The strategic value of this comparative focus is supported by existing research highlighting the way Asian cis women and trans Latina sex workers are stereotypically racialized and represented respectively as passive victims and offenders while both are constructed both as non-citizens/outsiders, and therefore targeted by law enforcement and immigration controls (Lam and Lepp 2019; Ham 2017; Dalton and Jung 2019; Bolivar 2017; Hoefinger et al. 2020). In Australia and New Zealand our focus will be on the realities of Asian cis women as they are the migrant group most targeted by the racial bordering politics of sexual humanitarianism in both countries. In France we will include in our comparison between the experiences of Asian cis women and Latina trans women the ways in which Nigerian cis women are constructed as specifically vulnerable to trafficking and exploitation, which will allow us to better understand the hierarchies of racialized victimhood operationalizing the implementation of the abolitionist law that was passed in April 2016. In the US, our analysis will focus on the comparison between the experiences of Asian cis women and those of Latina trans woman.

Context and method

The current study draws on ethnographic fieldwork and semi-structured interviews conducted between 2017 and 2020 in Australia (Melbourne and Sydney), France (Paris and Marseille), New Zealand (Auckland and Wellington) and the United States (New York and Los Angeles) in the context of the SEXHUM project, which investigated the relationship between migration, sex work, and trafficking drawing on migrants' own understandings and experiences of agency and exploitation.[1]

The methodological approach for SEXHUM is based on a combination of ethnographic observations, 240 in-depth, semi-structured interviews with 221 purposively sampled sex workers and trafficked persons, and semi-structured interviews with 80 key informants, including social service providers, law enforcement, and legal advocates across the national settings of the project. SEXHUM compensated sex workers and trafficked persons for their time in cash whenever it was possible in accordance with local national practices. Key informants were not compensated. Informed consent was obtained from all participants and study procedures were approved by Kingston University and endorsed by key academic organizations and institutions in the four national settings of the project. To protect confidentiality, all sex worker interviewees were provided with a pseudonym. Throughout the duration of the fieldwork period, the research team conducted ethnographic observations in strategic settings and events for sex workers or trafficked persons including sex work venues and organizing spaces, diversion courts and programmes, and anti-trafficking collaborations between non-governmental organizations and law enforcement.

To account for the ways in which race, gender and sexuality frame the research process and the realities it investigates, SEXHUM adopts an intersectional and self-reflexive approach to understand and analyse existing inequalities, hierarchies and divisions. This ethical and methodological approach is particularly important and relevant for SEXHUM because of the whiteness of the research team, which reflects existing privileges in academia and could potentially discourage and undermine the participation of racialized and marginalised social groups. The research team has addressed this issue by including the experiences of the widest possible variety of racialized participants, by collaborating with racialized community members in project data gathering, publications and dissemination events, as well as by relying on post-colonial and decolonial scholars and theories.

Having introduced the main focus and issues that will be dealt with in this article and outlined its methodological approach, we will now analyse more in detail the unfolding of sexual humanitarian racialized and sex-gendered bordering in each national context.

Australia

Australia's federal states legislate independently on the sex industry, displaying variations of all known models: decriminalization (NSW and Northern Territory), licensing (Victoria and Queensland) and criminalization (Western and South Australia). In Australia, SEXHUM focussed on NSW (Sydney) and Victoria (Melbourne) in order to analyse and compare the experiences of migrant sex workers under decriminalization (NSW) and legalization through licensing (in Victoria). Such comparison was crucial as Victoria was the only SEXHUM setting with a licensing policy framework, which is substantially different from decriminalization as it involves the regulation of the sex industry through criminal, rather than common law. In 1995, NSW decriminalized sex work and local councils replaced law enforcement as its regulatory body. Premises who offer sexual services need to obtain a developmental authorization (DA) from councils to operate lawfully (according to common law). If caught offering sexual services without a DA, owners and sex workers risk heavy fines or closure, yet they do not commit a criminal offence. The state of Victoria polices sex work through the 1994 licensing Sex Work Act. Premises providing sexual services need to get a license to operate legally. Anyone providing sexual services working in breach of the Sex Work Act, (e.g. by working in an establishment without a license) is liable to a criminal charge. In Australia, all non-citizens convicted of a criminal offence may face deportation. In Victoria, this includes migrant sex workers found to provide sex work in an unlicensed venue, regardless of their legal status. In NSW on the other hand, migrants in the unauthorized sector are liable to fines under common law, and do not risk deportation if holding a valid work visa. As a matter of fact, licenses are extremely pricey in Victoria, while developmental authorizations are hard to obtain by most councils in NSW. Under such circumstances, some establishments, often massage parlors, can be found offering sexual services without holding a license or a DA in breach of the Sex Work Act or of council regulations.

Nationwide, Australia's dominant sexual humanitarian discourses and interventions focus on the presumed exploitability of (Asian cis-female) migrant sex workers. National news, documentaries, and successful TV series repeatedly depict Asian sex workers (mostly Thai, Chinese and Korean) as passive victims pushed to sell sex against their will (Sodsai 2017; Gondouin, Thapar-Björkert, and Ryberg 2018). In NSW and Victoria, sexual humanitarian concerns relative to the exploitation of migrant sex workers emerge mostly in relation to Asian cis women working in unauthorized massage parlors (NSW) or in unlicensed brothels (Victoria) (Sodsai 2019), who therefore became the main focus of the SEXHUM project in Australia. Across Australia, these media-fueled moral panics translate into sexual humanitarian law enforcement raids and operations in sex work establishments (or those suspected to be such) targeting mostly Asian venues and workers, who risk being prosecuted and deported if found working in breach of state laws or without a valid visa, often in the name of finding victims of trafficking.

In Melbourne (Victoria), raids and checks on what the neo-abolitionist Project Respect (2017) estimates to be 500 'illegal brothels' (allegedly mostly Asian massage parlors) are regularly documented by the media. Remarkably, these interventions are called for by neo-abolitionist organisations (to reduce what they consider an inherently exploitative sex industry) and by owners and operators of licensed venues (to curb competition) (Oriti 2017; Sodsai 2019; Mitchell 2019; EROS 2017). In Sydney (NSW), council checks on (majority Asian) massage parlors suspected of offering sexual services without authorization also happen regularly and council officials employ private investigators (known as 'brothel busters') to gather proof that sexual services take place (Hansen 2019; Davidsson 2017).

Despite the allegedly exploitative, slavery-like conditions to be found in these establishments (Duff 2017; Project Respect 2017), official statistics and research confirm that the cases of trafficking and sexual exploitation in the sex industry have dramatically decreased in the past ten years (Macioti et al. 2020). As of November 2019, referrals for sexual exploitation to the national government funded Support for Trafficked People Program (STPP) run by the Red Cross were 30 per cent of all referrals, as opposed to 100 per cent in 2012 (Red Cross 2019, 4).

When interviewed for SEXHUM, both councils and police maintained that checks and raids are in place to curb exploitation. Yet, our data show that rather than helping exploited victims, these sexual humanitarian interventions impact negatively on the lives of the migrant sex workers involved. To shed light on a thus far under-researched yet excessively media-covered area, we focussed a substantial part of its fieldwork on documenting the experiences of migrant sex workers operating in so-called 'illegal' brothels or massage parlors. Between 2017 and 2020, out of a total of 60 in-depth interviews with (migrant) sex workers, SEXHUM conducted 22 interviews and over 500 hours of ethnographic research with Asian cis female migrant sex workers working in unauthorized and unlicensed massage parlors in Sydney and Melbourne, respectively.

Our data dispute the racialized sexual humanitarian moral panics framing Asian women providing sexual services in 'illegal' massage parlors as passive, easy prey for traffickers. Those we interviewed in Sydney were satisfied with their earnings and diurnal working hours and preferred working in these venues rather than in authorized 'full service' shops as they felt that the cover of being advertised as "massage only" brought less stigma upon them. They were aware of earning less money than in "full service", but preferred performing what they considered to be less strenuous sexual work (mostly hand jobs and oral) and being able to earn some money from their share of the regular massage fee[2], when not offering sexual services to a specific client. At the time they were interviewed, all respondents working in the unauthorized/unlicensed sectors had the right to stay and work in Australia, though the vast majority were on temporary visas.

In both Sydney and Melbourne checks by council and police are what these workers fear the most. Yet in NSW, because of decriminalization, non-citizens with valid work permits risk less than in Victoria, where they automatically face deportation for committing a criminal offence, even if holding permanent residence. In NSW condoms found in workers' possession are used as evidence that sexual services take place, in which case owners may get away by arguing they were unaware of it, incur fines and have to (temporarily) shut their shop. Workers on valid work visas instead risk being filed, fined and losing their workplace. In both states, if a worker is apprehended without a valid working visa and they are not identified as a victim of trafficking, they face detention and deportation. Sandy, a 43 years old Thai worker based in Sydney recalls:

> [The council] checked twice, they asked you to open the bag and if you had condom. I had, but I hid it, not in my bag. Some girls put in the bag, (...) and

THE SEXUAL POLITICS OF BORDER CONTROL   129

if they find it, doesn't matter if used or not used, (…) you pay a fine and go to court, or first time they tell you to go home but they have your name. (…) they know everything (…) And if you work illegal, they can send you home [deport you] and can't come back for 5 years (…) A friend was sent home [deported] (…) The council sent some guy to be a customer and catch her. (…) I try go only with regulars. (…) I am scared.

To understand the political and social relevance of the extreme bordering dynamics targeting Asian cis female migrant sex workers, these need to be contextualized within the mainstreaming of (right-wing) extremist, and anti-migration rhetoric and policies in Australia (Hogan and Haltinner 2015). In this perspective, the overall racialized bordering politics of sexual humanitarianism in both NSW and VIC can be seen as one further expression of the shift in Australia towards forms of 'extreme bordering' and authoritarian populism drawing on broader nationalist anxieties that have historically focussed on the "fantasy of an 'Asian' invasion" (Papastegiadis 2005).

The situation in the two Australian states indicates how in both licensing regimes (Victoria) and in decriminalized ones (NSW) racialized and gendered sexual humanitarian stereotypes of migrant Asian cis women as passive easy prey for exploiters fuel repressive controls by the authorities on migrant workers. Yet, because of the absence of criminal laws regulating sex work, (work visa holding) migrant sex workers in NSW are less vulnerable to policing and deportation than in Victoria. Representing migrant sex workers in the so called 'illegal' sectors as victims does not match the experiences of these groups, most of whom consciously decide to work in these establishments for a number of reasons, including in order to have more agency over the services they want to offer. Crucially, they should not have to hide condoms in fear of being caught, fined or deported, as this could lead to risky, unsafe practices (Selvey et al. 2018).

France

In France, the SEXHUM project focussed on the impact of the neo-abolitionist Law N° 2016-444 'against the prostitutional system' on the rights and lives of migrant sex workers. The three main aims of the law passed on 13 April 2016 were to decrease the number of sex workers by abolishing the previous criminalization of public soliciting, shifting criminality to clients by charging them with a fine, and instituting an exit programme (*parcours de sortie*) for people who no longer wanted to do sex work. Whereas these first two measures introduced by the law form its explicitly 'repressive' component, the third point was conceived as its 'social policy' aspect, providing sex workers with a financial aid for social and professional reintegration of 330 euro per month, and with a temporary residence permit of six months renewable for a maximum of three times.

In France, SEXHUM undertook 59 qualitative interviews with migrant sex workers and focussed on the experiences of Latina trans women (25), Asian (15) and Nigerian cis women (12) because these were the groups most frequently at the centre of public debates about their supposed vulnerability to violence, exploitation and trafficking (in the case of Asian and Nigerian cis women) or marginalized by such debates (trans Latina women).

Most research participants think that the criminalization of clients has a more negative impact on their wellbeing and safety than the previous anti-soliciting measures adopted by the government. They also experience considerably less control over their working conditions as a consequence of the decreased number of clients since the new law came into effect. Our ethnographic observations and interviews with sex workers show that the police often pressure them to report clients, while those who are undocumented are threatened with deportation if they do not comply (Giametta, Le Bail, and Mai 2018). Moreover, the study shows that at a local level, the law has not always suspended municipal bylaws and regular identity checks, which resulted in sex workers being pushed away from their usual work places and city centres into more dangerous, isolated and unknown places. Finally, as was the case with the introduction of the criminalization of clients on Sweden in the late 1990s (Svedin et al. 2012), the 2016 law increased rather than reduced the stigma associated with sex work, producing the effect of further silencing sex workers and discouraging them to report acts of violence to which they are subjected.

The most direct effect of the 2016 law on sex workers has been an acute financial precariousness. Many respondents, particularly the most disadvantaged and racialized ones, have been struggling to make ends meet at the end of each month and spending considerably more time working in order to do so. Economic precariousness produces and exacerbates a variety of issues including the increase of violence by people posing as clients; the worsening of working conditions and of mental and physical health; and finally, for migrant sex workers, the risk of being construed as fraudulent and therefore not worthy of the social protection mechanisms introduced by the 2016 law.

Notably, the 2016 law was perceived as specifically concerning migrant workers because it was advertised by the government as a necessary anti-trafficking measure and it promised a temporary leave to remain for those undocumented migrants who access the prostitution exit programme (Le Bail and Giametta 2018). The implementation of the law coincided with the shift of the bordering dynamics embedded in its sexual humanitarian approach towards more extreme bordering practices translating into the targeting of Chinese and Nigerian cis women and with the neglect of Latina trans women according to racialized and sex-gendered understandings of victimhood. Whereas Chinese women tend to be presented by the French politics of racialized sexual humanitarian bordering as silent victims of Chinese male-dominated mafias, Nigerian women have come to embody the ultimate figure of the victim of trafficking by an overpowering Black male criminality. Meanwhile, Latina trans women's on-going experiences of violence and abuse have not been addressed by sexual humanitarian concerns or interventions.

Our data confirm the findings of Le Bail and Lieber (forthcoming) that, as a consequence of the implementation of the 2016 law, Chinese street-based sex workers experienced an increase of identity checks as well as an increase of police operations targeting landlords renting to sex workers, who could be charged for procuring (*proxénétisme*). For instance, A Ling, a 44 years old Chinese woman, experienced these two combined effects of the law directly when the police targeted her home and colluded with her landlord:

> One morning when I arrived at work the door was open and there were police officers waiting for me to come home. There was an interpreter and there was my landlord there as well. They had already searched the flat, they took out my money and telephone and metro card from my bag, they told me to sit down and took my statement.

Although the 2016 law promises women recognized as 'victims' state-funded protection mechanisms to fight prostitution and human trafficking, when the women we interviewed applied for such mechanisms they felt patronized by the law's neo-abolitionist understanding of victimization. The latter does not take into account how sex work guaranteed many Chinese women their financial autonomy while avoiding the exploitative condition they often encounter in regular jobs. As a result, most Chinese sex workers feared immigration controls and deportation more than the risk of facing exploitation in the sex industry.

The Chinese and the trans Latina migrants we interviewed shared a systemic double stigma; both endured heightened forms of (police) control and (widespread) violence due to the way they are racialized and sex-gendered in the context of their sex work. Both Chinese cis and Latina trans women have been paying the consequences of the extreme bordering dynamics introduced by the criminalization of clients with their lives, as they are forced to work in further isolated locations in order to escape police control. In 2018, the killing of sex worker Vanessa Campos, a young Peruvian trans woman in the Bois de Boulogne, a historical location of sex work in Paris, triggered an international outcry against the violence to which trans women, particularly migrant sex workers, are exposed on a daily basis, and also against the laws prohibiting sex work (Miren 2018). Vanessa Campos was murdered in the Bois while trying to help out a client being mugged by a group of men knowing that neither the sex worker nor the client would easily press charges against them (Le Bail and Giametta

2018). Her story is emblematic of the differential politics of racialized victimhood and bordering charactering sexual humanitarianism. Whereas Chinese women tended to be criminalized and 'bordered' by excessive sexual humanitarian concerns and controls, trans Latina women's marginalization and vulnerability to violence tend to be ignored.

As we mentioned above, the experience of Nigerian women in France is strategic to understand the racialized politics of the sexual humanitarian extreme bordering scenario promoted by the 2016 Law, as they found themselves in a paradoxical situation. On the one hand, they were portrayed by racialized political and media discourse as the main potential recipients of the exit programmes for being ideally naïve and innocent victims-being the most associated with colonial tropes according to which "the West is conceived as the moral leader in the fight against the exploitation of non-Western women migrants" (Aanu Oloruntoba et al. 2018). On the other, they tended to be rejected from such programmes, as they were not considered genuinely willing to stop sex work. The story of Precious, a 27-year-old Nigerian woman who was detained for 45 days in a migration detention centre after being rejected from the perspective of regularization and support offered by the *parcours de sortie*, is emblematic of the racialized bordering politics of sexual humanitarianism, which denies the authenticity of racialized subjects and their "stories" (Giuliani, Giametta, and Petrovich Njegosh 2020) while mobilizing anti-trafficking discourses and initiatives to fight irregular immigration and punish racialized migrants.

The comparison between the experiences of Asian cis women, Latina trans women and Nigerian cis women highlights the ways in which sexual humanitarian rhetoric and interventions are embedded in the shift toward forms of increasingly "extreme bordering" in France. The national specificity of this shift needs to be contextualized within the convergence between state abolitionism and the official invisibilization of race within French republicanism, which deploys actually racialized and sex-gendered (cis-centric) criteria of victimhood as strategic vectors of extreme bordering. The comparison between the experiences of the three migrant groups analysed here exposes the racialized hierarchies of victimhood framing the extreme bordering politics of sexual humanitarianism in France, ranking Nigerian cis-women as more vulnerable than Asian cis women (while proportionally excluding them more from support by constructing them as fraudulent), while neglecting the vulnerabilities of Latino trans women.

New Zealand

In 2003, the passage of the Prostitution Reform Act 2003 (PRA) decriminalized prostitution in New Zealand in order to safeguard the human rights of sex workers and protect them from exploitation, while simultaneously promoting

THE SEXUAL POLITICS OF BORDER CONTROL 133

their welfare and occupational health and safety. However, the PRA also contains a Section (s19, PRA), which was added at the last moment during the Committee Stages of the Bill as an Anti-Trafficking clause (Hansard 2003, 6174), prohibiting migrants on a temporary visa to work as sex workers, or from owning or operating a brothel. The main aim of the SEXHUM project in New Zealand has been to understand whether and in what way Section 19 has actually protected migrant sex workers from exploitation and trafficking by gathering and analyzing their experiences of migration and work.

Of the 58 interviews completed in New Zealand, 46 are People of Colour, 29 of whom from Asian countries, with the majority (12) from mainland China. The focus on Chinese migrants was made in order to trace the echoes in contemporary sexual humanitarian concerns and interventions, which tend to target Asian cis women, of previous, historical racializations, as until 1951, Chinese were prevented from becoming citizens (Archives New Zealand 2020), even if born in New Zealand. It wasn't until 1953 that Chinese could vote in local elections then the General Election in 1954 for the first time. Over recent years there has been a rise in populism in New Zealand as there has been in other countries, with calls to restrict immigration. The 2017 election campaign saw an increase in anti-migrant rhetoric with the leader of the right-wing and populist New Zealand First Party claiming immigration was about ethnicity and race, and that the granting of work permits (to racialized migrants) had led to a "massive immigration influx [which] is distorting all the economic indicators" (Moir 2017). This racialized rhetoric continued unabashed even though it was shown that most work permits were granted to people from Germany, UK, Australia, South Africa and USA (Singh and Tan 2017).

As was the case in Australia, the mainstreaming of right-wing populism and its xenophobic slogans and policies created an enduring shift towards 'extreme bordering' rhetoric and interventions in New Zealand. After the announcement of the new Labour-led coalition government in October 2017, Immigration New Zealand (INZ) increased their investigations into migrant sex workers and their raids on brothels. They also increased sexual humanitarian bordering efforts by refusing suspected sex workers entry and preventing them from boarding aircrafts bound for New Zealand. The numbers are higher in later deportations and refusal of entry than previously, with 132 suspected sex workers prevented from entering New Zealand in the year to February 2018, compared to 45 in the year to April 2013 (McCann 2019; Tan 2013). In 2018 INZ denied accusations of racial profiling despite the fact that a significant (27) number of recent deportations of migrant sex workers involved migrants from Asia (Tan 2018).

Many of the sex workers we interviewed were aware of the protections offered by the PRA to permanent residents and citizens, and used these, particularly the ability to refuse clients and to enforce safer sex practices. As in previous studies (Abel and Roguski 2018; Armstrong 2018; Roguski 2012), there was no evidence of trafficking. At the same time, our data confirm the observation made by the CEDAW Committee that Section 19 of the PRA, brought in to prevent trafficking, may actually leave women more vulnerable to abuse and exploitation (including trafficking) because it inhibits them from reporting to the police out of a fear of deportation (CEDAW 2018, 7).

Joanna, a 54 years old Chinese woman describes her experiences of bullying and clearly relates them to the lack of the possibility for migrants to work legally in the sex industry:

> When we come to NZ from another country, it would be best to be able to have a visa that allows us to do this job so that nobody is able to bully us – boss or clients. With no visa, sometimes clients or bosses will bully us, and say that because we are not legal, we can't report anything to the police.

Sunny, a 30 years old Chinese female sex worker claimed that she would not report being victim of violent crime to the police for fear of being reported to Immigration and eventually deported.

> I do not think I would contact the police though if something went wrong, even if it wasn't at work, because I do not want them knowing what I do as I think they may tell Immigration, and I do not want them to know as I may get deported.

Our findings show that Section 19 also prevents migrant sex workers from approaching medical professionals. Many Chinese sex workers stated they would not see a doctor in New Zealand, but would prefer to travel back to their home country, even if it was just for a small matter. During the arc of the project (2016–20) clinical key informants have indicated a substantial decrease of migrant sex workers' attendance of sexual health clinics, which is strongly related to an increase in immigration controls and deportations.

Our research data show the enduring role that historical racialized hierarchies of Anglo-Saxon superiority, according to which "racial differences far outweighed any capacity to work", play in contemporary sexual humanitarian policies and interventions (Graham 1992, 114–116). Although Section 19 affects all migrants, it disproportionately affects migrant cis women from Asia. Our data demonstrate that racialized categories and hierarchies of supposed vulnerability are framing the identification of potential sexual humanitarian targets in New Zealand, which impact very negatively on the rights and lives of migrant sex workers by exacerbating their exploitability and deportability. Our data and findings also show that, similarly to Australia, the overall racialized bordering politics of sexual humanitarianism in New Zealand reflects a shift towards forms of extreme bordering that are aligned with the political revitalization of historical anxieties that established "if not literally a 'white New Zealand' policy, at least one which was carefully designed effectively to prevent the settlement of Asians" (O'Connor 1968). However, unlike in Australia, in New Zealand migrant sex workers are not included within the protection guaranteed by the PRA. Our findings strongly suggest that their full inclusion within such protection is the best and only way to reduce their vulnerability to exploitation and trafficking.

United States

The overall landscape of sex work, migration and trafficking in the US is characterized by an oppressive carceral regime that grew increasingly repressive under the Trump administration (Hoefinger et al. 2020, 6). Although prostitution is legislated at the state level, where, in most jurisdictions, all forms of sex work and all parties involved are criminalized (except in some small counties in Nevada), Trump and his administration implemented numerous policies and executive orders limiting rights for marginalized communities of migrants, queer and trans people (Murib 2018; Waslin 2020). Sex work has been targeted through sexual humanitarian interventions in the form of repressive legislation aimed at impeding all sex work through criminal law (Hoefinger et al. 2020).

In 2018, in the name of 'combating trafficking' the Allow States and Victims to Fight Online Sex Trafficking Act (FOSTA) and the Stop Enabling Sex Traffickers Act (SESTA) were passed in the US House of Representatives and Senate, respectively, with bipartisan support. This amended Section 230 of the Communications Decency Act to hold websites accountable for third party advertisements for sexual services on their platforms, pushing sex workers offline and further into precariousness and exposure, increasing their chances of being arrested and prosecuted, while reducing ways to work independently and safely (Blunt and Wolf 2020; Musto et al. 2021). Within an increasingly anti-migration environment of 'extreme bordering' – of actual borders, of bodies, of access to information and communication – people viewed by authorities as victims of sex trafficking (e.g. all sex workers) have been subject to arrests which function as a catalyst for court supervision and referral to social services, a process referred to in turn as "arresting to assist" and "arrest referral" (Musto 2016; Conner 2016). These trends have been described as a form of carceral protectionism (Musto 2016) and "penal welfare" (Gruber, Cohen, and Mogulescu 2016), where victims are de facto treated as criminals and where criminal interventions are reformulated as humanitarian programmes.

Transgender migrant sex workers and BIPOC (Black, Indigenous and People of Colour) sex workers are most affected by punitive sexual humanitarian interventions, and largely fall through the gaps of protective services for victims of trafficking (Fehrenbacher et al. 2020; Hoefinger et al. 2020). In both NYC and LA, trans Latina sex workers were a particularly targeted group and were therefore strongly represented in our interviews. In both sites, respondents recalled being singled out and arrested for 'walking while trans'; (assumed to be sex workers for being out in the street). Several had been in immigration detention, prisons and jails where they had experienced misgendering, discrimination and derision for speaking Spanish and for their gender identity, sexual assault, torture-like treatments, and were often denied hormonal therapies.

Human Trafficking Intervention Courts (HTICs) were established in New York in 2013 with the aim to reframe people charged with prostitution (in this case, mainly cis women) as victims of domestic violence and trafficking rather than as petty offenders (Gruber, Cohen, and Mogulescu 2016). People who are charged with prostitution-related misdemeanors, including survivors of trafficking and those who trade sex "by choice or circumstance", (Ray and Caterine 2014) are mandated to complete a series of 5–6 social service sessions (such as individual or group therapy, art therapy, life skills workshops, or yoga, for example). Once they complete the mandatory sessions, defendants can seek to attain an "adjournment for contemplation of dismissal" (ACD), which is not an admission of guilt, through the court; the charge is dismissed and sealed if they are not rearrested within the following 6 months (Ray and Caterine 2014; Yale GHJP 2018).

Our findings show that the ambivalent forms of sexual humanitarian control and protection (Musto 2016) and the limited opportunities of support provided by HTICs were eroded by the anti-migration 'extreme bordering' measures introduced by the Trump administration. SEXHUM's NYC-based researcher witnessed the intrusion of ICE officers inside the buildings of the Queens County Criminal Justice Court, where many migrant sex workers, including undocumented victims of trafficking, were trying to defend their cases (Fertig 2017). The impact of extreme bordering in NYC is also exemplified by the death of Yang Song, a 38 years old undocumented Chinese cis woman who fell to her death from a 4-story building during a sexual humanitarian anti-sex work raid, with only one session left before having her case closed in the Queens HTIC (Barry and Singer 2019).

In the US the SEXHUM project interviewed a total of 58 migrant and BIPOC sex workers and trafficked persons born in the US, or in Latin America, the Caribbean, Africa, or Asia including cisgender, transgender, and non-binary/gender-nonconforming people between the ages of 19–70 years old. 20 key informants were also interviewed in NYC and LA. A significant part of ethnographic fieldwork was undertaken in HTICs in NYC and in the anti-trafficking task forces in LA. The research team also conducted ethnographic fieldwork through the participation in sex worker, transgender, and migrant rights spaces and organizations, as well as by attending community-based social events, meetings, and political initiatives. Our research complements previous studies that highlight how defendants are mostly legal age (18 years or older) US-born cisgender women of colour and Mandarin-speaking Chinese cisgender women arrested in raids on massage parlors (Ray and Caterine 2014; Yale GHJP 2018).

Only a handful of trans participants had experienced the HTICs. Our data confirm that the long drawn-out court processes and social service sessions are out of step with the material reality and priorities of sex workers, while they unveil how the (sexual) humanitarian ethos of HTICs is structurally embedded in the enforcement of anti-prostitution laws. In this context, as NYC Legal Aid attorney Leigh Latimer pointed out, transgender defendants experience "differential treatment" in the booking, arraignment, and dismissal process, and in accessing the HTICs. She explains: "Because of the over-policing in the trans community [they] might see the prior criminal records – for drugs and things – used against them a little more as opposed to cis gender women". In LA, HTICs do not exist, but similar Law Enforcement Assisted Diversion (LEAD) programmes are overseen by the LA County Sheriff's Department Human Trafficking Bureau. The cis-centric bias characterizing sexual humanitarian understanding of victimhood tends to undermine trans people's recognition as victims of trafficking, thereby excluding them from a very important form of humanitarian protection (Fehrenbacher et al. 2020).

Many of our trans research participants explained that they resorted to sex work because they were excluded from mainstream legal forms of employment for being trans. At the same time, most were ambivalent regarding the opportunity of identifying themselves as victims of trafficking with authorities. This is both because when they report being victims of a crime, police tend to prioritize the prosecution of their sex work offenses, and because of the lack of targeted programmes responding to their complex needs and priorities, which mirrors research highlighting law enforcement refusal to file reports on the trafficking of LGBTQ persons (Boukli and Renz 2018). The experience of Claudia, a 38-year-old trans woman from Central America is emblematic of the abuse (from clients, exploiters and the police) many trans migrants endure for fear of being deported. In her own words:

> The therapist I am seeing at the moment is at the XY Project of the XY Center. I am hoping that they help me and I like the sessions very much. We are talking about difficult issues about my life that I don't want to talk about, as they are traumas from my previous life. Apart from what happened to me as a child, I was also abused here in the US. They drugged me in a disco and then they abused me. I did not denounce them for fear of being deported.

Claudia's interview excerpt and overall experience show the crucial and positive difference made by sex worker-led, trans-specific projects, such as the one supporting her asylum case in NYC in addressing the gaps in health care. They also show the negative health consequences caused by the forms of 'extreme bordering' framing sexual humanitarian, anti-trafficking interventions and by the criminalization of sex work, as well as the need for peer-led sex work projects to receive broader public health support and funding (Hoefinger et al. 2020).

Conclusion

Overall, the data and findings discussed in this article show that humanitarian problematizations of sexual behaviour play a strategic role in the deployment of increasingly repressive, racialized and extreme forms of bordering in neoliberal times. They demonstrate that there is a proportional relationship between the degree of racialization of migrant groups and their subjection to sexual humanitarian concerns, exclusionary controls and increasingly extreme bordering. Our findings show the intersectional role of sex-gendering in excluding racialized non-cis migrants from humanitarian and legal protection. Across our four national research settings we found shared patterns of racialization and cis-centric sex-gendering translating into differently exclusionary practices of extreme bordering targeting (and deporting) Asian (and, in France, Nigerian) cis- women as ideal 'passive' victims while excluding Latina trans women from humanitarian concerns and support.

The experiences of migrant sex workers analysed here show that the structurally racist coloniality of human rights (Maldonado-Torres 2017; Wynter 2003) and the limited degree of sexual humanitarian support they have provided to their target populations in times of relatively 'progressive' neoliberalism were further eroded by the political mainstreaming of right-wing extremism, leading to directly exclusionary anti-migration policies. In this worrying global context of rising authoritarian populism, increased xenophobia and neoliberal socio-economic polarization the sex industry acts as a "grey zone" (Yiftachel 2009) of informality and marginalization within which migrants can paradoxically both resist (or complement) increasingly exploitative forms of mainstream labour and encounter specific forms of exploitation.

Our findings strongly suggest that in order to respond to this paradoxical situation and enhance the possibility for migrants to find self-realization rather than exploitation and harm in the sex industry it is important to repeal all "repressive" and "restrictive" laws criminalizing or limiting both the sale and purchase of sexual services and to adopt instead an ethical and "integrative" approach that aims to "integrate the sex work sector into [the] societal, legal and institutional framework" (Östergren 2017, 15). More specifically, our comparative data and analysis demonstrate that there is an inversely proportional relationship between the degree of criminalization faced by migrant sex workers, including people in trafficking situations, and their ability to access justice and assert their rights and lives against increasingly extreme and racialized forms of bordering.

THE SEXUAL POLITICS OF BORDER CONTROL

However, even in our most integrative research setting, NSW, where migrants on temporary visas can work legally in the sex industry, sexual humanitarian concerns translate in extreme racialized bordering interventions exposing Asian migrant cis women to deportation and repressing their agency when they work in unauthorized massage parlors, where they can negotiate sexual services more freely and make more money precisely because of the 'grey' and hidden nature of their sexual labour. In New Zealand, the convergence between the mainstreaming of right-wing anti-migrant rhetoric and the impossibility for migrants on temporary visas to work in the sex industry translated in the racialized and extreme bordering of Asian cis women, many of whom faced exploitation because their work was illegalized by Section 19 of the 2003 PRA.

In France the passing of the 2016 abolitionist law introduced a further degree of criminalization of sex work by proxy through the criminalization of clients and legitimized the extreme bordering of migrant groups by sexual humanitarian interventions according to racialized hierarchies of victimhood that did not translate in proportional entitlement to humanitarian and social support while exacerbating their social-economic vulnerability. Finally the US, where sex work is criminalized outright, was the research setting within which the translation between the mainstreaming of xenophobic anti-migrant discourse into extreme, harmful and racialized forms of bordering was most visible and recurrent, as well as being the context with the highest number of trafficking victims and cases of exploitation, including African American citizens. These considerations and our overall findings indicate that, given the scale of involvement of migrant sex workers in the sex industry worldwide, any policy and social intervention on sex work can only have a chance of succeeding if it also includes prospective and actual migrants' legal right to access the international labour market, which would reduce their exploitability by the people who facilitate their labour migration trajectories (Bravo 2009). The New Zealand and NSW case studies specifically demonstrate how decriminalization policies need to include all national as well as migrant sex workers regardless of their visa status, in order not to reproduce racialized and sex-gendered borders putting migrant workers at heightened risk of exploitation, violence and criminalization and curbing on their access to justice.

Notes

1. SEXHUM – Sexual Humanitarianism: understanding agency and exploitation in the global sex industry – ERC Consolidator Grant 2015–682451. More information about the SEXHUM project is available on its website: www.sexhum.org
2. The share for massage fees only is usually 40% for the worker and 60% for the shop. One hour of regular massage ranges from $60 ($25/$35) to $80 ($35/$45),

depending on the shop. Payments for extra sexual services are kept by the workers in full.

Disclosure statement

No potential conflict of interest was reported by the author(s).

Funding

This work was supported by H2020 European Research Council [grant number ERC CoG 682451].

ORCID

Nicola Mai ⬤ http://orcid.org/0000-0001-6073-0820
P.G. Macioti ⬤ http://orcid.org/0000-0003-3742-5726
Calum Bennachie ⬤ http://orcid.org/0000-0001-9250-676X
Anne E. Fehrenbacher ⬤ http://orcid.org/0000-0002-0880-2660
Calogero Giametta ⬤ http://orcid.org/0000-0003-1351-9103
Heidi Hoefinger ⬤ http://orcid.org/0000-0002-1312-1229
Jennifer Musto ⬤ http://orcid.org/0000-0002-3925-6228

References

Aanu Oloruntoba, F., A. O. Ogwezzy-Ndisika, B. Adeshina, and K. Okechukwu Amakoh. 2018. "Transnational Gendered Narratives on Migration: The Nigerian Media and Female Migrants en Route to Italy from Libya." *Feminist Media Studies* 18 (6): 1130–1132.

Abel, G., and M. Roguski. 2018. "Migrant Sex Workers in New Zealand: Report for MBIE." Wellington, (NZ): Ministry of Business, Innovation and Employment (MBIE).

Archives New Zealand. 2020. *Citizenship*. Wellington, NZ: Archives New Zealand. https://archives.govt.nz/citizenship.

Armstrong, L. 2018. "New Zealand, in Global Alliance Against Trafficking in Women." In *Sex Workers Organising for Change: Self-Representation, Community Mobilisation, and Working Conditions*, edited by Maria Stacey and Borislav Gerasimov, 72–107. Bangkok, TH: Global Alliance Against Trafficking in Women. https://www.gaatw.org/resources/publications/941-sex-workers-organising-for-change.

Barry, D., and J. E. Singer. 2019. "'Jane Doe Ponytail': Her Life Ended in N.Y. Now Her Brother's Bringing Her Home." *The New York Times*, April 9 2019. https://www.nytimes.com/2019/04/09/nyregion/jane-doe-song-yang-flushing.html.

Bernstein, E. 2018. *Brokered Subjects. Sex, Trafficking, and the Politics of Freedom*. Chicago: Chicago University Press.

Blunt, D., and A. Wolf. 2020. "Erased: The Impact of FOSTA-SESTA and the Removal of Backpage on Sex Workers." *Anti-Trafficking Review* (14): 117–121.

Bolivar, A. 2017. "For Chicago's Trans Latina Sex Workers, A Cycle of Fear, Violence, and Brutality: From Employment Discrimination to Incarceration to Deportation, Trans Latina sex Workers Face a Triple Threat of Sexism, Racism, and Classism Through Policing." *NACLA Report on the Americas* 49 (3): 323–327.

Boukli, A., and F. Renz. 2018. "Deconstructing the Lesbian, Gay, Bisexual, Transgender Victim of Sex Trafficking: Harm, Exceptionality and Religion–Sexuality Tensions." *International Review of Victimology* 25 (1): 71–90.

Bravo, K. E. 2009. "Free Labor: A Labor Liberation Solution to Modern Trafficking in Humans." *Transnational Law and Contemporary Problems* 18: 545–616.

CEDAW. 2018. *Concluding Observations on the Eighth Periodic Report of New Zealand.* OHCHR. https://tbinternet.ohchr.org/_layouts/15/treatybodyexternal/Download.aspx?symbolno=CEDAW%2fC%2fNZL%2fCO%2f8&Lang=en.

Conner, B. M. 2016. "In Loco Aequitatis: The Dangers of Safe Harbor Laws for Youth in the Sex Trade." *Stanford Journal of Civil Rights & Civil Liberties* 12: 43.

Dalton, B., and K. Jung. 2019. "Becoming Cosmopolitan Women While Negotiating Structurally Limited Choices: The Case of Korean Migrant sex Workers in Australia." *Organization* 26 (3): 355–370.

Davidsson, R. 2017. "No Happy Endings in this Tale of Massage Parlours." *The Hatch*, August 3 2017. https://hatch.macleay.net/no-happy-endings-in-this-tale-of-massage-parlours/.

Duff, E. 2017. "Illegal Brothel Complaints Spike after NSW Government Blocks Sex Industry Reform." *Sydney Morning Herald*, April 30 2017. https://www.smh.com.au/national/nsw/illegal-brothel-complaints-skyrocket-after-nsw-governments-refusal-to-reform-sex-industry-20170428-gvv0vn.html.

EROS. 2017. "Strategies and Campaigns for 2017: Illegal Brothels." *Eros Journal* (4): 44.

Fehrenbacher, A. E., J. Musto, H. Hoefinger, N. Mai, P. G. Macioti, C. Giametta, and C. Bennachie. 2020. "Transgender People and Human Trafficking: Intersectional Exclusion of Transgender Migrants and People of Color from Anti-Trafficking Protection in the United States." *Journal of Human Trafficking* 6 (2): 182–194.

Fertig, B. 2017. "Outcry After Immigration Agents Seen at Queens Human Trafficking Court." *WNYC*, June 16 2017. https://www.wnyc.org/story/outcry-after-immigration-agents-come-trafficking-victim-queens-courthouse/.

Fraser, N. 2016. "Progressive Neoliberalism Versus Reactionary Populism: A Choice That Feminists Should Refuse." *NORA – Nordic Journal of Feminist and Gender Research* 24 (4): 281–284.

Giametta, C., H. Le Bail, and N. Mai. 2018. "The Impact of the 'Swedish Model' in France: Chronicle of a Disaster Foretold." *Open Democracy*, April 25 2018. https://www.opendemocracy.net/en/beyond-trafficking-and-slavery/impact-of-swedish-model-in-france-chronicl/.

Giuliani, G., C. Giametta, and T. Petrovich Njegosh. 2020. "Per un'analisi della memoria delle migrazioni in Europa: discorsi, (auto)rappresentazioni e propaganda." In *Stranieri nel ricordo. Verso una memoria pubblica delle migrazioni*, edited by D. Salerno and P. Violi, 173–202. Bologna: Il Mulino.

Gondouin, J., S. Thapar-Björkert, and I. Ryberg. 2018. "White Vulnerability and the Politics of Reproduction in Top of the Lake: China Girl." In *The Power of Vulnerability*, 116–132. Manchester University Press.

Graham, J. 1992. "Settler Society." In *The Oxford History of New Zealand*, edited by G. W. Rice, 112–140. Auckland, NZ: Oxford University Press.

Gruber, A., A. J. Cohen, and K. Mogulescu. 2016. "Penal Welfare and the new Human Trafficking Intervention Courts." *Florida Law Review* 68: 1333.

Ham, J. 2017. *Sex Work, Immigration and Social Difference*. London: Routledge.

Hansard. 2003. *Vote on the Prostitution Reform Bill 2000*. Hansard Parliamentary Debates, Vol609, p6608. https://www.parliament.nz/en/pb/hansard-debates/historical-hansard/.

Hansen, N. 2019. "Sydney Massage Parlours Found Guilty of Illegal Sex with Private Investigators." *The West Australian*, August 1 2019. https://thewest.com.au/news/nsw/sydney-massage-parlours-found-guilty-of-illegal-sex-with-private-investigators-ng-3b5633fa4d4103378a940108aec522f8.

Hoefinger, H., J. Musto, P. G. Macioti, A. E. Fehrenbacher, N. Mai, C. Bennachie, and C. Giametta. 2020. "Community-Based Responses to Negative Health Impacts of Sexual Humanitarian Anti-Trafficking Policies and the Criminalization of Sex Work and Migration in the US." *Social Sciences* 9 (1): 1.

Hogan, J., and K. Haltinner. 2015. "Floods, Invaders, and Parasites: Immigration Threat Narratives and Right-Wing Populism in the USA, UK and Australia." *Journal of Intercultural Studies* 36 (5): 520–543.

Lam, E., and A. Lepp. 2019. "Butterfly: Resisting the Harms of Anti-Trafficking Policies and Fostering Peer-Based Organising in Canada." *Anti-Trafficking Review*, Issue 12 (2019): 91–107.

Le Bail, H., and C. Giametta. 2018. *What Do Sex Workers Think About the French Prostitution Act? A Study on the Impact of the Law from 13 April 2016 Against the 'Prostitution System' in France. Synthesis*. Paris: Médecins du Monde.

Le Bail, H., and M. Lieber. Forthcoming. *Sweeping the Streets, Cleaning Morals: Chinese Sex Workers Claiming their Right to the City of Paris*.

Macioti, P. G., E. Aroney, C. Bennachie, A. E. Fehrenbacher, C. Giametta, H. Hoefinger, N. Mai, and J. Musto. 2020. "Framing the Mother Tac: The Racialized, Sexualised and Gendered Politics of Modern Slavery in Australia." *Social Sciences* 9 (11): 192.

Mai, N. 2018. *Mobile Orientations. An Intimate Autoethnography of Migration, Sex Work and Humanitarian Borders*. Chicago: Chicago University Press.

Maldonado-Torres, N. 2017. "On the Coloniality of Human Rights." *Revista Critica de Ciencias Sociais* 114: 117–136.

McCann, M. 2019. "Revealed: Hundreds of Suspected Sex Workers Stopped at NZ Border." *Newshub*, June 5 2019. https://www.newshub.co.nz/home/new-zealand/2019/06/revealed-hundreds-of-suspected-sex-workers-stopped-at-nz-border.html.

Mezzadra, S., and B. Neilson. 2013. *Border as Method, or the Multiplication of Labor*. London, NC: Duke University Press.

Miren, F. 2018. "A Migrant Trans Sex Worker's Murder Has Set Off Protests Around the World." *Vice*, September 21 2018. https://www.vice.com/en_us/article/nemz3m/vanesa-campos-sex-worker-murder-protests.

Mitchell, N. 2019. "Massage Parlour Brothels Busted: One Shut Down Every Week." *3AW News Talk*, November 21 2019. https://www.3aw.com.au/massage-parlour-brothels-busted-one-shut-down-every-week/.

Moir, J. 2017. "Winston Peters says Immigration is all About 'Ethnicity and Race.' *Stuff*, May 3 2017. https://www.stuff.co.nz/national/politics/92163124/winston-peters-says-immigration-is-all-about-ethnicity-and-race.

Murib, Z. 2018. "Trumpism, Citizenship, and the Future of the LGBTQ Movement." *Politics & Gender* 14 (4): 649–672.

Murji, K., and J. Solomos. 2005. "Introduction: Racialization in Theory and Practice." In *Racialization: Studies in Theory and Practice*, edited by K. Murji and J. Solomos, 1–12. Oxford: Oxford University Press.

Musto, J. 2016. *Control and Protect: Collaboration, Carceral Protection, and Domestic sex Trafficking in the United States*. Oakland, CA: University of California Press.

Musto J., A. E. Fehrenbacher, H. Hoefinger, N. Mai, P. G. Macioti, C. Bennachie, C. Giametta, and K. D'Adamo. 2021. "Anti-Trafficking in the Time of FOSTA/SESTA:

Networked Moral Gentrification and Sexual Humanitarian Creep." *Social Sciences* 10 (2): 58.

O'Connor, P. S. 1968. "Keeping New Zealand White, 1908–1920." *The New Zealand Journal of History* 2 (1): 41–65.

Oriti, Thomas. 2017. "Project to Support Women in Illegal Brothels." *ABC News*, February 24 2017. https://www.abc.net.au/radio/programs/worldtoday/project-to-support-women-in-illegal-brothels/8300966.

Östergren, P. 2017. *From Zero-Tolerance to Full Integration: Rethinking Prostitution Policies*. DemandAT Working Paper No. 10. https://www.demandat.eu/publica tions/zero-tolerance-full-integration-rethinking-prostitution-policies.

Papastegiadis, N. 2005. *The Invasion Complex: Deep Historical Fears and Wide Open Anxieties*. Willy Brandt Series of Working Papers in International Migration and Ethnic Relations 2/05. Malmö University. http://muep.mau.se/handle/2043/1861.

Project Respect. 2017. *Position Statement: Illegal Brothels*. https://d3n8a8pro7vhmx. cloudfront.net/projectrespect/pages/15/attachments/original/1504666071/010620 17_Position_Statement_Illegal_Brothels_-_FINAL.pdf?1504666071.

Ray, A., and E. Caterine. 2014. "Criminal, Victim, or Worker? The Effects of New York's Human Trafficking Intervention Courts on Adults Charged with Prostitution-Related Offenses." *New York Foundation*, October 1 2014. https://nyf.issuelab.org/resource/criminal-victim-or-worker-the-effects-of-new-york-s-human-trafficking-intervention-courts-on-adults-charged-with-prostitution-related-offenses.html.

Red Cross. 2019. *Support for Trafficked People Program. Data Snapshot: 2009 to 2019*. https://www.redcross.org.au/getmedia/7a957782-a7a1-4b25-97c0-86930dbf0f53/ARC-Support-For-Trafficked-People-Program-Data-Snapshot-2009-to-2019-small.pdf.aspx.

Roguski, M. 2012. *Occupational Health and Safety of MSWs in New Zealand*. Wellington, NZ: Kaitiaki Research. http://www.communityresearch.org.nz/research/occupation al-safety-and-health-of-migrant-sex-workers-in-new-zealand/.

Selvey, L. A., R. C. Lobo, K. L. McCausland, B. Donovan, J. Bates, and J. Hallett. 2018. "Challenges Facing Asian Sex Workers in Western Australia: Implications for Health Promotion and Support Services." *Frontiers in Public Health* 6: 171.

Singh, H., and L. Tan. 2017. "Top Source Countries for Migrant Workers are not Asian." *New Zealand Herald*, April 26 2017. https://www.nzherald.co.nz/nz/news/article. cfm?c_id=1&objectid=11842859.

Sodsai, P. 2017. "'Happy Ending' Massage Shops vs 'Legitimate' Ones: Can you Spot the Difference?" *SBS Thai*, October 6 2020. https://www.sbs.com.au/language/english/happy-ending-massage-shops-vs-legitimate-ones-can-you-spot-the-differ ence.

Sodsai, P. 2019. "The Majority of Illegal Brothels are Massage Shops' Say Police." *SBS Thai*, October 3 2019. https://www.sbs.com.au/language/english/the-majority-of-illegal-brothels-are-massage-shops-say-police.

Svedin, C. G., L. Jonsson, C. Kjellgren, G. Priebe, and I. Åkerman. 2012. *Prostitution i Sverige. Huvudrapport: kartläggning och utvärdering av prostitutionsgruppernas insatser samt erfarenheter och attityder i befolkningen*. Linköping, Sweden: Linköping University Electronic Press.

Tan, L. 2013. "Prostitutes Kept Out Despite Visas." *New Zealand Herald*, June 5 2013. https://www.nzherald.co.nz/nz/news/article.cfm?c_id=1&objectid=10888451.

Tan, L. 2018. "Sex Workers Reject Lisa Lewis as their 'Voice'," *New Zealand Herald*, June 20 2018. https://www.nzherald.co.nz/nz/news/article.cfm?c_id=1&objectid=12073 830.

Ticktin, M. 2008. "Sexual Violence as the Language of Border Control: Where French Feminist and Anti-Immigrant Rhetoric Meet." *Signs* 33 (4): 863–889.

Waslin, M. 2020. "The Use of Executive Orders and Proclamations to Create Immigration Policy: Trump in Historical Perspective." *Journal on Migration and Human Security* 8 (1): 54–67.

Wynter, S. 2003. "Unsettling the Coloniality of Being/Power/Truth/Freedom: Towards the Human, AfterMan, Its Overrepresentation—An Argument." *The New Centennial Review* 3 (3): 257–337.

Yale Global Health Justice Partnership. 2018. *Un-Meetable Promises: Rhetoric and Reality in New York City's Human Trafficking Intervention Courts. Global Health Justice Partnership of the Yale Law School and Yale School of Public Health and The Sex Workers Project*. New York: Urban Justice Center.

Yiftachel, O. 2009. "Critical Theory and "Gray Space": Mobilization of the Colonized." *City* 13 (2-3): 246–263.

Yuval-Davis, N., G. Wemyss, and K. Cassidy. 2019. *Bordering*. Cambridge: Polity Press.

Predatory porn, sex work and solidarity at borders

Piro Rexhepi ⓘ

ABSTRACT
This piece examines the exploitation of migrant sex workers in Greece through the marketization of nonconsensual video recording of sexual encounters where profit and pleasure are extracted from emerging predatory economies at border crossings. In the context of this special issue on Sexuality and Borders, the piece suggests that extraction of value from sexuality and sex work at borders relies on racial profiling of refugees, reinforcing, sorting and situating them in the colonial cartographies of space where the construction of desirability furnishes the consumer and producer with enduring orientalist fetishes of migrant male masculinity as untainted by the supposed metrosexualization of the European man. Blending history and fieldwork to uncover the production and proliferation of these sex tapes, the article also looks at the ways in which sexual play and pleasure seeking engender new social and spatial relations through solidarity that emerges in response to predatory porn industries.

To be queer in 2019 is to experience a kind of vertigo. It is to not know left from right. Beneath the nod of legal protection, the showy condemnation of homophobia, and the smooth gloss of Netflix shows, something bloody and sinuous writhes. I feel it move underneath under my feet, I feel its tug and its weight and its slippery crimson mass. Beneath the rainbow, the war machine.

Field Notes: Queer Vertigo by Sita Balani

Heterosexuals seem to cope with queer theory in its most abstract, intellectualized and disembodied form, but run scared when confronted with the materiality of lesbian, bisexual and gay lives, experiences and embodiments.

Coming out of Geography: towards a queer epistemology? by John Binnie (1997)

While in Greece during what came to be known as the "refugee crisis," some local and migrant friends of mine struggled with removing hidden video recordings of their sexual encounters with locals off the porn sites where they had been uploaded without their consent. In the process of trying to figure out how to expunge their circulation, a predatory porn market emerged whereby sexual encounters recorded with mostly Syrian, Albanian, Afghani or Iraqi migrants in Greece were sold for a profit online. Queer migrants had no way of removing these videos given that their undocumented position in Greece placed them in a precarious state. Indeed, what became clear to us as we navigated the online migrant porn industry was that it was this very precarity of the queer migrant, bound to the broader border economies, that made this particular kind of predatory porn desirable.

What I'm calling *predatory porn* here is a profitable digital industry of "amateur" non-consensual recordings of migrant queer and/or sex workers proliferated for a profit on online porn sharing platforms. In this process of exploitation, migrants that are otherwise marked for miming are momentarily monetized to emulate desirability generating new logics of digital dispossession and disembodiment of desire as vibrating commodity vectors for surplus value traded in the digital marketplace of what Christopher Patterson (2020) calls "open world empire." Like "predatory value" (Byrd et al. 2018) which is "generative of a dialectic of biopolitical sorting" (1) but also illustrative of the "constitutive and continuing role of both colonization and racialization of capitalism" (2) in contemporary modes of production of value, predatory porn relies on similar logics of exploitation. It is in the mobility of migrants at borders where this extraction is perhaps most palpable as *enclosure erotics* where libidinal exploits are not only conditioned by profit but also underwritten by racialized mappings of space, time and desire as measures of masculinity and modernity. In what follows, I want to think through some of the ways in which erotic sensibilities, encounters and economies of sex along the Euro-Atlantic enclosures are not just conditioned by racial capitalisms colonial re-enactment of borders through sexuality – but to also look at moments and circumstances when sexual play generates new social and spatial relations. That is not to say, there aren't moments when those conditions are collapsed in the overall erotic encounter, but to ask what kind of solidarities and radical care emerge in the "cracks and fissures"[1] of the coloniality of desire?

This is not an ethnographic piece in as much as it is not written with the intention of extracting knowledge but rather exposing the exploitation of queer migrants and/or sex workers that frequently goes unnoticed and underreported in the abstract academic concerns for "objectivity" at the border. My key concern here is how to interpret my relationships and encounters with my friends in a manner that does not endanger or exploit their already precarious position. All that is recounted here is done with the approval of all those involved. I also want to underline that although this paper focuses on migrant male same-sex workers it is by no means limited to this community as forcibly displaced women, trans and cis-hetero men come under similar forms of economic exploitation in border sex work economies. Throughout this piece, I have done my best to avoid hiding or leaving my own position outside of the politics that these questions propel as I myself engaged in plenty of sexual activity. I also watched some of the above-mentioned videos and, as I was in conversation with some of my friends who had ended up in them, I cannot separate those embodied encounters and filter them through *ethnopornography* alone. As relevant as this new field has been as a concept "to analyze the production, circulation, and corresponding consumption of 'facts,' studies, observations, images, and documentary texts that seek to represent the body, desires, and rituals of another individual (or a particular group, in the vein of ethnology and ethnography) in a way that has the potential to be read as 'erotic' and 'pornographic'" (Sigal, Tortorici, and Whitehead 2020) – it is still mediated by a relative distance which I can't say I embody here though the field itself has at times informed my reading of pornography.

Instead, I have followed Catherine Walsh's advice on decolonial praxis which has influenced me immensely to think of the kind of work we can do as "praxis of intellectually, spiritually, emotionally, and existentially entangled and interwoven" processes, always "contextual, relational, practice based and lived" (Mignolo and Walsh 2018, 19). On observing her own work, Walsh notes that her "proposition has never been to study or report about social movements, actors, and thinkers but rather to think with, and, at the same time, to theorize from the 'political moments' in which I also engage" (2018, 85). In this sense, this is queer and decolonial praxis in as much as I have tried to avoid straightening the contradictions and complexities of the queer questions and friends I bring into this piece to a theoretical coherence, tendencies that fail our feelings when measured against the academic writing, reviewing and publishing industry with its enduring coloniality that still seeks to sustain a sorting out of academic/activist and mind/body binaries. I join Kušić and Záhora (2020) more recent call "to bring in emotional and bodily experiences of academic work, and to help move towards different, more caring, and less conclusive ways of knowledge production," as a way of not just confronting the coloniality of knowledge production and proliferation but more importantly moving beyond it. One way of doing this is to dwell in what Elizabeth Freeman (2010, xi) calls "nonsequential forms of time" in order to avoid the temptations of temporal folding of bodies into a particular *chrononormative* arrangement of space.

These reflections are also a product of various texts and dialogues that have influenced me over the years on how to think about the politics of the body, desire, sexuality and de/coloniality in, from, and through the larger geopolitical context of the post-cold war intensification of colonial, carceral and racial capitalism along what has come to be known as the Balkan Refugee Route. Fatima El-Tayeb's work on the political racelessness and erasure that dominates the discourse on Europe and migration (2011), Tjaša Kancler's work on trans* imaginaries and decolonial perspectives on Europe's post-Cold War establishment of border buffer zones along its eastern and south-eastern peripheries (2014, 2017), Rahul Rao's work on the enduring and evasive coloniality of contemporary queerphobic politics of postcoloniality (2014), Sabiha Allouche's work on the racialization of queer migrants in Lebanon (2017), Saffo Papantonopoulou's work on the importance of non-US/EU centric approaches to understanding post-Ottoman socio-spatial relations, sexualities, sex work and subjectivies (2014), Madina Tlostanova's work on the enduring coloniality in both post-colonialism and post-socialism (2017) and Salman Sayyid's work on speaking and writing from an autonomous Muslim praxis and decolonial Islamic politics and positionality (2015) were immensely influential before, during and after my time in Salonika in thinking through some of the body-geo-politics and borders and sexuality in a new context of border fortification in the Balkans and the homonationalist itineraries that have dominated the post-socialist politics of sexuality.[2]

Sex and Salonika

Thessaloniki as it is known today, has many names. Solun in Southern Slavic languages, Thessaloniki in Greek, Selanik in Albanian and Turkish and Salonika as it was known by its own citizens until its post-Ottoman annexation by Greece in 1913. The subsequent Hellenization that followed the annexation would involve the eventual Europeanization of the city. This meant the expulsion of its Muslim population to Turkey between 1913 and 1924, followed by the deportation of its Jewish and Roma population to Nazi extermination camps during WWII and finally with the deportation and forced assimilation of its Slavic-Macedonian population between 1945 and 1949. I use Salonika as this is the name that locates the city less within the confines of Euro-enclosures geographies and more so in its (post)Ottoman Eastern Mediterranean histories.

Between 2016 and 2018, I was a member of "Empires of Memory: The Cultural Politics of Historicity in Former Habsburg and Ottoman Cities," a research group at the Max Planck Institute for Religious and Ethnic Diversity in Göttingen, Germany. The project aims to think through the various ways in which colonial/imperial pasts continue to bear marks on contemporary cultural politics in several post-Habsburg and post-Ottoman cities. I was interested in the project for several reasons. Spatially speaking, I had grown up between Sarajevo and Salonika, near Lake Prespa, Macedonia or the Republic of North Macedonia as it is now known. The two cities had always attracted my imagination. Sarajevo was of course the hip city in Yugoslavia, the Olympic city, the co-existence city, the Muslim metropolis of the socialist federal republic with proud anti-fascist and anti-colonial movements; a post-Ottoman and post-Habsburg city that assassinated its imperial overlord to be, the Archduke France Ferdinand in 1914. I think of this as a companion piece to my critical reflections on the coloniality of Sarajevo's multilayered past, which having already been expressed in *Interventions: International Journal of Postcolonial Studies* (Rexhepi 2018).

Salonika had a no less lustrous radical history, having been the site of the first revolution in the Ottoman Empire, one that was not geared towards nationalist self-determination but the founding of a free republic – as the Young Turks had, at least initially, promised. *As a matter of historical fact, the first move of the revolution had started in my local hometown of Resna, now Slavicized as Resen. It had been our local bey, Ahmed Niyazi, who directed the third Ottoman Corps to rebel against the Porte on 3 July 1908 and went on to take over the neighbouring city of Manastir (now Bitola), reaching Salonika within a week. In Resen this is somewhat of a local point of pride among the elderly, combined with prejudice against Salonika. We liked to think that while we started the revolution, Salonika got the credit for it since the proclamation of the Young Turk constitution took place there later that same month, on July 24, 1908, ending the absolute reign of Abdul Hamid II in 1909. A century later, through eugenics population exchange projects, the annihilation of its Jewish and Muslim populations, Salonika was Greek and European. These spatial and symbolic designations would be irrelevant would they not come to haunt the city.

I can't say that I arrived in Salonika without my own relationship to the city, not only through the historical imaginaries I detailed above, but also through personal experiences of visiting the city while growing up. In the 1990s, weekend trips and vacations to Salonika from neighbouring Macedonia were very common. If we drove to Istanbul, we would almost always stop in Salonika or around it to see a derelict mosque or tekke in what once had been a prominent Muslim and Jewish city. My parents still have a marble stone with inscriptions of the Yasin surah at home that we "picked up" on one of our visits to the ruins of the fifteenth century Bektashi Durbalı Sultan Tekke in Farsala, now revived again by Albanian migrants. My visits to Salonika continued later without my parents. When I was in high school and had moved to Skopje, I would take the train down for weekends. My last year in high school in 1997, Orhan, an older friend of mine, obtained a car and we drove down for our first gay sauna experience. These visits would increase and we ended up going down for the parties at the only gay bar in the city Ahududu (Turkish for Raspberry) where we made queer friends and were homosocialized (or *homosodomized* as my friend Orhan comically corrects this draft that I have sent him to review and approve). In that sense, like large port cities across the Mediterranean, Salonika is both a city of sex and a sexy city – a bit like the Beirut of the

Balkans for the gay scene, in that you will find queers visiting from Istanbul or those on a weekend trip from Prishtina or Belgrade.

But there was another side of Salonika that lurked in my imagination. One of the first Macedonian-made television series, *Solunski Patrdii [Salonika Sketches]*, was released in 1985 and was re-run on tv all the time as a matter of national pride, because it was our own tv series but also because, by the late 1980s Macedonian, nationalism re-integrated Salonika in the imagination of the people as part of their legible past. The series was situated in Salonika at the turn of the twentieth century with the great Turkish actress from Macedonia, Sabina Ajrula, playing Fatimah[3], a witty sex worker luring Macedonian peasants into her *chardak* on their market day in town. Fatimah would always appear elevated on her terrace surrounded by other beautiful women, as a clever and cunning bully of the bourgeoisie – her relationship to her clients was politicized both through class and orientalism. Fatimah made fun of her drunk admirer Jašar Beg, who represented the urban Ottoman dandy and was played by another legend of the Turkish cast in Macedonian cinema, Salatin Bilal. My grandmother and I were glued to the tv whenever the show aired. What I now think we both use to find interesting about the series as I try to approximate those feelings now writing from the future, were its early telenovela qualities, especially the back and forth flirting, the affairs and the cast costumes. In this category of films that emerged in the late 1980s and early 1990s, Yugoslav orientalism, or *Yugorientalism* as I like to call it, mediated a representation of the Ottoman Christian Raya as peasants and workers trying to make a living while their wealthy Muslim overlords frequently got drunk and were constantly mired in affairs of love and lust. I of course identified with the latter. I lived in a village, so peasants did very little for my imagination, I was one myself so to speak (the shame of which I am perhaps still trying to compensate for even by writing it here). As a queer child, I was of course taken in by the urban erotic protagonists and their intrigues which promised possibilities for erotic exploits.

Going back on YouTube and watching bits and pieces of the series as I was working on this paper, it is hard not to notice how much this series, and similar visual representations, must have shaped my own desire(s), as they were also very reflective of the dynamics in real everyday life in Macedonia in the two decades of late socialism/early post-socialism. Some of those dynamics are brilliantly captured by Sasho Lambevski (1999) in "Suck my Nation, Masculinity, Ethnicity and the Politics of (Homo)sex," illustrating how broader nationalist discourses are embodied in the queer economies of desire, with the depiction of Albanian and generally Muslim men as tops and Macedonians as bottoms, reducing all encounters to these roles and preventing, as Lambevski points out, "Macedonian and Albanian 'gay' men from establishing new forms of mutual friendship and love."[4] Being part of that scene myself, I remember more complex and contradictory relations but

Lambevski is right in that the broader contours of the erotic exchanges were dominated by those dynamics of class, place and race – in as much as Albanians in Macedonia were not simply treated as others merely because of their ethnicity or religion but as a racial other.

Orhan reminded me how not too long ago we had both made fun of a Macedonian guy who asked on his gayromeo profile for "new gays to stay away" as he was only online to "harness the natural scent of real Albanian men." We had a good laugh about that while Orhan made fun of my own Grindr profile that used to read something like "homonationalist tears collector, triple agent, provocateur, poet." He thought I was being political and pretentious and Saffo Papantonopoulou, a trans Greek-Egyptian woman whose interests in all things Ottoman and sex in Salonika had brought us together, thinks I was seeking academic affirmation on the apps. Maybe they are both right. I of course asked him if there was a time that we weren't being political on the apps but Orhan prides himself on being old-school gay and using the apps to just hook up for sex. I couldn't resist calling him out on the fact that he too politicizes the apps by positioning himself as a "cut top," code for a circumcised Muslim/Albanian top that meets Grindr expectations but doesn't really reflect who Orhan is, because Orhan is really a bottom. The Albanian man in this script is perceived as a traditional top embodying an archetypical male masculinity untainted by modernity and metro-sexuality, which the bottom seems to be affected by and embodied with. According to this script, the educated and clever Macedonian supposedly desires some of his recent past and wants the Albanian, who seemingly still resides in that recent past, to enact it. At the same time, the Albanian top can assert (and insert) himself into the Macedonian and give it to him intimately in the face of Albanians' historical subordinate second class citizen position.[5] The temporal anchors to this kind of desire, one that locates the top in the past and the bottom in the present, thus create a trans-temporal encounter that then comes to either resolve or reproduce some of the erotic and political tensions palpable in society.

In this post-Ottoman arrangement of affect, sexuality and desire, the supposed un-tamed Islamic sexual excess of Albanians was meant to be domesticated under larger and frequently limp civilizing projects such as the International Control Commission sent by European Powers in 1914 to modernize Albanians.[6] Across the post-Ottoman world, these legacies of coloniality and capitalism continue to exploit a great deal of erotic tension centred around the forbidden encounter with the refugee/racial/religious/ethnic/classed other as heterosexual forms of fidelity to post-colonial modernity.[7] Sabiha Allouche's (2017) work in Lebanon, for instance, illustrates how

> the interplay between refugees and the receiving state is summed up in the elitist discourse of a 'Syrian neo-invasion' that results in the revival of an

'authentic Lebanese masculinity.' Whereas the Syrian refugee is vilified as a 'rapist' in a heterosexual context, they are emasculated as 'necessarily bottom' in a same-sex one.

Allouche's work is important in that it illustrates how historical narratives are re-assembled and engaged to remake a new regional racist trope that integrates and structures post-colonial nationalist hetero- and homo-masculinities. Moreover, Madina Tlostanova argues that the entanglements of coloniality and borderization with desire and sexuality enact a re-classification of humankind. One that is meant to "stimulate desire and reconfigure the everyday, physical, political and sensible conditions of embodiment, [and] shape subjectivities for the hyperma- chine of capitalist production," as Tjaša Kancler (2017) points out. Much of the sex-work economy and hidden camera amateur migrant predatory porn emerged in the shadows, sides and stops of the Balkan refugee route during the "refugee crisis" of the 2010s. Salonika being the central node of the route as the port of departure for those moving north.

When I arrived in Salonika for the anti-racist festival in the summer of 2015, the city was percolating with organizing migrant movements, old houses and factories turned into migrant-run squats, anti-racist gatherings and with SYRIZA in power, an overall sense of solidarity seemed to have taken over the city. Saffo gave a talk in the anarchist community on destroying straight- ness as I and several other mutual friends moved around the city, making acquittances and joined whatever initiatives we came across to help in the refugee effort. I have published some of these accounts from 2015 and the summer of 2016 in *Critical Muslims*.

Salonika summer 2015, fall 2016, summer-fall 2017

I returned to Salonika in the aftermath of the EU-Turkish agreement that was meant curb and control migration in the Eastern Mediterranean. The gener- ous Max Planck allowance allowed me to seek out a residence I always had wanted to stay in, a small airbnb apartment in the building of the former inter-war Albanian consulate in the city, an ornate villa built in the 1920s next to the Yeni Dzami, the famous mosque built by the Dönmeh commu- nity[8] in what was then the modern Hamidiye neighbourhood, now known as Agia Triada. Saffo thinks this is probably where people who wanted to be excluded from the population exchange of the 1920s, would come to seek Albanian papers since Albanians were meant to be (but frequently were not) the only Muslims exempt from the deportations mandated by the 1923 Lausanne "Convention Concerning the Exchange of Greek and Turkish Populations."[9]

The first two weeks I fell into a self-indulgent weed-induced haze that helped me recover from several sleepless months in Göttingen, Germany, sorting out paperwork at the Max Planck Institute for Religious and Ethnic Diversity. Being in Thessaloniki, with my family nearby in Prespa, allowed me to feel myself and feel relatively safe for a few weeks. Out of guilt over being too idle, stoned as I was, I still betrayed my failed attempts at the "queer art of failure" Halberstam (2011) and did work. I mostly re-visited sites and museums that I had visited over the years and wrote down and erased different ideas about what I thought was going on. I walked around the city with an inflated sense of self, not in the mental but physical sense – the kind of bloating you experience as you start to de-stress. I walked in and out of squats I had visited with my friend Saffo the year before. I also visited squats built around the old city walls where refugees live now in ruins of houses built for the refugees of the population exchange nearly a century ago in the 1920s.[10]

I also met several dubious characters for interviews about the cultural history of the city. Some of the meetings were cordial, others awkward, as some meetings with straight strangers can go. In almost all of them, various Greek academics, artists and activists would always start by saying that they believe the "name" issue with Macedonia is nationalist propaganda and that I am free to say I am from Macedonia and not Skopje, as people from Macedonia are expected to announce themselves in Greece not to offend Greek sensibilities about Macedonia being Greek and "our" theft of their name. Initially, I would reassure them that as an Albanian from Macedonia, I did not think I had a dog in that fight but I then realized that mentioning my *Albanian-ness* would set a whole different apologetic drama into motion given the racist treatment of the large Albanian migrant community in Greece as well as the historical erasure of Albanians from the national history. So, to make things move along faster into the subjects that I was meeting them for, I usually removed my oversized sunglasses (everyone wears them religiously in the city) and nodded in something like a mixture of acknowledgement and approval. While most meetings were pleasant, there were moments of meeting nationalists in places where you would expect to find them, archeological, ethnographic and ethnological museums where they guard the "national treasures" of *Hellenism*.

I returned to Mark Mazower's (2007) *Salonica City of Ghosts* and visited some of those sites. I also returned to queer sites that I had known from earlier visits: a cruising ground that extended from the Macedonia Palace hotel to the YMCA park behind the Archeological Museum and the Statue of Alexander the Great square where good looking people know walk and take pictures of their pets. I remember cruising there in the late 1990s and early 2000s but since cruising is now digital, I also activated my Grindr account. You knew someone was Albanian when the exchange would turn to "you send it first," "no you send a pic first, because I asked first". That would go on for about two days, by which time the erotic anticipation of an instant hook-up had turned to jokes about gay Greeks and you had become too familiarized to fuck.

I had managed to go through several love affairs the previous summer, but in the fall the city had quieted down and revealed a more coherent queer community – or rather communities. I remember meeting Sam the Syrian as he was locally known. On days that he was not working we would get stoned and watch music videos. I am not sure there was enough chemistry for anything more. But we liked each other and became friends. I think he thought it was funny that I was "possessed by politics" and I liked him because he had a real capacity to relate to people in a sarcastic and sexy way. We drove our neighbours crazy since I was living alone and he started bringing some of his friends to my Airbnb. Through him I also met K, an Albanian migrant whose papers had expired, and who was abusing weed and sometimes meth when he could find it. He loved linguistics and his profile picture showed him seated in a squat with a spliff in his mouth – performing the Albanian gay "gango." He was one of those anti-fascist queers that remain beautiful in all their depressive affective states of refusal and resignation. On some of the better evenings we spent together, we treated ourselves to dinner at Mitsos in the old town and walked back stoned to Agia Triada through Salonika's seafront promenade. We loved sex because we both believed that it was the only thing through which queers discover themselves as the one activity where we weren't obliged to enact hetero norms.

We frequently hung out with Sam. We laughed at our online profiles and agreed that we had all exaggerated a bit but Sam's had nothing to do with who he really was. Like my friend Orhan in Macedonia, he had one of those profiles of being a total top. He also used "married top" as bait and to maintain consistency (as he liked to keep things real) he wore a wedding band on his left hand. In real life he described himself as a "twilight zone bottom" and spoke at length about how important it is for bottoms to nurture their microbiome with probiotics for optimal gut health and ultimately a good release. Sam and K knew each other through the local sex scene and the fact that they had both ended up in online hidden amateur porn videos where they were invariably tagged as "married top" or "migrant top" by a notorious xtube troll who went by the screenname Takatapino.

In the category of predatory porn, Takatapino would secretly record sexual encounters with migrants and sex workers against their knowledge and then boast about having the largest migrant porn collection in Greece. Judging by the fact that both Sam and K had ended up on one of his various posts. Bragging about his large private collection was his way of soliciting buyers on the darknet for profit. Sam and K had already confirmed this when they first tried to remove their videos from his xtube channel. After they reported the videos to a site several times without any results, they set themselves on figuring out how to get to him by setting up fake profiles as consumers interested in purchasing his videos. With the help of local hackers, they eventually took down his site. Yet, every time someone took him down, he would change his profile and re-post the videos – sometimes he would remove them but once they were online it was difficult to expunge them. Tracking online clients in Greece who posted video recordings without the approval of sex-workers became one of Sam and K's missions. They knew the digital porn community and had developed a detection method, which combined various subsequent verification methods – including luring the offenders with promises of a "good fuck" or posing as potential buyers. Most videos, however, continued to escape content moderation even in instances where it was obvious that the videos are recorded and posted without consent and with titles and tags that were demeaning and dehumanizing of migrant sex partners and sometimes sex-workers.

One such example is the xtube profile Dark Side, a user who claims to have "a special dote on immigrants (arabs, east europeans, africans etc.) in greece in their twenties!" liking "to – record and take photos from my sex sessions when i can. It's evolved in a some kind of … hobby besides sex!" Dark Side names his videos "cheap male hooker doing everything for the dollar," "Afghan fucker drills my hole" next to "Albanian Fucker Ravishing my ass." [11] They also boast of having the largest archive of recorded sex in Greece: "I'm somewhat proud of my PRIVATE COLLECTION … which is built rather … quickly! I'm sure is the BIGGEST IN GREECE in terms of quality (the way vids are made, and quality) and quantity (MANY LONG LENGHT VIDEOS with … ALL THE SEX SESSION RECORDED, and with … MULTIPLE PARTENERS) From 9/2011(when i start quality recording) until … today 07/2014 I have 1000 GB FULL HD videos with … 100 different tops recorded, without take into account the multiples time with the same person or the threesomes!!!"

Sam and K believed that people like Dark Side and Takatapino are responding to a gay market demand for migrant porn under the larger gay erotic economy of married daddies, str8 amateur porn and webcam bait. Sam would frequently say that if he was going to be an internet porn star, he wanted to get paid for it and do it on his own terms, with casting and costumes designed and directed by him. Some of this he did on his webcam. K and I teased him that if he ever got around to doing them, they might turn out more like Turkish soap operas than the "capitalist realist" (to borrow from Mark Fisher 2009) porn where everyone looks like an indifferent heterosexual. We also had some more serious conversations about migrant porn not being an exception to other capitalist libidinal exploits that emerge in the precarity of borders, where migrants have also been utilized to stabilize a whole set of right wing panics ranging from a new Ottoman invasion to the demographic decline of populations – the seemingly still virile migrant posing a threat to the integrity of the national masculinity.

But there were two interrelated issues at play here with direct consequences for the safety and livelihood of migrants. On the one hand, sex workers were being exploited since their labour was only compensated for the initial encounter – the video recording of which would result in more profits to the local client, but to which profit the migrant sex worker had neither rights to nor remedies for. This was not unrelated to the content of the videos. Judging from comments on the sites, what made migrants attractive to their clients and their online consumers was their virility and anonymity, an "absence" so to speak. It was the intrusion into the intimacy of the "beast" shot from angles that resemble those early BBC documentaries on observing animals surreptitiously as they go about their business, an enduring gaze of euro-colonial binaries of civility and savagery that continue to dominate the human-animal split in Eurocentric erotics and epistemology.[12] Unaware of the cameras, in their natural state, free of social inhibitions, the migrant top has taken the bait inside the house of the host and performs the role of the "ungoverned body" that undermines the respectable gaze; in the distance, they furnish fantasies of transgression, sexualized and desired against the bleak post-industrial state saturated as it is in dystopic nostalgia and decline.[13] Their still existing hope, traded as virility, becoming the queer capital targeting consumer desire in the online gig economy. The central gravitation of these predatory porn economies in both their monetary and libidinal sense and sexuality: both border and migrant. This is where casual orientalist and raced desires about the migrant masculine man are mobilized in structural forms of exploitation – since orientalist desires produce migrants as visitors not just from a different place but also a different time – compensation and care are indefinitely deferred.[14] Is not accidental then that part of what excites the client and online consumer is the inability of the migrant to have recourse or rebel given his anonymous and precarious position. "Progressive" amateur porn videos on the other hand, mostly coming from Germany, Italy and France, fare worse. In seeking to transform migrants for queer capital from sites marked for death to bodies marked for desire they try to subvert the roles and recording rules but remain otherwise thoroughly voyeuristic at best or banal in their attempt to address the "Syrian Refugee Relief".[15]

One of the more produced versions of this genre is *XConfessions.com* inspired short by Bruce LaBruce's *Refugees Welcome* (2017). In it, Moonif, a gay Syrian refugee poet played by Jesse Charif is saved from rapist skinheads by Pig Boy, played by the Czech actor Von Roháč in the character of an anarcho-queer-poet turned saviour. The opening scenes show Roháč reading one of his poems somewhere that seems like a queer cafe in Berlin with Moonif wandering about in and out of spaces in confusion seemingly trying to situate himself and his homoerotic sensibilities. In the following scene, Moonif is attacked and raped by several skinheads and Pig Boy appears as a super-hero beating the rapists and taking Moonif to his apartment to care after his wounds. As he proceeds to undress him and clean his wounds, a dialogue emerges between the protagonists, "I am a foreigner, but not like you I guess" says the Czech host to the Syrian man who responds that it was the skinheads who were the monsters. "Do I look like a monster to you?" asks the Czech saviour, "a good monster" responds the Syrian. The setting of the film puts on display all that today defines anarcho-queer ambiance and affect, from tattoos, piercings and haircuts to Nein posters in dim lit spaces with the refugee projected in constant awe and awakening around them. The Syrian poet recites his poetry as his Czech comrade moves from washing to kissing and licking his feet and eventually topping him. In the following scene, both men wake up next to each other with church bells ringing in the background. As they proceed to make love again, the Syrian poet is triggered by the church bells with images of churches and mosques coming in and out of the frame so as to announce at once the guilt which both subjects seem to embody and a premonition of a bad omen. One of the skinheads that the Czech top beat up the night before has been found dead and now Moonif and Pig Boy have to leave town. In the final scene they are shown to be hitchhiking South with signs pointing to Dresden in what we assume the final destination to be South and not West as most queer escape narratives dictate. The film closes with a shot of the Czech top fucking the Syrian bottom as they wait in the crossroads. The East European in the film plays multiple propositions, on the one hand his racialization seeks to blur the differences even when they are explicitly recognized, they are enacted to combat queer of colour critique by suggesting a more "complicated" constellations of racialization. The triangulation of Nazis, Islam and Catholicism is interesting as it captures the dominant anarcho-queer German politics of secularism but also part of "new cohort of Turkish- and Arab-background public intellectuals in Germany" as Esra Özyürek (2014) points out, that "like the children of Nazis before them, children of Muslims can rebel against their fathers and sexually liberate themselves," producing "a new interpretation of German history not as an anomaly, an evolutionary modernization story gone terribly wrong, but as an historical model that other nationalities should also pass through and come out of." A very German future built on, as Fatima El-Tayeb (2020) recently points out, on colonial amnesia by folding all its external colonial exploits into a European internalist story. "Absent from the concerted rewriting of European twentieth-century history after the end of the Cold War, which combined postfascist and postsocialist narratives into a Western capitalist success story, was a third factor in dire need of reassessment: Europe's colonial past. The refusal to engage with this past as internal to Europe's history also shaped the continent's vision of its future, manifest in a steadily growing postcolonial population that remains "un-European" and in futile attempts to once and for all define and fortify Europe's physical, political, and identitarian borders .... This malleability is particularly obvious in the perception of refugees and undocumented migrants, especially those classified as "economic migrants" (primarily North and West African Muslims and East European Roma) whose death by the thousands at Europe's southern (and increasingly eastern) border is willingly accepted" (2020, 76).

When I sat down to write this piece by looking at field notes, Grindr messages, pictures, short videos I had made in Salonika and emails from the period, I was trying (and I still am) to understand some of the encounters that emerged in Salonika without too many overstatements about fragile but determined new possibilities for solidarity through sex, sexuality and sex-work. Yes, queers are disrupting borders by constantly creating our own intimacies outside of the colonial/capitalist matrix through friendships and interactions of choice and circumstance. In this regard, I have made an attempt here to render the prolonged radical post-Ottoman sensibilities that permeated our friendship, but also my own critical Muslim imaginary and its queer and decolonial attachments and interventions. The very presence of such imaginaries and attachments questions the teleology of a utopian coming together by interrogating the nostalgia visible in the left across the region, but it also insists on thinking of regions and political positions as spaces where new movements can arise that don't negate the past as neutralized and colorblind, and refuse to domesticate sex, sexuality and sex-work as classless "identity politics."

In/conclusive remarks

So how can we think and understand the relation between these histories and geographies of queer desire and queer capital circulating as porn plasticity absorbing the border and its sexuality? While the main focus in this paper has been the exploitation of migrant male same-sex workers, the kind of economic exploitation that takes places in sex work economies in and around borders is by no means limited to these communities as forcibly displaced women, trans people as well as cis-hetero men are also targeted by predatory value extraction. What is important here is not so much what a porn video can or cannot do but how predatory economies of sex reveal an intensified reclassification of race, class and sex in the face of migration and border controls. Unsurprisingly, Greece became the actual and metaphorical local where such encounters could be imagined, enacted and exploited given its mediated geopolitical position as a migrant Mediterranean hub and one of the key enclosure sties of Fortress Europe.

Predatory porn is only a small segment of the multi-billion euro industry of "refugee crisis" that is invested in the exploitation of the physical, emotional, economic and material exhaustion of refugees. From EU revenue streams that rose from €5.6 billion Euros for 2014–2020 to €21.3 billion for 2021–2027[16] funnelled to Balkan governments to subcontract surveillance, security, tracing and policing "services" down to local transportation, food, health and sanitation business that pray on the precarity refugees to generate profits. What these figures do not illustrate are the infinite ways in which migrant labour is exploited under the broader auspices of the humanitarian-industrial complex. More importantly, what the predatory porn industry illuminates is how this libidinal extraction of value relies on racist colonial imaginaries of people and spaces. In many ways, the construction of desirability that emerges in the non-consensual recordings and proliferation of predatory porn furnishes the consumer and producer with certain fetishes of masculinity that assume the migrant male to embody some imagined archetypical pre-modern heterosexuality – untainted by the supposed metrosexualization and modernization of the European man. The predatory video recording of the sexual encounter, like the secret surveillance infrastructures of migrant movement installed by local authorities in collaboration with the EU, satisfies a euro-voyeuristic gaze that extracts both pleasure and profit from precarity at its enclosure sites while simultaneously profiling, reinforcing, sorting and situating people in the colonial and racial cartographies of space.

That these encounters rendered here happen at the geopolitical gates of European enclosures, if we think of the Balkan refugee route as one such geopolitical site of borderization, of sequestering, sorting and storing migrants, or what Mbembe (2019) calls an "archipelago of carceral spaces," is illustrative of the enduring reliance on border buffer zones to solidify the relationship between race and space. Within this carceral geography of borderization, Salonika is a key refugee site in both the historical and contemporary context. From an historical perspective, the population exchange between Greece and Turkey in the interwar period, for instance, illustrates best how a racialized global cartography that started to take shape since the colonial expansions of the 15the century, were being enacted as eugenic geopolitics that b/ordered the racial segregation of the world by the beginning of the twentieth century – a period that Robert Vitalis (2015) calls the beginning of a "White World Order." Aslı Iğsız has recently pointed out, how the population exchange created a "racialized alignment of different groups with designated geographies of belonging, such as the assumption that incoming Muslims from Greece belonged to Turkey and likewise that the Greek Orthodox from Turkey belonged to Greece" which "signaled a modern fusion of the eugenicist logic with demography, mobilized through racialized thinking and statistics, and implemented as spatial segregation" (Iğsız 2018). Today, this process is visible in what Mbembe (2019) sees as the "ghettoizing of entire regions of the world" that contribute to the re-classification and refraction of bodies through fertility and mortality with population politics again becoming a new approach to georacial designs. In this sense, there is a particular kind of predatory and pornographic whiteness that emerges in the borderlands underwritten by colonialism/capitalism that is intimately tied to the immediate "racial" border.

The mobility of the queers seeking pleasure, survival and each other across borders however unsettles this georacial sorting, stratification and straightification as they traverse the refugee routes making both care and cracks into the global walls of whiteness, rearranging the stress of survival as a way of forwarding new possibility for queer play, community and intimacy – this may be what Hi'ilei Julia Kawehipuaakahaopulani Hobard and Tamara Kneese (2020, 2) call "radical care" or "a set of vital but underappreciated strategies for enduring precarious worlds" deployed as "critical survival strategy." In the background of predatory porn, erotic encounters along the Euro-Atlantic enclosures illuminate interactions and possibilities that imagine and enact different kinds of intimacies, embodiments and particularities of space, solidarity and shared histories through sexuality.

Notes

1. For more on this (see Mignolo and Walsh 2018).
2. For more on post-socialist sexuality, see Rexhepi (2017a, 2017b).
3. Today, most people in Macedonia will recognize her by her recent role as the "milk mother" of Suleyman the Magnificent, the character of Afife Hatun in the popular Turkish popular series *Magnificent Century [Muhteşem Yüzyıl]* (2012–2014).
4. Ajkuna Tafa narrates part of Lambevski's reflections in "Skopje-Sarajevo-Salonika: A Post-Ottoman Trilogy," https://www.youtube.com/watch?v=miUB-80VRIA.
5. For more on this, see Neofotistos (2008).
6. For more on this, see Rexhepi (2017c).
7. Non-normative histories of gender and desire have been relegated to near total erasure, from *burrneshas* as Jeta (Jetim) Luboteni (2019) points out in "A Heavy Word: Discourses on Albanian Sworn Virgins," to the booming bejtexhi homoerotic poetry of the 19th century as I have argued (2016) "Islamic Sexualities and the Construction of Europeanness" and their contemporary disavowal in (2016) "From Orientalism to Homonationalism."
8. For more on the Dönme and a consideration of how the Geni Dzami/Yeni Camii has emerged as a site of Neo-Ottoman memory in recent years, see Walton (2016).
9. For more on this, see Manta (2009).
10. In the 1920's Thessaloniki was emptied of its Muslim population with their former homes and neighbourhoods being appropriated for the newly arrived Christian migrants from Asia Minor. Most of the new settlements were situated

THE SEXUAL POLITICS OF BORDER CONTROL 161

in Ano Poli or the upper or Turkish part of town as is known locally. Those migrants arriving while their "host" families had not departed yet, in some instances they would share the living space until such time that the Muslim families would leave, in others, migrants would build make-shift homes by the city walls that encircle the neighbourhood. The ruins of these make-shift homes have historically served as shelter for the undercommons of the city and more recently for refugees.

11. https://www.xtube.com/profile/dark_side_-25411782/about-me.
12. For more on colonial history and racialization of the colonized male body, see Anderson (2000).
13. For more on the broader connections between animality and pornography as well as the digital but also the human looking/gaze, see Malamud (2012).
14. Race and racializing as Tilley and Shilliam (2018) point out is "productive and material, rather than confined to the ideological realm."
15. See, for instance, "Providing Syrian Refugee Relief" "Germany has been really good about taking in Syrian refugees. And this refugee was more than happy to take me in … to his ass. He's been through a lot, but he's thrilled to be some-place where he can bleach his roots and get hard German cock whenever he needs it. And I'm just happy to do my little part to provide Syrian Refugee Release … I mean 'Relief'" https://www.xtube.com/video-watch/providing-syrian-refugee-relief-preview-31678702.
16. For more on this, see Rexhepi (2020).

Disclosure statement

No potential conflict of interest was reported by the author(s).

ORCID

Piro Rexhepi 🄯 http://orcid.org/0000-0001-9691-1842

References

Allouche, Sabiha. 2017. "(Dis)-Intersecting Intersectionality in the Time of Queer SyriaRefugee-Ness in Lebanon." *Kohl: a Journal for Body and Gender Research* 3 (1): 59–77.
Anderson, Kay. 2000. "'The Beast Within': Race, Humanity, and Animality." *Environment and Planning D: Society and Space* 18 (3): 301-320.
Binnie, Jon. 1997. "Coming Out of Geography: Towards a Queer Epistemology?" *Environment and Planning D: Society and Space* 15 (2): 223–237.
Byrd, J. A., A. Goldstein, J. Melamed, and C. Reddy. 2018. "Predatory Value: Economies of Dispossession and Disturbed Relationalities." *Social Text* 36 (2 (135)): 1–18.
El-Tayeb, Fatima. 2011. *European Others: Queering Ethnicity in Postnational Europe*. Minneapolis: University of Minnesota Press.
El-Tayeb, Fatima. 2020. "The Universal Museum: How the New Germany Built its Future on Colonial Amnesia." *Nka Journal of Contemporary African Art* 46 (1): 72–82.
Fisher, Mark. 2009. *Capitalist Realism: Is There No Alternative?* New Alresford: John Hunt Publishing.

Freeman, Elizabeth. 2010. *Time Binds: Queer Temporalities, Queer Histories*. Durham: Duke University Press.

Halberstam, Jack. 2011. *The Queer Art of Failure*. Durham: Duke University Press.

Hobart, Hi'ilei Julia Kawehipuaakahaopulani, and Tamara Kneese. 2020. "Radical CareSurvival Strategies for Uncertain Times." *Social Text* 38 (142): 1–16.

Iğsız, Aslı. 2018. *Humanism in Ruins: Entangled Legacies of the Greek-Turkish Population Exchange*. Stanford: Stanford University Press.

Kancler, Tjaša. 2014. "Arte, Política y Resistencia en la Era Postmedia." PhD Diss. University of Barcelona.

Kancler, Tjaša. 2017. "Body-Politics, Trans* Imaginary and Decoloniality." Accessed March 22, 2017. https://www.academia.edu/31557368/Body-politics_Trans_Imaginary_and_Decoloniality.

Kušić, Katarina, and Jakub Záhora. 2020. "Fieldwork, Failure, International Relations." https://www.e-ir.info/author/katarina-kusic-and-jakub-zahora/.

Lambevski, Sasho A. 1999. "Suck My Nation-Masculinity, Ethnicity and the Politics of (Homo) Sex." *Sexualities* 2 (4): 397–419.

Luboteni, Jeta (Jetim). 2019. https://feminist.krytyka.com/en/articles/heavy-word-discourses-albanian-sworn-virgins.

Malamud, Randy. 2012. "Pornographic Animals." In *An Introduction to Animals and Visual Culture*. The Palgrave Macmillan Animal Ethics Series, 94–114. London: Palgrave Macmillan. https://doi.org/10.1057/9781137009845_5.

Manta, Eleftheria K. 2009. "The Çams of Albania and the Greek State (1923–1945)." *Journal of Muslim Minority Affairs* 29 (4): 523–535.

Mazower, Mark. 2007. *Salonica, City of Ghosts: Christians, Muslims and Jews 1430–1950*. New York City: Vintage.

Mbembe, Achille. 2019. "Bodies and Borders." Lecture Given at Universität zu Köln, July 17. Online. Accessed December 6, 2019. https://www.youtube.com/watch?v=JqreV_1FqtU.

Mignolo, Walter D., and Catherine E. Walsh. 2018. *On Decoloniality: Concepts, Analytics, Praxis*. Durham: Duke University Press.

Neofotistos, Vasiliki. 2008. "'The Balkans' Other Within': Imaginings of the West in the Republicof Macedonia." *History and Anthropology* 19 (1): 17–36.

Özyürek, Esra. 2014. *Being German, Becoming Muslim: Race, Religion, and Conversion in the New Europe*. Vol. 56. Princeton: Princeton University Press.

Papantonopoulou, Saffo. 2014. "'Even a Freak Like You Would Be Safe in Tel Aviv': Transgender Subjects, Wounded Attachments, and the Zionist Economy of Gratitude." *WSQ: Women's Studies* 42: 278–293.

Patterson, Christopher. 2020. *Open World Empire: Race, Erotics, and the Global Rise of Video Games*. Manhattan: NYU Press.

Rao, Rahul. 2014. "The Locations of Homophobia." *London Review of International Law* 2 (2): 169–199.

Jelača, Dijana, Maša Kolanović, and Danijela Lugarić, eds. 2017a. *The Cultural Life of Capitalism in Yugoslavia: (Post) Socialism and Its Other*. New York: Palgrave.

Rexhepi, Piro. 2017b. "Borders." *Critical Muslim* 21: 45–56.

Rexhepi, Piro. 2017c. "Unmapping Islam in Eastern Europe." In *Eastern Europe Unmapped: Beyond Borders and Peripheries*, edited by Irene Kacandes and Yuliya Komska, 53–78. New York: Berghahn Books.

Rexhepi, Piro. 2018. "The politics of postcolonial Erasure in Sarajevo." *Interventions* 20 (6): 930–945.

Rexhepi, Piro. 2020. "Carceral Geographies along the Balkan Refugee Route." In *Racial Capitalism, Intersectionality of Sexuality, Struggles and Bodies as Borders*, edited by Tjaša Kancler and Marina Gržinić. *Časopis za kritiko znanosti, domišljijo in novo antropologijo* 281: 80–92.

Sayyid, Salman. 2015. *A Fundamental Fear: Eurocentrism and the Emergence of Islamism*. London: Zed Books.

Sigal, Peter Herman, Zeb Tortorici, and Neil L. Whitehead, eds. 2020. *Ethnopornography: Sexuality, Colonialism, and Anthropological/Archival Knowledge*. Durham: Duke University Press.

Tilley, Lisa, and Robbie Shilliam. 2018. "Raced Markets: An Introduction." 534–543.

Tlostanova, Madina. 2017. "Transcending the Human/Non-Human Divide: The Geo-Politics and Body-Politics of Being and Perception, and Decolonial Art." *Angelaki* 22 (2): 25–37.

Vitalis, Robert. 2015. *White World Order, Black Power Politics: The Birth of American International Relations*. Ithaca: Cornell University Press.

Walton, Jeremy F. 2016. "Geographies of Revival and Erasure: Neo-Ottoman Sites of Memory in Istanbul, Thessaloniki, and Budapest." *Die Welt Des Islams* 56: 510–532.

Sexuality and borders in right wing times: a conversation

Alyosxa Tudor ⓘ and Miriam Ticktin

ABSTRACT

We respond to prompts about the relationships between race, migration, and sexuality, as these intersecting differences have been forced into the same frame by the violent practices of right-wing regimes, and brought into relief by Covid19. Even as we have long known that sexual politics are a way to govern bodies, and to distribute uneven states of vulnerability, we are seeing new incarnations of government. What we aim to point out is how people who are seen as "different" are being attacked, maimed, dispossessed and murdered. But perhaps more importantly, we insist on the specific nature of right-wing times because these regimes not only encourage attacks on people, but on the very idea that such people should exist and be recognized and understood; that there are areas of scholarship that centre them, or areas of law that try to address the inequalities that dispossess them.

In their prescient 2019 symposium on sexuality and borders, Billy Holzberg, Anouk Madörin and Michelle Pfeifer identified a deepening relationship between sexuality and mobility; they pointed to the increasingly important role of sexuality in the production and maintenance of border regimes, and how racialized border regimes in turn mediate expressions of sexuality. That is, they acknowledge sexuality as a dominant frame by which mobility is captured and regulated.

The symposium made an important intervention, but then we were hit by the Covid19 pandemic and the effects of the many virulent, anti-immigrant, authoritarian and racialized regimes were made even more manifest. Instead of haunting us, right wing sentiment has materialized into a form of mass death of Black and brown people and migrants – not just through the biopolitical logic of "letting die", but by actively exposing and cultivating infection in meat packing plants, prisons, detention centres as well as in front line workers. Holzberg, Madörin and Pfeifer anticipated that this would be furthered by its intersections with sexuality; and in our conversation, we explore how, specifically, with the idea that right-wing times have rendered these intersecting relationships both slightly different, but nevertheless all more urgent to understand.

Those most vulnerable have borne the brunt of inadequate healthcare and housing, combined with newly invigorated forms of police and other forms of violence: perhaps top amongst these are trans people of colour. The massive rally for Black Trans lives in Brooklyn, New York in June 2020, in the midst of the pandemic, acknowledged this vulnerability; with 15,000 people dressed in white, packed into the plaza in front of the Brooklyn Museum and spilling out into the transecting streets, people reacted to the many recent deaths of Black trans women, several of which came in the wake of rollbacks to transgender healthcare protections. Other murders occurred in prison or on the street. As Angela Davis (2020) stated in an interview, if we want to develop an intersectional perspective, the trans community is showing us the way; the trans community has taught us how to challenge our foundational sense of normalcy, and as Davis underscored, if we can challenge the gender binary, then we can resist prisons, and jails, and police. And, we would add, we can challenge the very idea of borders and nation-states.

In what follows, we respond to prompts about the relationships between race, immigration, and sexuality, as these intersecting differences have been forced into the same frame by the violent practices of right-wing regimes, and brought into relief by Covid19. Even as we have long known that sexual politics are a way to govern bodies, and to distribute uneven states of vulnerability (Stoler 2010), we are seeing new incarnations of government. With the concepts of tolerance, multi-culturalism or integration, liberalism works to manage, govern and control difference. That is, it abandons and excludes those who exceed the bounds of acceptable or recognizable difference, but it works by cultivating and creating difference that it can exploit. Illiberalism, on the other hand, works to expunge difference; to repress it, excise it. Current forms of illiberalism protect purity, based on blood-lines and heteronormative families. What we aim to point out is how people who are seen as "different" are being attacked, maimed, dispossessed and murdered. But perhaps more importantly, we insist on the specific nature of right-wing times because these regimes not only encourage attacks on people, but on the very idea that such people should exist and be recognized and understood; that there are areas of scholarship that centre them, or areas of law that try to address the inequalities that dispossess them. We note that these areas of thought and law, too, are under attack.

Finally, the feature that perhaps most drives contemporary right-wing movements is their attachment to the nation, and to nationalisms. Our conversation centres this attachment in its intersection with sexuality, and together, we work to undo it – to further a form of anti-nationalism. We end by joining with and amplifying the voices of many people who have used this devastating moment to reimagine new and better ways of being together and in the world.

(1) How can we analyze and investigate the relation of racism and migration in research on sexuality and borders? Is there a difference on how we think of the entanglement of racism and migration in the US and in Europe? What are transnational overlaps and context specific peculiarities?

MT: In the US, questions of racism and migration rarely meet, either academically or politically. That is, the debates about racism take African Americans as their primary subject, referencing the history of slavery. The debates on migration stay focused in large part on Latinx communities, and on the border itself. Yet the way racism plays into immigration policy – and has from the start, characterizing immigrants in the language of essential Otherness, and working to exclude them (through the Chinese Exclusion Act, or the Japanese Internment camps) – has been translated into questions of citizenship, deservingness and integration. And the way immigration policy relies on anti-black racism is rarely mentioned; indeed, people do not address the fact that many immigrants are black, and that they are currently deported at 3 times higher rates than other immigrants for having supposedly committed a crime (Paik 2020).

While in Europe, colonialism is what brings – or at least threatens to bring – the languages of immigration and racism together, in the US, one rarely hears about colonialism in relation to immigration, despite the long history of imperial relations with Latin America. And certainly the ways in which settler colonialism, and the decimation of indigenous communities, prefigures the treatment of both African Americans and immigrants is rarely even considered.

But, these struggles are increasingly visibly intersecting, for better and for worse. In both cases, sexuality is foregrounded as the connecting force. On the negative side, they are meeting in and through the deeply racist desire to control sexuality and reproductive capacity; in particular, through the practice of forced sterilization. The recent revelation about the sterilizations of immigrant women in ICE detention has opened up the intertwined histories of African American, indigenous and immigrant communities and the underlying eugenics policies that have shaped US state engagement with all of them.

In September 2020, nurse practitioner Dawn Wooten served as whistle-blower for the sterilizations being performed at Irwin County Detention

Center (ICDC) in Georgia. In addition to witnessing the lack of testing and medical care for those who had been exposed to Covid19, and the general unsanitary and neglectful living conditions, Wooten said that nearly all the detained women who went to see the assigned gynecologist returned without ovaries and/or uteruses. These operations were performed without proper consent, in a coercive manner – often the women did not even know they had had hysterectomies.

This echoes the long history of Black Americans being forcibly sterilized, named already in the 1974 case Relf v. Reinberger when two Black sisters, aged 12 and 14 were forcibly sterilized because their mother, who was illiterate, was made to sign a form she did not understand. In the south, poor Black women were regularly forced to agree to sterilization when doctors threatened to withhold care or welfare benefits, including during childbirth. This eugenics policy was federally funded and mandated, resulting in approximately 150,000 Black women involuntarily sterilized. It was not accidental that the whistleblower was African American in the case of the Irwin County Detention Center; Wooten was aware of the abuses of sexual and reproductive rights in Black communities, and able to recognize these as violent practices.

As activists and scholars have documented, women carry condoms as they cross the US-Mexico border, knowing that US Customs and Border Control officials regularly rape immigrants with impunity (Falcon 2006). Yet this latest set of acts has made clear that such forms of sexual violence are actually also – and perhaps primarily – a part of genocidal violence.

If these struggles are being forced into the same frame by violent practices – if indeed as Nadine Naber states, "oppressive powers make the connections for us" (2017) – it also points to new possibilities for solidarity. For instance, when we acknowledge how Black men and other men of colour are all grouped under the same category of "sexual predators", creating a racialized, rapacious masculinity, this opens the way to collective organizing, against a shared form of racism. While negative stereotypes of Black men's sexuality have long circulated – with lynchings as the ultimate punishment for this so-called sexualized violence against white women – similar strategies of demonization are clear in Trump's labelling of Mexicans immigrants as "rapists". Of course, Arab men have borne the brunt of this formulation since September 2011, as "monster-terrorist-fags" (Puar and Rai 2002).

But if we follow this same logic, we have to acknowledge that this is not about Black folks, nor about Latinos or Arabs – indeed, this is not a singularly American logic; it is a form of transnational sexualized racism, in which transnational and globalized racialized regimes are consistently used to stigmatize and dehumanize people by way of sexual panics. One of the more recent, infamous cases is that of Cologne on New Year's Eve in 2015, when Muslim men – initially labelled "refugees" – were accused of being sex offenders, attacking white German women. I wrote about a similar case in Paris that took place in 1999, when young French men of Arab origin were being accused of being gang rapists (Ticktin 2008). But there are countless such cases, going back to colonial times. Overall, we see that these forms of violence are transnational, even as right-wing politics continue to use the nation as the container of hatred.

AT: I have long grappled with the question how to conceptualize the race/ migration nexus (Erel, Murji, Nahaboo 2016) for a European context without giving up a postcolonial understanding of racism and racialization. I am not alone in this pursuit. It has been a constant issue in critical scholarship (e.g. Mayblin and Turner 2020) and heated controversies over the role of whiteness for analyses of the relationship of migration and racism have emerged. A few years ago, a colleague "cited" me in a German newspaper article (Terkessidis 2017).[1] He implies that I don't recognize the murder of Theodoros Boulgarides, committed in 2005 by a (state supported) Neo-Nazi terror cell in Germany, as racist. The Neo-Nazis targeted migrants, and the victims mostly had a migration history from Turkey – Boulgarides was the only victim with a migration history from Greece. In the newspaper article, my colleague accuses me of adding to the pain of the bereaved family by seeing the victim as "white". The problem is, however, that I had never talked about the case, I literally have never said the words that were put into my mouth.

I assume this misquotation demonstrates a desire for categories and certainties that is projected onto my knowledge production. And I understand this desire which comes with critical questions on the possibilities of finding accurate words for naming structural violence. Indeed, how can we find formulations that are strong enough to make clear that people are being killed because of being ascribed as migrants?

Central strands of European migration studies scholarship have had the tendency to ignore post/colonial racism and racialization and instead are caught in an understanding of migration that is disconnected from postcolonial analysis. To mitigate this, I suggest differentiating between racism and what I call *migratism* to analyse the complex connection of racialization and migration in postcolonial Europe. *Migratism* makes it possible to think of migration as an analytical rather than descriptive category and resists equating the ascription of race with the ascription of migration (Tudor 2014, 2018a). Most importantly, the conceptualization of migratism is epistemological – it is not about boxes, but rather about critically examining certain pregiven categories. It is about offering a perspective that allows us to think and do things we were not able to think and do without it. Migratization – the ascription of migration – intersects in complex ways with racialization but is not the same. A failure to differentiate between racialization and migratization renders Europeans of colour abject in discourses on migration, nation and – paradoxically – racism.

While "the migrant" in the US often is excluded in critical race theory, as you point out, Miriam, and of course the term "immigrant" also has a history of being used as euphemism for white European settlers in the contexts of the Americas (Dunbar-Ortiz 2021), in continental Europe, "race" has often been displaced as something not relevant, as if "migration" was happening here and "race" was happening elsewhere. This type of race-ignorant scholarship has been prevalent in continental Europe and comes with a mixture of conscious denial and unconscious disavowal of European colonial history and its multiple sites of occupation, dispossession and genocide (El-Tayeb 2011).

However, it is also present in the UK, both in earlier scholarship and in more recent academic takes on Brexit. What makes me really uneasy about this is the incapacity to theorize transnational forms of racism and white supremacist nationalisms in Europe in these approaches. As our examples in this conversation show, the interplay of race, migration and belonging to the nation state works differently in continental Europe, the UK and the US. But there are also similarities that can be traced back to the functioning of race in European settler colonialism and slavery (Hall 1991). I think what we both try to do in our work – going beyond the nation state in order to investigate the entanglement of race and migration – helps to address these tensions.

If one of the supra-national similarities of hegemonic conceptualizations of race and migration is the replication and assertion of white supremacy, another in connection to the nation state is the idea that sexual violence is brought in from "elsewhere", from the "outside", what you so aptly call "sexual violence as the language of border control", Miriam (Ticktin 2008). However, of course, in our current situation, approaches that are really interested in tackling gender and sexual violence need to centrally take into account how border regimes make women, lesbians, trans, queer and non-binary people, sex workers or not, vulnerable to violence. It is not migration that is the problem, but nationalism, white supremacy and the highly policed borders that require dangerous border crossings. This insight turns investigating, criticizing and opposing border regimes into a key topic for gender and sexuality studies, especially for strands that are concerned about gender and sexual violence. It is crucial to analyse the border industrial complex as relying on and stabilizing violent gender and sexual regimes *and* at the same time using gender and sexuality as arguments for its necessity. As Schmidt-Camacho (2005, 281) makes clear, to understand "gender violence as a central feature of both nation-formation and capitalist development rather than seeing it as an expression of their failure", means that any approach to gender and sexual violence needs to address the violence of the nation state and its regulatory regimes, like borders, migration laws, deportations, detention centres etc.

(2) How might the vocabulary of borders and sexuality help us to make sense of the current pandemic?

MT: What you make so beautifully clear, Alyosxa, is that this is not simply a question of sexualized and racialized violence, but that such violence cannot be thought of outside of border regimes; that we need to recognize the inherent violence of borders and nation-states themselves. Borders require forms of dehumanization to allow capital to flow, keeping certain people in place and others out of place. In this sense, we need to look directly at the form of the nation-state to address all these forms of violence.

Turning to nation-states, then, I think we can learn a lot about Covid19 by thinking about how national borders and pathologies are co-constitutive, and how these tend to rely on a language of sexualized invasion or contagion.

From the beginning, COVID-19 was framed as a narrative of war: political leaders regularly made triumphant pronouncements about defeating this enemy, winning this war. As part of this story, there is the necessary Invasive Other – the evil foe who infiltrates or penetrates and must be exterminated so "we" can "win". This language has been used to conflate invasive pathogens and people and to close national borders, mixing up medical and political quarantine.

When we use the language of invasion, we make containment and elimination the goal; but more importantly, the term enables the extension and displacement of the initial enemy, in this case, the virus, onto entire classes of people. This was illustrated by Trump's use of "Chinese virus" or "Wuhan virus", which conflated the idea of invasive pathogens with invasive people, opening the way to violent attacks against people of Asian origin. Indeed, it follows a long pattern of turning people of colour (from Arabs, Muslims, Sikhs to Black folks) into sexualized and racialized terrorists, trying to penetrate the homeland (Puar 2007).

More specifically, we use the idea of "invasive" to describe many things today: from people to pathogens, from plants to ideas (Ticktin 2017a).[2] But once something is described as invasive – even if it is of a very different kind or order – it is often patrolled and controlled through similar technologies, practices and policies, and these overlaps can have deadly consequences. Indeed, once different types of "invasive others" are conflated – through conceptual, moral or aesthetic likeness – practices used against one type of invasive may be used against another. Trump has said of immigrants, "these aren't people, they are animals, and we are taking them out of the country at a level and a rate that has never happened before" (Hirschfeld Davis 2018).

Metaphors not only render certain likenesses thinkable, but also shape and authorize certain kinds of action. Refugees are currently being forcibly detained in the dangerous zones they are fleeing, and immigrants – from children to adults – are being kept in cages.

The language of invasion has a sordid history. In World War II, for example, new technologies of quarantine and delousing for the purposes of hygiene were eventually used to exterminate Jews, who were described as lice, and a threat to the hygiene of the nation (Raffles 2007, 2017). In fact, it does not seem accidental that the chemical ultimately used in the gas chambers – Zkylon B – had previously been used for delousing Mexican immigrants in the US in the 1930s (Anderson 2017).

The point is that when people are likened to parasitic and other forms of threatening life, capable of infection and contamination – there are mandated responses, first and foremost of which is cleansing or elimination.

HIV/AIDS is a case in point. Rather than actually treating the viral infection, people have sought to control HIV/AIDS by regulating the movement of people who are HIV positive into and out of nation-states; in other words, by trying to contain and exclude them. In the US, from 1988 until 2010, there was a restriction on immigration and travel to the United States for non-U.S. citizens living with HIV/AIDS. This conflated certain racialized, sexualized populations with disease; HIV/AIDS became a disease of errant populations, and the nation-state was configured as a victim, trying to fight off unwanted penetration.

Framing the problem as the need to shut the borders of nation-states against invasive others is not only wrong, but deadly.[3] "National quarantines" make no sense, as nation-states are clearly not "safe spaces"; those caged in prisons and detention centres have revealed this far too clearly, as have the videos of the police in the US, lynching black men and women such as George Floyd and Breonna Taylor and most recently in France, Michel Zecler, instead of protecting them. Using the pandemic to remove the right to asylum – and, under Trump, closing the door to all immigration in the United States – only serves a white-supremacist neoliberal agenda that is deepening inequality and literally killing people, not saving them.

Understanding this virus requires that we rethink taken-for-granted political categories. While we may still need forms of medical isolation or quarantine, these cannot map onto existing political borders. Most importantly, viruses do not invade. They are not living entities; they are just bits of information that our cells bring to life (Napier 2020). And viruses are already an integral part of our body-worlds. Indeed, they have been a driving force in the evolution of the species: a non-negligible percentage of human DNA comes from viral infections (Brives 2020). Neoliberal regimes that defund health care, practices of deforestation, and the domination of agribusiness are key practices that make us differently and unequally susceptible to already circulating virus variants; but these are part of racial capitalism, which go well beyond nation-states (Adams 2020; Napier 2020; Wallace 2016).

Queer and feminist theory have led the way to understandings of the body as embedded in and part of larger ecologies, as inseparable from them. These theories challenge the idea of independent liberal selves. As Julie Livingston (2020) writes, "The body is an act of exchange and a site of vulnerability in a complex and more-than-human world". It is, as she so aptly notes, a tentacular relationship, where the air we breathe and exhale eventually gets inhaled by someone else, somewhere else; where the water that goes through our bodies to keep us alive may next nourish a farmer's field. Or, as Mel Chen notes (2020), where the smoky air, from the climate-change-enhanced wildfires of California, gets inhaled by an unmasked, infected pedestrian, creating a doubly potent inhalant for the next passerby. We are interconnected, co-constituted.

Recognizing that we live in a connected world is the only way to survive today: we are in a life and death embrace with each other that no one can wriggle out of. This is a not a dystopic statement; if we do recognize this, we might not only survive, but eventually might flourish in much more substantive ways than what our extractive and exploitative racial capitalist system currently allows. Indeed, we must take advantage of the fact that through COVID-19 our connections have been rendered visible in a way that is impossible to ignore. This goes back to your call for an anti-nationalist epistemology, Alyosxa.

AT: I think we can draw connections here to the situation in Europe and the question who has, who loses and who never had proper citizenship rights and with it, sexual and gendered rights – be that in a nation state or in "Europe". In spring 2020, when the first COVID wave hit Western Europe, charter flights from Romania brought thousands of workers (Erizanu 2020), both white Romanians and Romanian Roma, to the UK and Germany as seasonal workers.[4] Images of big crowds of people waiting at the airports show the absolute lack of protection. These people are seasonal, cheap workers, staying in mass accommodation, and in the British case after Brexit, are not even allowed to settle in the UK – the post-Brexit point system for preventing immigration of so called "low skilled" workers already has a built-in potential for short-term, exploitative work conditions (Walsh 2020). It is a disposable migrant workforce with people coming from already vulnerable and precarious situations.[5]

It is not surprising that in Germany in April 2020 in a meat plant more than 400 Romanian workers tested positive for Covid-19 (SWR aktuell 2020). These workers are not even employed by the factory; they work for subcontractors, earn only a few Euros per hour, work 260 hours a month, mostly in night shifts, share mass accommodation, will be transported back to Romania after a few months and pay thousands of their hard-earned income to the agencies that act as brokers. The ones who tested positive were quarantined. Many Germans who commented on social media sites regard the migrants as being the ones who bring contagion to the region, who don't "understand" social distancing and "misbehave" in public. They were constructed as the "perverts", compared to the normative Germans sheltering in their households with their families.

As I want to stress, this example sheds light on both the normativity and privilege of the "household" and on uncomplicated belonging to the nation (Grewal et al. 2020): there is a mismatch between the confinement in mass accommodation – that cannot be described in terms other than "labour camps" – vs. the expectation that the Romanians practice social distancing (among each other) in public. Gender and sexuality come in through the interconnection of the family and the nation state. Both depend highly on normative gender and sexuality (Manalansan 2006; Luibheid 2008). And as you also point out, Miriam, historically in the US, this becomes very clear in kinship under slavery and settler colonialism: the family that remains together as a household is a privilege of white settlers/slaveholders (Spillers 1987; Arvin, Tuck and Morrill 2013). Children being separated from their parents at borders in the US under Trump underlines the continuation of these practices (Batra Kashyap 2019).

As we can see in the example of the migrant workers, mass accommodation and the lack of privacy are markers of already existing precariousness. Both shelter in place – having a private place – and being confined with chosen loved ones is a privilege. Migrants worldwide are being exposed to danger and death[6], during the crisis but not only then. This is why no-border movements are so important. Moreover, even if borders can be crossed legally for work migration, the normalization of the idea that a migrant (worker) has fewer rights than a citizen and can be "sent back" any time as they "don't belong" needs constant political and epistemological pushback. It is the precarious crossings, precarious movements, precarious exclusions from uncomplicated belonging that put people in danger. Interestingly, similar to anti-trafficking arguments, many voices that criticized the unbearable and exploitative situation of these seasonal workers that became evident during the first COVID wave, aim to restrict migration and they often come from a place that opposes migration and calls for well-paid jobs for the local population "instead", but mask this with opposition to the exploitative conditions (Mai 2018).[7] Critical scholarship therefore cannot only call for closing these facilities down – as they are often the only chance for many people to work abroad and earn the money they need to sustain themselves and their loved ones – but needs a broader analysis of risk, exploitation, nationalism, border regimes and consumerist privilege and expectations.

Our examples underline what intersectionality as an epistemology teaches us: That racialization and migratization multiply the danger that comes with sexism, misogyny and queer- and transphobia – they not only add but make it into a specific vulnerability. In the household, women, queer, trans and gender-nonconforming people are subjected to domestic violence. In the labour camp, detention centre, refugee camp or other precarious migration situations, there are also women, queer, trans and gender-nonconforming people who are subject to the violence of their employers, superiors, co-workers, of guards, border controls, police and the hostile dominant society.

In the Global North, the social crisis provoked by the pandemic is based on narrow understandings of the household, the family and good citizenship, and this feeds into a context where not only sexual and gendered rights are being undermined (Breslow 2020) but also critical knowledge production is being attacked. In the US, the government under Trump attempted to erase at a moment of a pandemic that specifically kills people affected by anti-Black racism (Pilkington 2020) vital transgender civil rights protections in health care (Sanger-Katz and Weiland 2020). This was not only an attack on trans people in general but trans people in the Black community in particular as you also point out, Miriam. In the UK, after years of transphobic media debates during the process of a public consultation on the changes to the Gender Recognition Act (GRA) (Mermaids 2020), the government in June 2020 announced to ignore the results of the consultation that are overwhelmingly pro-trans and cited "protecting women" as the reason (Milton 2020; Tudor 2020b).[8] Moreover, during this exceptional situation of a global pandemic that hit both the US and the UK in particularly devastating ways, making them into two of the countries with the highest casualties compared to their population numbers – a fact that is certainly connected to the countries' right-wing governments – critical race studies were attacked in both contexts. In the US, the government published in September 2020 under the misleading title "Executive Order on Combating Race and Sex Stereotyping"[9] an order to prevent critical teaching about white and male privilege and institutional racism and sexism. In the UK in October 2020, the Tory Minister for Equalities Kemi Badenoch denounced "critical race theory" (naming the term for the first time in the House of Commons chamber) and argued in a debate on Black History Month that schools teaching on "white privilege as an uncontested fact" were breaking the law (Murray 2020).

I think of anti-nationalist epistemology as one of the key concerns of studying sexuality and borders – the possibility and necessity to think beyond the paradigm of the nation state. Fields of knowledge production like gender studies, critical race theory and attempts to decolonize the curriculum, indeed are by definition not projects of nationalist respectability (Tudor 2021). And this refusal of nationalist respectability is where the risk lies. We have seen in times of right-wing imposed austerity and crisis that specifically the social sciences and humanities are under threat, in the UK for example the proposed government rescue packages for struggling universities came with conditions: 1. "[S]uch rescue packages would see the government exerting more control over what was taught and how money was spent"; 2. "Universities would be expected to end courses seen as being of 'low value', with an emphasis on either high-quality research or courses with good job prospects"; 3. "[A]ny funding for student unions should be for the 'wider student population rather than subsidising niche activism'" (Coughlan 2020).

What is happening is that in a moment of crisis governments in the UK, the US, Hungary and Romania for example attempt to severely diminish academic freedom and also queer and trans rights. What this means in the UK is first, that Tory governments over decades have created a situation in which universities struggle financially and now they offer a buyout that gives the government control over what would be taught. Second, it is a threat and opens the possibility to cut back the arts and humanities and unwanted research and teaching fields like gender studies under the made up argumentation that they are "low value" or not "high-quality research". And third, the term "niche activism" in this context is a direct threat towards student unions and societies representing gendered, sexual and racialized minorities. In short, when looking at this "offer" the UK government made in a moment of crisis, we are looking in the face of one of the many endings of democracy.

(3) How might we use this extreme moment of right-wing politics and violence to both critique and imagine otherwise?

MT. If, as you so compellingly write, Alyosxa, the squashing of all forms of knowledge that challenge nationalist ideologies points to an ending of democracy, I want to suggest that it also presents an opening – or a series of openings – onto new political formations.

For instance, in this time of Covid19, to stay healthy, people are forging new egalitarian forms of connection well beyond the nation-state. But these end-times are opening the way to new forms of "home" and solidarity as well. I want to first talk about Covid19, and then turn to the idea of abolitionist sanctuary, which can also be thought of as a new set of queer-inspired egalitarian spaces.

I have argued elsewhere that COVID-19 has enhanced experiments in what I will call a burgeoning *feminist commons* (Ticktin 2020).[10] Such formations not only foreground new, horizontal forms of sociality but insist that these are the only way to survive. That is, they acknowledge our porousness, accepting that we must fight for the well-being of everyone, if we are to be healthy ourselves.

I will briefly mention one example of that here: the intimate formations that some have called "pods", others "bubbles". People are forging intimate connections with others who are not part of their immediate or nuclear families and yet with whom they may not have any previous or deep emotional ties. That is, these are neither the heteronormative households, nor the form of mass accommodation that you mentioned earlier, Alyosxa. They break this binary, and create something else in between. But in quarantine times, these can function as life-or-death commitments. Not dissimilar to the history of the "families we choose" (Weston 1997), and the ways queer folks have created forms of kinship based on affinity or need, not on blood or biology, COVID has generated the need for new relationships with friends, comrades, neighbors, coparents, lovers and ex-lovers – relationships that require deeper trust and sharing in new, respectful ways that limit exposure to risk, while still enabling sociality (Chang 2020; Kohn 2020).

To be sure, pods are not inherently progressive formations; they respond to the retreat of the state – and to the loss of the publics that feed institutions such as public schools – and sometimes, they respond by further privatizing resources, rather than rendering them part of a commons. The "parents pods" forming among the wealthy to school their kids are a case in point (Moyer 2020). Similarly, enforced forms of togetherness during COVID-19 have resulted in increased rates of domestic violence (Taub 2020). These are the counterpart to the commons-pods. But here, I focus on the potential of pods to undermine – rather than further deepen – inequality.

Choosing quarantine pod-mates can be determined by proximity and location, shared need or circumstance (i.e. kids playing together, shared outdoor space, shared rent), or political or other forms of queer or extended kinship. Pods enable and require different affective structures. Whether or not pod-mates love or even like each other, they must agree to live by consensus: is a certain action okay with everyone in the pod? All of this must be constantly discussed, debated, revealed, agreed upon – conflict is always on the horizon. Such practices of intimate sociality based on shared risk require different ways of inhabiting and sharing space and resources.

Living in communal arrangements is in itself not new: there are communes, ecovillages and cohousing arrangements. But quarantine pods may not actually live together; they are formed to share a different type of vulnerability, namely, exposure to one another in times of sickness. They are grounded on a different sense of risk and trust: if one is not open, honest and respectful, one could be putting one's pod at risk of sickness, long-term disability, or death. Sharing and living with the risk of contagious illness is also not new – queer communities pioneered various models during the first outbreaks of HIV/AIDS in the 1970s and 80s. To be sure, there are differences: while HIV is less contagious, it is lethal when untreated; COVID-19 is more contagious, but much less lethal. This broadens the circle of concern enormously, even as it dampens the stakes, making pods a commoning practice that has the potential to become very widespread.

Turning to my second example of experiments in re-imagining these endtimes, I want to return to an important point you made earlier, Alyosxa, which is that gender and sexuality multiply the danger of migration and/or racialization; as you said, they not only add but make it into a specific vulnerability. What if we took your insight and suggested that this specific vulnerability offers a location from which to create a new set of political possibilities?

For instance, feminist, queer and trans POC have been at the forefront of a new movement that brings immigrant and black lives together in the struggle for what is being called "abolitionist sanctuary" (Paik 2020), or "expanded sanctuary". That is, they are bringing together the movements for migrant justice and racial justice, which, as we already discussed, rarely explicitly join together, finding ways to combine their different goals and temporalities, and ultimately imagining a queer space of home that challenges the nation. Indeed, we could say this is a scaled up version of the pods.

If abolitionism - the driving philosophy of #BLM – is about a long-term politics of care that changes subjectivities, communities, and infrastructures, sanctuary is often seen as a mechanism of immediate protection; of shelter from the law and from deportation. But sanctuary is also a politico-legal technology and a form of architecture that challenges nation-state borders by creating spaces inside the nation-state not subject to its laws.

In the US, the campaign for *expanded sanctuary* (or abolitionist sanctuary) challenges the ways that sanctuary supports immigrants at the expense of others.[11] It asks how spaces of solidarity with undocumented people can also address the broader challenges of inequality in American cities, which include poverty, police violence and mass incarceration, and the targeted murders of queer and trans people.

This movement suggests that we need sanctuary until there is no separation between being inside a space of sanctuary, and outside of it (Ticktin 2017b); indeed, until we have replaced our current violent reality with the abolitionist vision of an egalitarian, respectful spatial and political order that is based on equal access and sharing of the commons for everyone. This challenges the "household" as the basis of any liberatory political formation.

Once again, it is not accidental that Black, Latinx, queer and trans communities have been at the forefront of these movements, bringing together racial and immigrant justice with justice for LGBT folks, and for all those who are discriminated against. Those who are subject to the various, intersecting oppressions – those situated at this specific point of vulnerability- can see where such points of oppression meet and strike hardest. Together, they are helping to create new queer, anti-national spaces of care and flourishing.

AT. Community care as a response to heightened exposure is also what Stella Nyanzi (2013) compellingly analyzes. Thinking together colonialism, Ugandan postcolonial nationalism and queer- and transphobia, in her article on HIV/AIDS prevention in post-conflict Uganda, Nyanzi (2013) shows how sexual and gendered minorities and refugees are often excluded from official prevention programmes. Especially those in displacement are hit by the overlapping regimes of sexual morality, state violence and the heightened exposure to gender and sexual violence, illness and death. Nyanzi (2013, 450) remarks that the refugee-run self-organized support group *Les Saints* that aims to fill the gap the official sexual health providers leave, uses *wacheche* as a common denominator, which is according to her "a colloquial label for sex workers and same-sex-loving or gender non-conforming people in Uganda". Even if the term is colloquially not necessarily used as critical of the state and its borders, Nyanzi certainly introduces it in that way in her knowledge production.

Building on Nyanzi's approach, I suggest extracting a political and epistemological claim for decolonized and transnational trans/gender studies and for countering anti-immigration, anti-sex-work and transphobic argumentations. Let's imagine the term "wacheche" would come to have an international career like political and identity-based concepts like "lesbian" and "trans", or epistemological and political traditions of thought like "queer" with origins in the US. What would *wacheche theory* help us to understand about the entanglement of non-normative genders and sexualities and their connection to racialization and migrant status, about the violence of colonialism *and* (decolonial or Western) nationalism alike? Of course, I am not making the point on wacheche studies in order to argue we should replace "queer", "lesbian" or "trans" with "wacheche", but in order to remind us of the traveling or non-traveling of these terms and the variability of the dominant meaning that is attached to them, as also Zethu Matebeni and Thabo Msibi (2015) underline.

In Spring 2020, we could see the drama of national time unfold: every nation state started counting from their own first COVID cases and ignored the radical interconnection of what was evolving. I am struck by the fact of how the national has become, often even in critical analysis, the unquestioned paradigm. What happens in other countries does not seem real to most people. It was mostly migrant and diasporic subjects who have been operating in *non*-national time, seeing this coming from following transnational analysis. Especially in the US, it is my impression, "the transnational" only becomes visible to scholars and activists when it enters the national.

It becomes evident that racism – and what I theorize elsewhere as "migratism" (Tudor 2018a) – both create populations that are not under the

THE SEXUAL POLITICS OF BORDER CONTROL

protection of the nation state in the crisis. And have not been all along, as shown in the exposure of migrant workers, and also in the fact that in the UK for example, it is mostly Black and ethnic minorities who die of COVID, both in the regular population and among health care staff, as Yasmin Gunaratnam (2020) points out. We must take this seriously in our responses not only to COVID, but to the current situation in general. But of course, people who have been excluded from the nation state in so many ways are not sitting around and waiting for it to protect them. This is why turning this around, turning oppression into resistance through community care, as you say, Miriam, creating "new queer, anti-national spaces of care", is so important.

Notes

1. The following two paragraphs were first published as blog post for *Feminist Review* (Tudor 2018b). In the version here they are extended and updated in order to make a broader point on the state of European migration research.
2. The ideas about "invasive others" in this paragraph and the next were initially published in my special issue, *Invasive Others*, and reworked in the Op-Ed with Suzette Brooks Masters, "Coronavirus Cannot become an Excuse to label Groups of People Invasive" (2020), https://immigrationimpact.com/2020/03/20/coronavirus-racism/#.YC4S4mgzaUk. The ideas are updated and revised here.
3. I first discussed borders in relation to Covid19, in "No Borders in the Time of Covid-19" in *American Anthropologist*, Public Anthropologies Series on Covid-19, July 2, 2020. http://www.americananthropologist.org/2020/07/02/no-borders-in-the-time-of-covid-19/. The paragraph and the next take up these ideas in reworked forms.
4. An earlier version of these thoughts (Tudor 2020a) was published in the blog series *Confronting the Household* (Grewal et al 2020) for the *Feminist Review Blog* and at the panel series *Under the Blacklight: The Intersectional Vulnerabilities that COVID Lays Bare* hosted by Kim Crenshaw: https://www.youtube.com/watch?v=NoFGUrkGbmo&t=606s&fbclid=IwAR0qm4AEkoXUBMjsHQxIC2MHp2 9zFy1g-cWgs3KjgfsC_JnF_FICHcwTIPs0 [December 12, 2020].
5. As Roma have been subject to discrimination and violence for centuries and therefore mostly live under the most precarious conditions in Romania (Oprea 2012; Tudor 2017; Parvulescu and Boatcă 2020), it is very likely that a high proportion of Romanian migrant workers are Roma, and are also marginalized within the group of Romanian labour migrants (Yıldız and De Genova 2018).
6. See for example reports of migrant workers in India trapped in lockdown (Pandey 2020).
7. See for example the Facebook discussion on the site of a local newspaper that reported on the COVID cases among the seasonal workers in the meat plant: https://www.facebook.com/badischeneuestenachrichten/posts/142147655472 7451 [December 1, 2020].
8. Some of the thoughts in the next paragraphs were first conceptualized in my discussion of transphobia in the UK during the BLM protests (Tudor 2020b).

9. https://www.whitehouse.gov/presidential-actions/executive-order-combating-race-sex-stereotyping/ [December 12, 2020].
10. In the next 3 paragraphs, I take up one part of the argument from my short piece, updated for the purpose of the conversation. "Building a Feminist Commons in the Time of Covid19" *Signs: Journal of Women and Culture in Society* symposium, "Feminists Theorize Covid-19" October 2020. http://signsjournal.org/covid/ticktin/.
11. What I write is informed by a workshop I co-organized in 2018 on "Expanded Sanctuary" with academics, community partners, and #BLM, queer and immigrant activists, at the New School. Organizations leading the way for expanded sanctuary include Mijente, the Black Youth Project or BYP100, and Baji (Black Alliance for Just Immigration).

Disclosure statement

No potential conflict of interest was reported by the author(s).

ORCID

Alyosxa Tudor ⓘ http://orcid.org/0000-0002-1103-9643

References

Adams, Vincanne. 2020. "Disasters and Capitalism … and COVID-19." *Somatosphere.* Accessed December 12, 2020. http://somatosphere.net/2020/disaster-capitalism-covid19.html/.

Anderson, Bridget. 2017. "The Politics of Pests: Immigration and the Invasive Other." *Social Research: An International Quarterly* 84 (1): 7–28.

Arvin, M., E. Tuck, and A. Morrill. 2013. "Decolonizing Feminism: Challenging Connections Between Settler Colonialism and Heteropatriarchy." *Feminist Formations* 25 (1): 8–34.

Batra Kashyap, Monika. 2019. "Unsettling Immigration Laws: Settler Colonialism and the US Immigration Legal System." 46 *Fordham Urb. L. J.* 548 (2019). Accessed December 12, 2020. https://digitalcommons.law.seattleu.edu/faculty/818.

Breslow, Jacob. 2020. "The Non-Essential Transphobia of Pandemic Disaster Politics." *Engenderigs.* Accessed December 12, 2020. https://blogs.lse.ac.uk/gender/2020/05/14/the-non-essential-transphobia-of-pandemic-disaster-politics/.

Brives, Charlotte. 2020. "The Politics of Amphibiosis: The War against Viruses Will Not Take Place." *Somatosphere.* Accessed December 12, 2020. http://somatosphere.net/2020/the-politics-of-amphibiosis.html/.

Chang, Cindy. 2020. "Not Going Coronavirus Outbreak Alone: Some Find Quarantine Buddies to Lessen Isolation.' *Los Angeles Times.* Accessed December 12, 2020. https://www.latimes.com/california/story/2020-04-01/coronavirus-isolation-quarantine-buddies.

Chen, Mel. 2020. "Feminisms in the Air." *Signs Blog.* Accessed December 12, 2020. http://signsjournal.org/covid/chen/.

Coughlan, Sean. 2020. "Emergency Loans for Universities about to Go Bust". *BBC News.* 16 July 2020. Accessed December 12, 2020. https://www.bbc.co.uk/news/education-53429839.

Davis, Angela. 2020. "Black Trans Lives Matter: Movement Pushes for Justice & Visibility Amid "Epidemic" of Violence." *Democracy Now!*, June 16.

Dunbar-Ortiz, Roxanne. 2021. *'Not "a Nation of Immigrants". Settler Colonialism, White Supremacy, and a History of Erasure and Exclusion*. Boston: Beacon.

El-Tayeb, Fatima. 2011. *European Others. Queering Ethnicity in Postnational Europe*. Minneapolis, London: University of Minnesota.

Erizanu, Paula. 2020. "Stranded Or Shunned: Europe's Migrant Workers Caught In No-Man's Land." *The Guardian*. Accessed December 12, 2020. https://www.theguardian.com/world/2020/apr/16/stranded-or-shunned-europes-migrant-workers-caught-in-no-mans-land.

Falcon, Sylvanna. 2006. "National Security and the Violation of Women: Militarized Border Rape at the Us-Mexico Border." In *Color of Violence: The Incite! Anthology*, 119–129, edited by INCITE! Women of Color Against Violence. Cambridge, MA: South End Press.

Grewal, Kiran, Clare Hemmings, Leticia Sabsay, and Alyosxa Tudor. 2020. "Confronting "The Household". *The Feminist Review Blog*. Accessed December 12, 2020. https://femrev.wordpress.com/2020/05/26/confronting-the-household/.

Gunaratnam, Yasmin. 2020. "When Doctors Die." *Discover Society*. Accessed December 12, 2020. https://discoversociety.org/2020/03/30/when-doctors-die/.

Hall, Stuart. 1991. "Europe's Other Self." *Marxism Today*. 18, 18–19. Accessed December 12, 2020. http://banmarchive.org.uk/collections/mt/pdf/91_08_18.pdf.

Hirschfeld Davis, Julie. 2018. "Trump Calls Some Unauthorized Immigrants "Animals" in Rant." *The New York Times*. Accessed December 12, 2020. https://www.nytimes.com/2018/05/16/us/politics/trump-undocumented-immigrants-animals.html.

Kohn, Isabelle. 2020. "The Pandemic Pods Choosing Friendship Over Public Health." *Mel Magazine*. Accessed December 12, 2020. https://melmagazine.com/en-us/story/the-pandemic-pods-choosing-friendship-over-public-health.

Livingston, Julie. 2020. "To Heal the Body, Heal the Body Politic." *Public Books*. Accessed December 12, 2020. https://www.publicbooks.org/to-heal-the-body-heal-the-body-politic/.

Luibhéid, Eithne. 2008. "Queer/Migration: An Unruly Body Of Scholarship." *GLQ: A Journal of Lesbian and Gay Studies* 14 (2): 169–190.

Mai, Nicola. 2018. *Mobile Orientations: An Intimate Autoethnography of Migration, Sex Work, and Humanitarian Borders*. Chicago: University of Chicago.

Manalansan, Martin. 2006. "Queer Intersections: Sexuality And Gender In Migration Studies." *The International Migration Review* 40 (1): 224–249.

Matebeni, Zethu, and Thabo Msibi. 2015. "Vocabularies of the Non-Normative." *Agenda* 29 (1): 3–9.

Mayblin, Lucy, and Joe Turner. 2020. *Migration Studies and Colonialism*. Cambridge: Polity.

Mermaids. 2020. "Mermaids' Manifesto for GRA Reform." Accessed December 12, 2020. https://mermaidsuk.org.uk/mermaids-manifesto-for-gra-reform/.

Milton, Josh. 2020. "Boris Johnson Is Scrapping Long-Overdue Plans To Allow Trans People To Self-ID Despite Overwhelming Public Support, Report Claims." *Pink News*. Accessed December 12, 2020. https://www.pinknews.co.uk/2020/06/14/trans-self-id-uk-boris-johnson-liz-truss-gender-recognition-act-leak-sunday-times/.

Moyer, Melinda Wenner. 2020. "Pods, Microschools and Tutors: Can Parents Solve the Education Crisis on Their Own?' *The New York Times*. Accessed December 12, 2020. https://www.nytimes.com/2020/07/22/parenting/school-pods-coronavirus.html.

Murray, Jessica. 2020. "Teaching white privilege as uncontested fact is illegal, minister says." *The Guardian*. 20 Oct 2020. Accessed December 12, 2020. https://www.theguardian.com/world/2020/oct/20/teaching-white-privilege-is-a-fact-breaks-the-law-minister-says.

Nadine Naber. 2017. ""The U.S. and Israel Make the Connections for Us": Anti-Imperialism and Black-Palestinian Solidarity." *Critical Ethnic Studies* 3 (2): 15–30.

Napier, David. 2020. "I Heard It through the Grapevine: On Herd Immunity and Why It Is Important." *Somatosphere*. Accessed December 12, 2020. http://somatosphere.net/forumpost/herd-immunity-covid19/.

Nyanzi, Stella. 2013. "Homosexuality, Sex Work, And HIV/AIDS In Displacement And Post-Conflict Settings: The Case Of Refugees In Uganda." *International Peacekeeping* 20 (4): 450–468.

Oprea, Alexandra. 2012. "Romani Feminism In Reactionary Times." *Signs: Journal of Women in Culture and Society* 38 (1): 11–21.

Paik, A. Naomi. 2020. *Bans, Walls, Raids, Sanctuary: Understanding U.S. Immigration for the Twenty-First Century*. Berkeley: University of California.

Pandey, Geeta. 2020. "Coronavirus in India: Desperate Migrant Workers Trapped in Lockdown." *BBC News*. Accessed December 12, 2020. https://www.bbc.co.uk/news/world-asia-india-52360757.

Parvulescu, Anca, and Manuela Boatcă. 2020. "The Longue Durée of Enslavement: Extracting Labor from Romani Music in Liviu Rebreanu's Ion." *Literature Compass*, 17. Accessed December 12, 2020. https://onlinelibrary.wiley.com/doi/full/10.1111/lic3.12559.

Pilkington. Ed. 2020. "Black Americans Dying of Covid-19 at Three Times the Rate of White People." *The Guardian*, 20 May 2020. Accessed December 12, 2020. https://www.theguardian.com/world/2020/may/20/black-americans-death-rate-covid-19-coronavirus.

Puar, Jasbir, and Amit Rai. 2002. "Monster, Terrorist, Fag: The War on Terrorism and the Production of Docile Patriots." *Social Text* 20 (3): 117–148.

Puar, Jasbir. 2007. *Terrorist Assemblages. Homonationalism in Queer Times*. Durham: Duke University.

Raffles, Hugh. 2007. "Jews, Lice, and History." *Public Culture* 19 (3): 521–566.

Raffles, Hugh. 2017. "Against Purity." *Social Research: An International Quarterly* 84 (1): 171–182.

Sanger-Katz, Margot, and Noah Weiland. 2020. "Trump Administration Erases Transgender Civil Rights Protections in Health Care." *The New York Times*. Accessed December 12, 2020. https://www.nytimes.com/2020/06/12/us/politics/trump-transgender-rights.html.

Schmidt Camacho, Alicia. 2005. "Ciudadana X: Gender Violence and the Denationalization of Women's Rights in Ciudad Juarez, Mexico." *CR: The New Centennial Review* 5 (1): 255–292.

Spillers, Hortense. 1987. "Mama's Baby, Papa's Maybe: an American Grammar Book." *Diacritics* 17 (2): 65–81.

Stoler, Ann Laura. 2010. "Beyond Sex: Bodily Exposures of the Colonial and Postcolonial Present." In *Genre et Postcolonialismes: Dialogues Transcontinentaux*, edited by Ann Berger, and Eleni Varikas, 191–220. Paris: Editions des Archives Contemporaines.

SWR aktuell. 2020. "Nach 82 Neuen Corona-Fällen - Scharfe Kritik an Fleischfabrik." Accessed December 12, 2020. https://www.swr.de/swraktuell/baden-wuerttemberg/karlsruhe/birkenfeld-fleischfabrik-102.html.

Taub, Amanda. 2020. "A New Covid-19 Crisis: Domestic Abuse Rises Worldwide." *New York Times*. Accessed December 12, 2020. https://www.nytimes.com/2020/04/06/world/coronavirus-domestic-violence.html.

Terkessidis, Mark. 2017. "Über Rassismus reden: Da war doch was?' *Die Tageszeitung*. Accessed December 12, 2020. http://www.taz.de/!5382405/.

Ticktin, Miriam. 2008. "Sexual Violence as the Language of Border Control: Where French Feminist and Anti-Immigrant Rhetoric Meet." *Signs: Journal of Women in Culture and Society* 33 (4): 863–889.

Ticktin, Miriam. 2017a. "Invasive Others: Toward a Contaminated World." *Social Research: An International Quarterly*, special issue on "The Invasive Other" 84 (1): xxi–xxxiv, Spring 2017.

Ticktin, Miriam. 2017b. "The Sanctuary Movement and Women's Rights: Sister Struggles" *Truthout*, April 19, 2017. http://www.truth-out.org/opinion/item/40416-the-sanctuary-movement-and-women-s-rights-sister-struggles.

Ticktin, Miriam. 2020. "Building a Feminist Commons in the Time of COVID-19." *Signs Blog*. Accessed December 12, 2020. http://signsjournal.org/covid/ticktin/.

Tudor, Alyosxa. 2014. *from [al'manja] with love. Trans_feministische Positionierungen zu Rassismus und Migratismus*. Frankfurt a.M.: Brandes&Apsel.

Tudor, Alyosxa. 2017. "Dimensions of Transnationalism." *Feminist Review* 117: 20–40.

Tudor, Alyosxa. 2018a. "Cross-Fadings of Racialisation and Migratisation: The Postcolonial Turn in Western European Gender and Migration Studies." *Gender, Place and Culture* 25 (7): 1057–1072.

Tudor, Alyosxa. 2018b. "The Desire for Categories." *The Feminist Review Blog*, https://femrev.wordpress.com/2018/03/19/the-desire-for-categories/.

Tudor, Alyosxa. 2020a. "Racism, Migratism, Covid' *The Feminist Review Blog*. Accessed December 12, 2020. https://femrev.wordpress.com/2020/05/26/racism-migratism-covid/.

Tudor, Alyosxa. 2020b. "Terfism is White Distraction: On BLM, Decolonising the Curriculum, Anti-Gender Attacks and Feminist Transphobia." Accessed December 12, 2020. https://blogs.lse.ac.uk/gender/2020/06/19/terfism-is-white-distraction-on-blm-decolonising-the-curriculum-anti-gender-attacks-and-feminist-transphobia/.

Tudor, Alyosxa. 2021. "Decolonizing Trns/Gender Studies: Teaching Gender, Race and Sexuality in Times of the Rise of the Global Right." *Transgender Studies Quarterly* 8 (2): 93–208.

Erel, Umut, Karim Murji, and Zaki Nahaboo. 2016. "Understanding the Contemporary Race-Migration Nexus." *Ethnic and Racial Studies* 39 (8): 1339–1360.

Wallace, Rob. 2016. *Big Farms Make Big Flu: Dispatches on Infectious Disease, Agribusiness, and the Nature of Science*. New York: Monthly Review Press.

Walsh, Peter. 2020. "The UK's Post-Brexit Point-based Immigration System." *UK in a Changing Europe*. Accessed December 12, 2020. https://ukandeu.ac.uk/explainers/the-uks-post-brexit-points-based-immigration-system/.

Weston, Kath. 1997. *Families We Choose: Gays, Lesbians, Kinship*. New York: Columbia University.

Yıldız, C., and N. De Genova. 2018. "Un/Free Mobility: Roma Migrants in the European Union." *Social Identities* 24 (4): 425–441.

Afterword
Entangled politics: borderscapes and sexuality

Radha S. Hegde

ABSTRACT

The volatility of the present moment requires scholars to direct nuanced intellectual attention to the intertwined space of borders and sexuality. While these subjects have historically come into visibility in academic research as separate and self-contained fields of study, the emphasis has to be shifted to their constitutive connection and intersection. In their examination of contexts, institutions and representations that perpetuate forms of exclusion, this special issue advances a strong and necessary critique of the materialities and politics of sexuality and borders in the global present.

The subject of borders defies containment, and the conjunction of borders and sexuality even more so; as such, the scholarly challenges posed are many. It is only with collaborative energy and interdisciplinary work that we can begin to unravel the multi-sited and multilayered complexity of this subject. It is this belief that prompted the vibrant dialogue about that took place in the conference at New York University in the spring of 2019. As the editors of this special issue note in the introduction, it was their intention to leave the terrain conceptually open to see what scholarly connections would be made in response to the call for papers on the theme of *Sexuality and Borders*. The broad-ranging set of essays presented here addresses the important and rather undertheorized intersection of borders and sexuality from a variety of global locations. Collectively, these essays succeed admirably in showing how race, gender and sexuality are systematically disciplined by borders and their attendant logics of securitization. The volatility of the present moment requires scholars to direct this manner of nuanced intellectual attention to the intertwined space of migration, borders and sexuality. I offer my rationale and a few reflections.

First and foremost, border regimes and their regulation of gender and sexuality are pressing concerns that define the global present. At the same time, the practices and processes of bordering and the implications on the politics of sexuality have distinct echoes of colonial pasts. The special issue recognizes this need for historicizing border politics. The debate over who can be rightfully admitted into the nation and questions of belonging remain crucial issues of national contestation. While global causes such as the neoliberal economy, political unrest and the consequences of climate change have intensified the need to migrate, these trajectories are also accompanied by a marked increase in anti-immigrant hostility. Issues concerning gender and sexuality which occupy a central role in the imaginary of a xenophobic nationalism are incorporated into logics of border control. There is a long history of references to the sexual appetite and deviant sexualities of the colonized, migrant men and their proclivity to sexual violence, their violent lust for white bodies, and the stigmatization of queer bodies. These types of representations continue and other recent instances are analysed in depth by the authors in this special issue. Bordering regimes and mythologies of nationalism mutually sustain each other, by consolidating racialized narratives of sexual danger, risk and contamination.

The urgency of the issues explored in this special issue reveals and reminds us about how deeply academic work matters. Ideologies become powerful when they are incorporated into the everyday functioning of societies. For scholars of gender and sexuality, the status quo, represents a state of saturation when social hierarchies become a naturalized part of the everyday. This normalization of power structures needs to be problematized, addressed and critiqued. Border regimes and their control of raced and gendered bodies work in tandem with social systems and their stratified arrangements. Assumptions and presuppositions about gender identities and sexuality are continually, and often insidiously, reworked. For example, in many parts of the world, neoliberal economic policies and nationalist ideologies have reformulated and reignited heteropatriarchal ideologies and practices with seemingly new justifications. At this moment in time, addressing forms of systemic prejudice and analysing the elision of particular types of bodies constitute a necessary decolonial intervention.

Borders in their multiple material manifestations and their institutional and symbolic significance constitute a dense site of study. Several scholars from across disciplines have advanced compelling arguments and demonstrated empirically that borders perform diverse functions and are laden with multiple meanings. With the discourse on borders proliferating from all directions and with increased technologization, the character and infrastructural capacity of the border is also expanding. This has intensified the flexing of state power at the border and accelerated processes of attaching labels of risk to particular raced and gendered bodies. Migrant bodies have been subjected to all manner of scrutiny and their admissibility to the national community tested for conformity to heteronormative visions of the imagined nation. The archives of immigration history are replete with accounts of immigrants and asylum seekers excluded on the basis of their sexual orientation, gender stereotyping, morality or sexually transmissible diseases. As the examples discussed in this issue show, the enactments of power and policing at the border amplify and solidify existing systems of racial and sexual discrimination. The narratives and material experiences are complex and require transnational conceptual frames as demonstrated in this special issue.

Given the shifting nature of the border and the opacity of its processes, the study of borders demands innovative lines of inquiry. The intersection explored in this special issue is already embedded within multiple hierarchies, agendas, and histories. When ideologies attach themselves to bodies and institutions, they stabilize configurations of power and solidify biopolitical agendas. The scholarly challenge is to map, track and analyse how this happens and reveal the logics that are reclaimed or sustained to justify the stigmatization and invisibility of bodies. For this end, I believe, along with scholars engaged in feminist, critical race, queer and postcolonial studies, that our questions and methods should be guided by a vision of just futures rather than an adherence to canonical requirements and disciplinary boundaries. It is not enough just to point to the discriminatory processes set into motion by border regimes, but to show through careful methodological and analytical attention, how systems manipulate and regulate lives and identities. The production of decolonial knowledge is demanding and premised on resisting and decentring default positions. This special issue responds to the challenge.

The study of borders, migration and sexuality has historically come into visibility in academic research as separate and self-contained fields of study. However, the emphasis has to be shifted to their constitutive connection, juxtaposition and intersection where contestations of public and private life take place. By bringing critical theoretical perspective to bear on the manner in which sexuality and race are naturalized or disciplined, these essays collectively expose the political workings of bordering processes in the contemporary moment.

In the entanglement of borderscapes and sexuality in different geographical sites and political contexts, we see the weight of dominant ideologies and their oppressive control of bodies and lives. In their examination of contexts, institutions and representations that perpetuate forms of exclusion, the authors featured here make a strong case for scholarship that resists and challenges the status quo. Today with the pandemic exposing the deep inequities of global societies and the precariousness of human life, there is an urgent need for scholarship that provides a robust critical response to vital social and political intersections. This special issue offers a strong and impassioned intervention into the materialities and politics of sexuality and borders.

Disclosure statement

No potential conflict of interest was reported by the author(s).

Index

Note: Page numbers followed by "n" denote endnotes.

Abdur-Rahman, A. 45, 57
abolitionism 177
African immigrants 13, 45, 47–48, 51, 54–55, 59
African immigration 13, 43
Africanness 50, 53
Ahmed, Sara 8, 106, 109
AIDS 94, 105–106, 109–118
Allouche, Sabiha 148, 151
American exceptionalism 13, 43, 54, 59
Anderson, B. 11
Anderson, Glenn M. 46
Andrijasevic, R. 11
Anzaldúa, Gloria E. 2
Arpaci, Murat 108
Asian cis women 125, 127, 129, 132–133, 139
Australia 4, 7, 15, 125–129, 133–135
authenticity 87–90, 98, 100, 132; paradigms 89, 98
authentic Lebanese masculinity 152

Bargu, Banu 112–113
Bayramoğlu, Y. 14
Bennachie, Calum 15
Binnie, John 145
biopolitics 5, 13, 43, 48, 59–60, 107, 109
Blackness 13, 43, 45, 49–50, 53–59, 106
borderization 152, 159
borderlands 2, 74, 79, 107; of reproduction 13, 65, 68, 74, 76, 78–79
borders 2–7, 9–17, 23–24, 30–31, 47–48, 54–55, 57–60, 65–69, 73–76, 78–80, 105–109, 113–118, 123–124, 145–146, 155–156, 158, 164–166, 169–171, 173–174, 184–186; regimes 2, 7–8,

101, 108, 164, 169–170, 173, 185–186; surveillance 115–116
borderscapes 108–109, 184, 186

Canada 4, 14, 85–87, 91–93, 95–98
Chávez, Karma 12
Chavis, Ben 27
Chen, Mei-Hua 11
Chen, Mel 172
cis-heteropatriarchy 30–31
citizenship 2, 6, 17, 45–47, 52–59, 66, 72, 86–87, 89, 100, 166
contagion 2–4, 10–11, 14, 170, 173
contagious diseases 106–107
containment 3, 10, 16–17, 170, 184
contemporary border controls 8, 14–15, 17
COVID-19 8, 16, 118, 170, 172, 175–177
critical race theory 169, 174
cross-border relationships 87, 89–90, 96
cultural identity 24, 26–28

Davis, Angela 165
Davis, Jenny L. 36
decriminalization 126, 128
deculturization 39n1
de facto sovereignty 30
deviant sexualities 10, 110, 185
discursive border 107
double consciousness 58
Douglas, Mary 8
Driskill, Qwo-Li 36

East Jerusalem 67–69, 71, 73–74, 76, 78, 80
El-Tayeb, Fatima 157

190 INDEX

entangled politics 184
eugenics policies 8–9, 166–167
everyday Indigenous futurity 37

Fairclough, N. 109
Family Unity and Employment
    Opportunity Immigration Act 46
Farris, S. R. 6
Fehrenbacher, Anne E. 15
Ferguson, R. A. 54
fertility clinic 67–72, 74–76, 78–79
fertility treatment 13–14, 66–68, 72, 74,
    76–77, 79
Foucault, Michel 5, 57
France 4–6, 9, 15, 125, 129–130, 132,
    138–139, 156, 171
Freeman, Elizabeth 147
Friedman, Sara 89

gender 24, 31–35, 37–39, 45, 54, 59, 65,
    165, 169, 173, 178
Gender Recognition Act (GRA) 174
Giametta, Calogero 15
Global North 12, 106, 108, 174
Gunaratnam, Yasmin 179

Halberstam, Jack 153
Harjo, Laura 37–38
Hegde, Radha 17, 108
Hoefinger, Heidi 15
Holm, Tom 27
Holmes, Cindy 38
Hong, G. K. 54
human trafficking 11, 113, 115, 131
Human Trafficking Intervention Courts
    (HTICs) 136–137
Hunt, Sarah/Tłaliłila'ogwa 33

Illouz, Eva 88
immigrants 46, 48, 51, 54, 57–59, 88, 108,
    166, 169–171, 177, 186
immigration 13, 17, 46, 51, 55, 57, 60,
    133–134, 165–166, 171
Indigenous futurity 38
Indigenousness 25, 27–28, 30–31,
    34, 38
Indigenous peoplehood 12, 23, 25,
    27–28, 36
Indigenous peoples 24–25, 27–30,
    32–33, 38–39
intimacy 3, 14–15, 85, 87–90, 94–95,
    97–101, 156, 160

Israeli fertility clinics 13, 67–69, 72, 74,
    79–80
Israeli health insurance 67, 76
Israeli hospitals 67, 70, 73–74, 76–78
Israel/Palestine 6, 65–80, 108

Kancler, Tjaša 148, 152
Kneese, Tamara 160
Kosnick, Kira 108
Kušić, Katarina 147

LaBruce, Bruce 156
Lambevski, Sasho 150
Latina trans women 125, 130–131
LGBTQ 35–36
Livingston, Julie 172
Luibhéid, Eithne 8
Lyons, Scott Richard 25

Macioti, P.G. 15
Mai, Nicola 11, 15
Mama, Amina 57
marriage 11, 14, 46, 85–90, 97,
    99–101
marriage fraud 14, 85–88, 90, 92,
    97–98
marriage gender bind 93
mass accommodation 172–173, 176
Matebeni, Zethu 178
Mazower, Mark 153
Mbembe, Achille 112, 159–160
McKittrick, K. 58
media 3, 14, 28, 53, 70, 75, 106, 108,
    111–114, 116–118, 127
mediated anxieties 14, 105–107, 113
medical space 69–70, 78–80
Medicine, Beatrice 36
migrant groups 124–125, 132,
    138–139
migrant sex workers 11, 14–15, 17,
    105–107, 109, 113–118, 125–131,
    133–136, 138–139, 156
migrant women 114, 116
migrant workers 108, 117, 129–130, 139,
    173, 179
migration 2, 9, 11, 14–15, 57–58, 88, 90,
    106, 123, 125, 133, 135, 166,
    168–169, 173
migration scholarship 101
migratism 168, 178
Miranda, Deborah 35
Monroe, James 32

INDEX

Mountz, Alison 10
Msibi, Thabo 178
Musto, Jennifer 15

national regimes 4, 7, 13
necropolitical violence 112–113
nervousness 51
New Zealand 4, 15, 125, 132–135, 139
Nyanzi, Stella 178

Obeidallah, Dean 53
occupation 6, 72, 76, 78, 169
Özyürek, Esra 157

Palestinians 66–67, 69–70, 72–76, 78–79
Patterson, Christopher 146
Pearson, J. Diane 27
peoplehood 13, 24–28, 30, 37
Perera, Suvendrini 7, 112
physical borders 108, 111
population exchange 152–153, 159
porous borders 70, 79
predatory porn 15, 145–146, 152, 154,
    159–160
Price, Flora 26
Project South 8–9
Prostitution Reform Act 2003 (PRA)
    132–135, 139
Puar, Jasbir 6
public anxieties 105–106, 109,
    112, 114
Pugliese, Joseph 7
Pyle, Kai 38

queer analysis 13, 59
queer migrants 11, 146, 148
queer sexualities 110, 112, 117

Rabinowitz, Dan 108
race 24, 26, 45, 47, 49–50, 53, 55–57,
    59, 88–89, 132–133, 158–159, 165,
    168–169, 184, 186
racialization 4–6, 13, 43, 124, 138, 146,
    148, 157, 168, 174, 177–178; colonial
    histories of 4
racialized logics 13
racial taxonomies 58
racism 2, 55, 57, 114, 166–169, 178
radical sovereignty 12, 23–24, 27, 29–30,
    37–39
Rao, Rahul 148
Reddy, Chandan 48

reproduction 4, 7–9, 13–14, 56, 65–68,
    74–76, 78–80, 124
reproductive control 4, 7, 13
reproductive technologies 13, 65–66,
    68, 79
repro-politics 74
rhetorical appropriation 31, 34
rhetorical borders 12, 23
rhetorical imperialism 24–28, 30–34,
    36, 39
rhetorical sovereignty 26, 29–30,
    35–36, 39
Rifkin, Mark 34, 40n7
right-wing politics 168, 175
Rubin, Gayle 2

Schmidt-Camacho, Alicia 169
Seemangal, R. 53
self-presentation 87
settler colonialism 2–4, 7, 12–13, 24–25,
    27, 30, 66, 68, 75, 79, 166, 173
settler-state 24, 26, 28, 30, 32
SEXHUM project 125, 129, 136
sexual discourses 3–5
sexual humanitarianism 15, 123–125, 129,
    132, 134
sexuality 2–6, 9–10, 12–13, 15–17, 34–38,
    45–47, 53, 55–57, 112, 116, 123,
    146–148, 151–152, 158, 164–167, 173,
    177–178, 184–186
sexual services 124, 126–128, 135,
    138–139
sexual violence 5–7, 167, 169, 178, 185
sex work 3–4, 11, 15, 109, 113–116,
    123–125, 127, 129–131, 135, 137–139,
    145, 148
sex workers 11, 113–114, 118, 126,
    128–133, 135–137, 146, 154, 156,
    169, 178
Sharma, N. 11
Simpson, Leanne Betasamosake 30, 38
social crisis 174
sovereignty 29–30, 32
sperm smuggling 68, 74–76, 80
Spillers, Hortense 8
Stoler, Ann 5
strategic intimacies 11, 14, 86–87, 90–91,
    93–101
surveillance technologies 3–4, 108

Ticktin, Miriam 5, 15
Tlostanova, Madina 148

trafficking 11, 15, 123, 125, 127–128, 130–131, 133–137
transactional relationships 100
transnational conversation 3
Tudor, Alyosxa 4, 15
Turkey 4, 14, 105–110, 113–117, 148, 159, 168
two-spirit 24, 35–36, 38–39
two-spirit people 32, 36–37
two-spirit reclamation 12, 23
Tyler, Imogen 9

UK 65, 133, 169, 172, 174–175, 179
United States 4, 10, 13, 26, 29, 44, 46, 51, 56–57, 59, 171
US Immigration 45
utopian non-place 68, 70–71, 74, 76, 79–80

violence 7, 54, 56, 107, 112–114, 116, 130–132, 139, 165, 168–170, 174–175, 178
virus embodied 110

Wilson, Alex 37
Wolfe, Patrick 25, 34
women 5–6, 8–9, 14, 16, 31–32, 73, 75, 78, 90–91, 113–115, 131, 167, 169, 171, 174
workers 127–128, 150, 165, 172–173
Wright, C. 11

Yilmaz, Seçil 108

Záhora, Jakub 147
Zengin, Asli 113